HUMAN LIFE

THE PASTORAL PSYCHOLOGY SERIES,
NUMBER 9

HUMAN LIFE:
PROBLEMS OF BIRTH, OF LIVING, AND OF DYING

Edited by
WILLIAM C. BIER, S.J.

FORDHAM UNIVERSITY PRESS · NEW YORK

Printed in the United States of America

Table of Contents

PREFACE   vii

I. THE WORTH OF HUMAN LIFE: LIGHT FROM RELIGION
AND CONTEMPORARY EXPERIENCE   1

The Value of Human Life in Judaeo-Christian Perspective   3
    Gerard H. Ettlinger, S.J.
Life Evaluations in Developing Countries   14
    Joseph B. Schuyler, S.J.
The Value of Human Life in Technological Society   29
    Victor Ferkiss

II. PROBLEMS OF BIRTH: POPULATION PROBLEMS   43

The World Population Situation: Current Trends and Issues   45
    Mary G. Powers
Population Control: Methods and Morality   53
    Charles E. Curran
Responsible Parenthood in the Contemporary World   73
    Sidney C. Callahan

III. PROBLEMS OF BIRTH: EUGENIC PROBLEMS   87

Genetic Engineering   89
    Marc A. Lappé
Genetic Screening and Counseling   95
    Andrew L. Szebenyi, S.J.
Eugenic Abortion   104
    John R. Connery, S.J.

IV. PROBLEMS OF LIVING: LEGITIMATE EXPECTATIONS FOR
Human LIFE   113

Basic Human Freedoms   115
    Robert O. Johann

Personal Human Development   125
    William J. Richardson, S.J.

V. PROBLEMS OF LIVING: SEVERE LIMITATIONS OF HUMAN
    EXPECTANCIES   139

    The Physically Handicapped   141
        Leonard Diller
    The Psychologically Disabled   152
        William F. Lynch, S.J.
    The Economically Disadvantaged: The Constricted Life of   159
        the Poor
        James R. Kelly

VI. PROBLEMS OF DYING: THE PROLONGATION OF LIFE   179

    Defining Death   181
        Robert C. Neville
    Artificial Prolongation of Life: Means and Morality   192
        David Hendin
    Truth-Telling and Decision-Making in the Case of the   201
        Terminally Ill
        Ned H. Cassem, S.J.

VII. PROBLEMS OF DYING: THE TAKING OF LIFE   211

    The Medical Profession: Euthanasia   213
        Eric J. Cassell
    The State: Capital Punishment   223
        Donald R. Campion, S.J.
    The Individual: Suicide   229
        William W. Meissner, S.J.

VIII. LIFE BEYOND DEATH: EXPECTATIONS OF IMMORTALITY   253

    Immortality in Humanistic Perspective   255
        Paul Kurtz
    Immortality in Oriental Religious Perspective   264
        Robert E. Kennedy, S.J.
    Immortality in Judaeo-Christian Perspective   276
        Leo J. O'Donovan, S.J.

Preface

A series of Pastoral Psychology Institutes, under the sponsorship of the Psychology Department at Fordham University, was begun in 1955. With the single exception of 1967 when no Institute was offered, they have been presented on alternate years since their inception. The volumes in the Pastoral Psychology Series are an outgrowth of the Institutes, with the current volume containing the papers presented in the 1975 Institute.

These Institutes, intended originally for the clergy and initially open only to them, began with a series of topics in which the behavioral sciences were able to make a contribution to clergymen in their attempt to deal with problems encountered in pastoral work. In more recent years the Institutes have been opened to other professionally qualified and interested persons in addition to clergymen, and the topics selected for treatment have been broadened accordingly.

The first two Institutes, those of 1955 and 1957, dealt rather briefly with a series of topics which were combined for publication into a single volume, the first in the Pastoral Psychology Series, entitled: *Personality and sexual problems in pastoral psychology*. Subsequent Institutes were devoted to single topics which received more extensive treatment. The 1959 Institute concerned itself with addiction, before the drug problem assumed its current proportions, and the proceedings appeared as volume two in the series: *Problems in addiction: Alcohol and drug addiction*. The 1961 Institute focused on the teenager and provided the material for volume three: *The adolescent: His search for understanding*. Marriage was the topic of the 1963 Institute and of volume four in the series: *Marriage: A psychological and moral approach*. The 1965 Institute concerned itself with the place of woman in the Church and in the modern world, and the proceedings appeared as volume five under the title:

Woman in modern life. The 1969 Institute addressed itself to the question of conscience because of the central position which this topic had come to assume both in the Church and in the world. This Institute provided the material for volume six in the series with the title: *Conscience: Its freedom and limitations.* In 1971 the topic was alienation, one of the pervasive characteristics of modern man, and the proceedings appeared as volume seven: *Alienation: Plight of modern man?* The last previous Institute, that in 1973, turned its attention to another peculiarly modern problem, namely, the extraordinary increase in the number of elderly people in the population, and appeared as volume eight under the title: *Aging: Its challenge to the individual and to society.*

A consistent feature of the Institutes has been their interdisciplinary approach. From the beginning of the series there has been an invariable emphasis on the contributions of the behavioral sciences, including, after psychology, particularly psychiatry and sociology. Frequent contributions have also come from such disciplines as theology, philosophy, political science, and social work. More limited contributions, depending usually on the particular topic under consideration, have been made to the Institute series by anthropology, economics, the legal profession, and the judiciary.

All the Institutes have conformed to the same overall pattern of arrangement. They have been conducted from a Monday through a Friday of a week in the latter half of June. The Institute reported in the present volume ran from the 16th to the 20th of June 1975. This time was initially selected and subsequently continued because it fits, with a minimum of inconvenience to both contributors and participants, between the end of the academic year and the start of summer school or other summer commitments. It also has the not inconsiderable advantage of being held at a time when the facilities of the campus are not taxed, and hence are available for the Institute.

The Institutes have provided a concentrated week-long experience focused on a pre-selected topic, and the interchange in both formal discussion and informal conversation between the contributors, who presented the papers, and the participants, who attended, has consistently emerged as a particularly valuable feature of the Institutes. However satisfying discussions of this kind are for those present, experience with them indicates that their significance is greatly—one is inclined to say almost entirely—conditioned by the immediate context in which they occur. They represent a face-to-face situation, where expression, gesture, and tone of voice are important elements, and where the atmosphere of spontaneous interchange is all-important. Almost all of this is lost in the printed word. In our experience, it is virtually impossible to recapture this atmosphere subsequently, and thus, this volume, like its predecessors, regretfully forgoes the attempt to do so. This experience, which is a living one, is the bonus which is reserved for those who are able to spend the week required to attend the Institute, as opposed to those who must be content with the reading of the published volume. We believe, however, that the published proceedings have a contribution to make to a far larger group than those present at the Institute sessions, especially since the more recent Institutes have addressed currently relevant and even pressing topics and have been broadened beyond the problems encountered in pastoral work. The reception accorded previous volumes in the Pastoral Psychology Series would seem to attest the validity of this conviction.

The topics chosen for the Institute series have combined an attention to the perennial, as for instance personality and sexual problems and marriage, and to the contemporary. With the continuation of the series, more attention has been given to immediately current problems. Thus it can be said that the topics chosen for the more recent Institutes have been not only timely, in a period of rapidly changing times, but even occasionally ahead of the times, as, for instance, the choice of addiction for the 1959 Institute and of the role of woman in the modern world for the 1965 Institute. It has been the aim of the planners of the Institute series to select topics which not only are current, but which lend themselves to, and indeed require, the kind of interdisciplinary approach which the Institute series is in a position to provide.

In selecting *Human life* and emphasizing particularly the two ends of the life cycle for the 1975 Institute, the planning Committee considered that it had achieved both the above-mentioned objectives. Recent advances in medicine have created new moral and pastoral problems, particularly at the beginning and the end of the life cycle.

With respect to birth, medical advances, which have greatly reduced infant mortality and which have extended life expectancy, have combined to create an enormous increase in world population. With the consciousness that all living men and women constitute one interdependent world, and with the growing realization that the earth's resources are indeed limited, a completely new urgency has arisen for some form of population control. What methods are available, and what are morally acceptable? One of the Institute papers addresses itself to this question. Now that new techniques, particularly amniocentesis, have become available for assessing the condition of the unborn, genetic counseling—unknown a generation ago—has become a reality. This creates new moral and pastoral problems, and several of the papers address themselves to this question.

Then, at the other end of the life cycle medical advances have given rise to another set of moral–pastoral problems. Life can now be sustained, even for extended periods, long after human consciousness has gone. Hospital attendants give water and nourishment to these "human vegetables." Should they continue to do so? For how long? Has a patient a right to ask to die? When is a person dead, and by what criterion? These are current moral and pastoral problems which are addressed in the Institute.

A glance at the table of contents reveals that the material presented in this volume is divided into eight sections. Section I seeks to provide some background on the value of human life as seen in the light of religion and contemporary experience. Sections II and III are devoted to the beginning of the life cycle, Section II addressing population problems and Section III eugenic problems. Sections IV and V are devoted to the middle of the life span, Section IV considering legitimate expectancies for human life, and Section V considering selected cases in which normal life expectancies are severely limited—the physically handicapped, the psychologically disabled, and the economically disadvantaged. Sections VI and VII turn to the end of the life cycle, Section VI being devoted to the (mostly artificial) prolongation of life, and Section VII to the taking of life—by the medical profession (euthanasia), by the state (capital punishment), and by the individual (suicide). Finally, Section VIII pushes beyond the life span as experienced in this world and inquires about man's expectations of immortality—as seen in humanistic, Oriental religious, and Judaeo-Christian perspective.

As editor of the Proceedings and Chairman of the Institute Committee, I am pleased to pay grateful tribute to my fellow Committee members, all of whom are connected with Fordham University, and all of whom shared with me the responsibility for the planning and the conduct of the Institute out of which these Proceedings came. They are: Mr. H. George Fletcher, Director of Fordham University Press; Rev. Joseph G. Keegan, s.j., at the time of the Institute Associate Professor and now Associate Professor Emeritus of Psychology; Dr. James R. Kelly, Associate Professor of Sociology; Rev. Daniel J. Sullivan, s.j., Associate Professor of Biology; and Rev. Andrew C. Varga, s.j., Assistant Professor of Philosophy.

The delay of the better part of a year in the publication of the Proceedings is owing to unforeseen duties at the University assigned to the Editor during the 1975–76 academic year, which almost completely precluded any work on the manuscript. That the Proceedings are now available is owing to the editorial assistance provided by Father Keegan, to whom I express my gratitude and appreciation. I also acknowledge the generous and willing cooperation of Fordham University Press, in facilitating publication in remarkably short time.

December, 1976   WILLIAM C. BIER, s.j.

HUMAN LIFE

I
THE WORTH OF HUMAN LIFE: LIGHT FROM RELIGION AND CONTEMPORARY EXPERIENCE

The Value of Human Life in Judaeo-Christian Perspective

GERARD H. ETTLINGER, S.J.

*Father Gerard H. Ettlinger, S.J. received his A.B.
and M.A. degrees from Fordham University and
the D. Phil. degree from Oxford University. From
1972 to 1974 he was Assistant Professor of Greek
Patristics at the Pontifical Oriental Institute, Rome.
He joined the Fordham University faculty in 1974,
where he is currently Assistant Professor in the
Theology Department. Father Ettlinger is the
author of a critical edition of the Greek text of*
Eranistes *of Theodoret of Cyrus, and is a contributor to* Sources Chrétiennes, Traditio, The
Classical Bulletin, *and* Studia Patristica. *He is a
member of the Catholic Theological Society of
America, the American Philological Association,
and the Mediaeval Academy of America.*

In the last forty years the Judaeo-Christian religious tradition has been
forced by the press of events to reconsider seriously its assessment of the
meaning and value of human life. Many factors have played a role in
shaping this re-evaluation: political theories and their consequences,
from the rise of National Socialism in Germany through the most recent
events in Indochina; technological, and more recently, ecological developments, from the spread of nuclear armaments, through the population
explosion and its ramifications, to the possibility of controlling the
development of life in its earliest stages and at its ultimate point in this
world. All these questions will be discussed in their modern aspects,

3

so to speak, at later stages of this Institute, and therefore I shall confine myself to the basically religious foundations of the Judaeo-Christian perspective. The concept of "tradition" can be employed as a slogan to deny the possibility of change and development, but in the best strands of the Judaeo-Christian heritage, this usage has always been seen as defective and erroneous. But if this heritage did not come fully developed from the minds of twentieth-century thinkers, then there is a place for a legitimate study of the basis of this tradition (in the best sense of the word); I would only add the additional qualifier "Graeco-Roman."

My approach then will be historical, and will attempt to show briefly *what* this perspective is in its origins, and, more importantly, *why* it developed as it did. This is not a denial of the validity or value of the contributions made by other cultures or traditions, nor a rejection of later and modern developments—it is quite simply a limitation of the scope of this paper to a study of the foundations of the Judaeo-Christian perspective as found in the Old and New Testaments and in the earliest Christian interpreters of these documents. The post-scriptural Jewish tradition developed according to its own principles, which cannot be discussed here (cf. Klein, 1967–68). Thus the historical approach to these questions should not conflict with, but rather complement, the more immediately verifiable and empirical data of contemporary findings.

JUDAIC PERSPECTIVE

The Old Testament is the story of one people's struggle for life in a world in which death and disaster were commonplace realities. On the most fundamental level sheer physical existence was highly prized, and "You shall not kill" (Dt 5:17) is perhaps the most concise and striking expression of this outlook. Yet God included capital punishment as a sanction for His commandments, and His chosen people did not hesitate to put entire populations to death whenever this fostered the spread of the lifestyle oriented to the true God. There is at least an apparent contradiction here, which undoubtedly had its roots in contemporary sociological and anthropological factors; yet the mentality indicates a religious dimension, which developed throughout the history of Israel and received a further transformation, for Christian eyes, with the coming of Christ.

The Old Testament opens with several accounts of man's creation by God; these attempt to explain man as he was known by the writers of those accounts. They are not philosophical explanations of an ideal humanity, and therefore the beauties of paradise and the greatness of man are immediately located in a world where evil, the pains of birth and of life, and death itself are overwhelmingly real. This existential view of man dominates the earliest parts of the Old Testament, and helps to explain why the struggle for life goes on in a context of the frailty of that life and of its ultimate dissolution. At this stage life was seen as a gift from God, in union with whom man must live, and on whom the spread of that life, as embodied in the very existence and growth of the nation, depends. Life is good and death is evil, and man chooses one or the other by accepting or rejecting God and His ways:

> See, I have set before you this day life and good, death and evil. If you obey the commandments of the Lord your God which I command you this day, by loving the Lord your God, by walking in his ways, and by keeping his commandments and his statutes and his ordinances then you shall live and multiply . . . [Dt 30:15–16].

When this life is over, the shadowy existence, if one may call it that, of Sheol awaits. The somewhat mysterious continuation of human existence after death envisioned by the Egyptians has no meaning for this outlook; nor is there a part of the human person which will enable him to live on in a real sense after this life. Job's wife tells him to "curse God and die" (Jb 2:9), and thus expresses the extreme, pessimistic conclusion to be drawn from this view of human life. But Job refuses to reject his God and his present life, disastrous though it is; this is an example of the faith which enabled Israel to fight for its national identity and existence in Egypt and Babylon, and the individual to ask God to help him overcome death: "Consider and answer me, O Lord my God; lighten my eyes, lest I sleep the sleep of death" (Ps 13:3).

The later writings of the Old Testament, especially the Wisdom literature, hint, perhaps under the influence of Greek philosophy, at an afterlife and some type of personal immortality—it is late in this period that the resurrection of the individual to a new life can be viewed as the ultimate stage of human existence (Dn 12:2).

This discussion of the Old Testament view of life began with the notion of sheer physical existence in the present world; but the religious dimension of the Hebrew approach to the question of life bases the value of human life on considerations beyond that level, even before the concepts of immortality and resurrection are, or can be, formulated. The practical consequences of the Hebrew evaluation of life will be noted in the last portion of this paper.

CHRISTIAN PERSPECTIVE

Great stress has been placed on the Hebrew view of life, since the Christian perspective grew out of it by adding its own particular insights.

New Testament theology (like that of the Old Testament) is a vast subject, and the differing approaches of the various authors cannot be summarized in one clear list of details. But two aspects of Old Testament thought are at the core of the primitive Christian evaluation of the meaning of human life: the notion of a life lived in fidelity to God, and the belief in a personal immortality and a future resurrection—all to be consummated in and through Jesus Christ.

However one may choose to explain the resurrection of Jesus, it cannot be denied that this "salvation-event," which comprises the resurrection from the dead, full glorification with His Father, and the sending of His Spirit, was decisive in forming the early Christian view of life. According to this view, human life is not meaningless or hopeless; rather it looks forward to a glorious end, which is not only foreshadowed, but even caused by the end of Him in whom faith and fidelity are now centered. In the New Testament and especially in St. Paul, the basic gift given to man through Christ's work is the gift of life.

The other aspect of Old Testament thought—life lived in fidelity to God—is now focused on Jesus as the mediator between God and man; true life is now possible through union with Him, and the means to this end can be summed up in the commandment of love. Detailed obligations do not vanish, it is true, but the love of God, and of neighbor and of oneself in God, is now the basis of a full life in the kingdom which begins here and now, and reaches its peak in the future. The religious dimension of the Old Testament is, according to the Christian view, more fully developed, and thus human life is endowed with a value—with a sanctity, so to speak—which the ancient Egyptian, Near Eastern, and Graeco-Roman civilizations were never able to envision.

From the creation accounts of Genesis to Revelation's vision of the new Jerusalem, human life is seen as a gift from God, which is to be used with love for, and in the service of, the giver, and which will find its ultimate fulfillment in Him. Death is a part of the reality of this human life; but its cause lies in man and in his tendency away from God and toward nothingness, and it too finds its meaning in the context of God's will that man should have life.

This view of human life enabled the Christians of the post-scriptural period to face martyrdom, to accept it, and even to seek it out as they did. It is perhaps inaccurate and unfair to speak only of Christians as being affected in this way, since the history of the Maccabees shows the people of Israel inspired in the same way prior to the Christian revelation. Yet the central focus here is on the Christian martyrs, and it cannot be denied that extreme views did exist; but these were ordinarily rejected as heretical (which in this case may be synonymous with unhealthy), and a hatred of human life as such or a morbid longing for the next life are not the main forces motivating the early Christians to martyrdom.

Ignatius, a bishop of Antioch around A.D. 100, was put to death in Rome, and his letter to the Romans clearly expresses his desire to be one with Christ by dying for Him. But this letter, and the other letters of Ignatius to various churches in Asia Minor and Greece, are exhortations to life—to the full Christian life of love and unity in Christ which will bring those who lead such lives to the fullness of life. There is a decidedly other-worldly quality in the actions and the writings of the early Christians, but human life is never rejected or condemned—it is instead to be transformed, through love, and through hope in the resurrection.

THE VIEWS OF AUGUSTINE

From the second through the fifth centuries, Christian authors make many specific statements about the value of human life, but this factual material will be presented at the end of this paper; for the moment a brief consideration will be made of St. Augustine, who expressed some of the most profound early Christian thoughts on human life. Augustine's influence on Western thought cannot be minimized, although it has at times been deplored. Whether the difficulties result from misinterpretations or from a too literal following of Augustine, with a consequent rejection of the notion of development, is not important here; the fact is that Augustine, as a Christian bishop and a sensitive human being, has left some remarkable statements on human life and death in this world and in the hereafter.

In his *Confessions* Augustine tells of the unexpected death of a friend with whom, on the latter's sickbed, he had a falling out over his (Augustine's) negative remarks on baptism and Christian belief. "My heart was darkened over with sorrow, and whatever I looked at was death" (4.4). This incident took place in Augustine's twenty-ninth year, and the sense of death never left him; the intensity of his reaction is mirrored years later in the *City of God*, when he speaks of death as a reality of human life. Augustine began writing the *City of God* in 413 at the age of 59, and finished it in 427, when he was 73 years old. It is therefore a work of his maturity and old age, far too complex to classify or summarize here, and one which contains elements of all his massive learning, both sacred and secular.

In defending Christianity against paganism, Augustine divides mankind into two groups, the good and the evil, corresponding to the two cities, the one of God and the other of man. The ultimate basis for the division is love, and it is here, in a notion which is central to the whole of his thought, that Augustine comes directly into contact with the question of human life.* For God is the source of all life, and thus creates only one city, His own. To belong to this city, man must love God, the source of all life, and then his neighbor and himself in that love which he has for God. It is man who creates the other city by perverting love (and thus himself), making the object of his love some lower, mutable reality, which can ultimately be reduced to himself apart from God. Thus self-love, or pride, is at the root of the perversion, by which man tends away from the source of life and of goodness, and seeks nothingness and death. Augustine here is face to face with the problem of evil, and it is this turning away from God and from life which explains original sin and death. Everything which comes from God, including man and human life, is good, insofar as it comes from God and shares in His life; evil is a negation of this reality, and therefore ultimately a denial of God.

For Augustine, therefore, man was created for life, both here and hereafter. He vigorously defends the goodness of man, body as well as soul, and maintains that if man himself had not chosen the way of corruption and nothingness, human life would simply have been transformed into its ultimate perfection in God. But man did so choose, and, as a result, his life here is a constant movement toward the consequences of that choice—namely, death:

> Indeed, from the very moment that a person begins his existence in this body that is destined to die, there is never a point when death is not coming on. . . . Perhaps man is at once both in life and in death, that is to say, he is in life, living it until it is wholly removed, but at the same time in death because he is dying from the moment that his life is diminished . . . [13.10].

Augustine's rhetorical training and his love of paradox are in evidence here, but they do not diminish the force of his sense for the evanescence of human life.

We have shown how God's love is, for Augustine, the source of life, and how man's true love for God and man continues and develops that life. It is this basic insight which prevents Augustine's extreme sensitivity to death from overwhelming him and transforming him into a rather morbid pessimist. For him death is a reality, but God's love has conquered it through Christ, and here the basic Christian focus on Christ and His resurrection joins with Augustine's vision of God as the source of all life. Thus he will distinguish two deaths, one of the body and the other of the soul (13.2.12). The first comes to all men, and will be done away with at the end of time by the resurrection of the body. The

* The source of the material in this and the following paragraphs is Augustine, *City of God* and, unless otherwise noted, it is taken from Books 11–14.

second affects only those who are not called by God in Christ to eternal life and who love wrongly in this life. The former consists in the desertion of the body by the soul and is not eternal. The latter consists in the desertion of the soul by God (a desertion caused by man himself), and will last for eternity—it is, quite literally, hell.

All mankind must suffer the first type of death; those who suffer the second type as well suffer what Augustine calls "total death," a notion which becomes clear in the light of the final resurrection of the body. For God wills that man should live, and when the bodies of the good are restored to life at the end, they will rejoin their souls to enjoy eternal life with God. The souls of those who have undergone total death—those of the evil—will rejoin their bodies, to live a life which in actuality is no life at all, but rather death—for it is an eternity of separation from God (cf. 19.11). Thus love is at the heart of Augustine's development of the meaning and value of human life.

The descriptions of eternal life and death (or heaven and hell) are taken from the last four books of the *City of God*, where both the treatise and the realities of Augustine's thought reach their fulfillment. The goal and high point of human life are obviously in the other world, and Augustine never loses sight of this. At various points in the work, therefore, he describes the miseries of the present life and the tragedies inherent in it (e.g., 22.22). Still he constantly maintains that this life is good and not to be scorned, and condemns those who would reject the body or deny resurrection to it—for the fullness of even eternal life man must be composed as he is here, of body and soul (cf. 22.10–21, 26–28). Finally, in seeking words to describe the inexpressible happiness and beauty of eternal life, he decides that the most fitting image is this life, and gives a rather enraptured picture of the joy and beauty which man can experience even in this imperfect world (22.24).

This study of Augustine shows that his thought reflects the Judaeo-Christian tension between belief in this world as a good creation of God's and the longing for fulfillment through union with God; this tension is resolved through belief in personal immortality and resurrection; the centrality of love as giving value to human life is also abundantly clear. One may perhaps differ with certain aspects of Augustine's thought on man and human life; but he believes most firmly in its basic goodness and therefore sees it as an ultimate value to be preserved, despite the problems which he finds in the existential reality.

SCRIPTURAL AND PATRISTIC QUOTATIONS

The remainder of this paper will consist of scriptural and patristic statements exemplifying the principles just discussed. The general pro-

hibition against the taking of human life summed up in the commandment "You shall not kill" has already been noted, as was the apparently
contradictory practice which allowed the taking of life when God's will
or plan demanded it. This is not confined to the Old Testament, however, for St. Augustine himself held that the taking of life was legal
in some cases (*City of God*, 1.21), and judged that acts committed in a
"just war" were moral, although his personal reaction to them was not
one of encouragement, as will be shown below (cf. *City of God*, 4.15).
There is little or nothing said in this period about the prolongation or
termination of life in sickness or old age, perhaps because medical
theory had little to offer in this area. Old age, however, is highly
esteemed, and the care of widows and orphans is considered a community duty at all stages of the tradition. The Judaeo-Christian evaluation of human life becomes especially clear in the area of birth and
childhood.

The legal code of the Old Testament is based on the *lex talionis*, a
life for a life; thus, if an ox, for example, which is a known threat, kills
a man or a woman, not only is the animal to be killed, "but its owner
also shall be put to death" (Ex 21:28–29). With respect to abortion,
the earliest Hebrew tradition mentions only one case, in which, it must
be noted, the cause of the miscarriage is accidental; the law demands a
life for a life only where "harm follows" (Ex 21:22–24). Since this is
distinguished from the situation where "no harm follows," even though
the miscarriage occurs in both cases, concern is clearly for the life of
the mother, not for that of the unborn fetus. This approach is close in
spirit to earlier Near Eastern legislation, such as that of the code of
Hammurabi, and Assyrian, Sumerian, and Hittite texts (Dölger, 1934,
pp. 4–6). These tend to base the punishment for causing a miscarriage
(usually a fine) on the social status of the mother, although one form of
a Hittite law enjoins a larger fine in the case of a more developed
embryo (Dölger, 1934, pp. 5–6).

The Septuagint version of the Exodus text reflects the influence of
Greek philosophy on Hellenistic Judaism, and the emphasis shifts from
the mother to the fetus; thus a distinction is made between the fetus as
"formed" or "not formed," and it is only in the first instance that life
for life is demanded. Aristotle is perhaps the best-known source for this
type of distinction, for he allows abortion when a couple has too many
children, but only "before sense and life have begun" (*Politics*, 7.14,
1335B). The oath of Hippocrates had included the promise not to "give
to a woman a pessary to cause abortion" (*Hippocrates*, pp. 298–99),
but Aristotle's distinction indicates a shift from the seemingly absolute
position of the oath. Philo reflects the Septuagint version of Exodus and
links abortion of the formed fetus with infanticide (*De specialibus*

legibus, 3.108–109); yet he also seems to follow Greek philosophical and medical theories which hold that the embryo is part of the mother, and that it is a question of murder only when the embryo is a person independent of the mother (3.117–118). All the basic issues which influence early Christian teaching are present here: Is the embryo part of the mother, or is it a person in its own right? If the latter is the case, when does it become so?

The New Testament contains no explicit statements on this subject, but, as Noonan has said, "The Gospels give preeminence to a single value in human behavior: love" (Noonan, 1965, p. 36). It is the law of love, as outlined above, which gives value to human life, and the ultimate sign of this judgment is the willingness of Jesus to give His life for all men. His disciples are to follow His example, and should not only be unwilling to take another's life, but should even be ready to lay down their lives for others: "By this we know love, that he laid down his life for us; and we ought to lay down our lives for the brethren" (1 Jn 3:16). To prove that this is the true spirit of Christianity with respect to the taking of human life, early Christian authors often cite the Lord's words forbidding not only killing, but even anger itself:

> You have heard that it was said to the men of old, "You shall not kill; and whoever kills shall be liable to judgment." But I say to you that every one who is angry with his brother shall be liable to judgment . . . [Mt 5:21–22].

It would seem that the pagan world of the early Christian era had little difficulty in accepting abortion and infanticide (Noonan, 1967–68, p. 303), and the literature is filled with denunciations of these practices. A few examples will suffice to show the general attitude of the Christians.

The *Didache*, one of the earliest extant post-scriptural writings, contains the following commandments (among many others): "Do not murder. . . . Do not murder a child by abortion, nor kill it at birth" (2.2a, b). Athenagoras of Athens, a second-century apologist, defends the Christians against pagan charges of murder and cannibalism in this way:

> Again, what sense does it make to think of us as murderers when we say that women who practice abortion are murderers and will render account to God for abortion? The same man cannot regard that which is in the womb as a living being and for that reason an object of God's concern and then murder it when it has come into the light. Neither can the same man forbid exposing a child that has been born, on the grounds that those who do so are murderers, and then slay one that has been nourished [*Legatio*, 35.6].

About the year 200 Clement of Alexandria also views abortion as oper-
ating contrary to God's providence, and says that the use of drugs to
cause abortions destroys not only the embryo, but also one's humanity
itself—the Greek word is "philanthropia" (*Paedagogos*, 2.10.96.1).

In the Latin tradition Tertullian (*c.* A.D. 200) is one of the earliest
authors to speak on this subject. He holds that the soul comes to a
child in the womb and makes it a living being from the start (*De anima,*
25); he distinguishes this stage of life from true humanity, which is
present when human form is fully developed in the womb. Thus Tertullian can call abortion "murder" (*De anima,* 37; *Apologeticus,* 9.8).
Minucius Felix, writing either shortly before or shortly after Tertullian,
uses much the same language (*Octavius*, 30.2).

Augustine treats abortion as homicide in some works, whereas elsewhere he speaks of it as a sin against marriage (Noonan, 1967–68,
pp. 311–312). But as is often the case with Augustine, the true spirit of
his thought comes out in a totally different context; speaking about the
resurrection from the dead in the *Enchiridion,* he discusses the classical
distinction and says that the unformed aborted fetus will not rise, while
the formed one with human life will. The latter is therefore a person in
Augustine's eyes, and shares in the life given by God and transformed
by Christ (23.84–86).

Abortion is not the only problem surrounding life at birth faced by
the early Christians, for the practice of exposing newborns—enshrined
in literature by the Oedipus story—was still a reality in the Christian
era. The *Didache* has already been cited against the practice of killing
a child "at birth," and similar references can be found in many early
authors. But the legislation of the early Christian empire is the best
proof of the tenacity of these practices, and even in the fifth century
laws were passed condemning and punishing them (*Codex Theodosianus,* 4.9.2, for the year 412).

Augustine's notion of a just war was mentioned earlier, and it is in
such areas that modern thought has especially clarified and developed
earlier statements. To Augustine's credit, however, it should be said
that he views the taking of life under these circumstances as a necessary
evil (*City of God,* 4.15); he is undoubtedly influenced here by the
reality of the horrors in a barbarian invasion and the need to resist, but
he never loses his basic belief in the sanctity of human life. Indeed he
finds joy at that terrible time in the fact that lives—including those of
pagans—were spared because of the sanctuary offered by Christian
churches, a sanctuary which was respected even by the barbarians (*City
of God,* 1.1).

There are many other authors who could be quoted on these problems, and many distinctions and clarifications which could be made con-

cerning the religious dimensions of the practical statements just cited. This survey has been sketchy, but one which, it is to be hoped, has shown the foundations and the direction of the Judaeo-Christian perspective on the value of human life.

REFERENCES

Aristotle. *Politics* (H. Rackham, trans.). The Loeb Classical Library. Cambridge: Harvard University Press, 1959.

Athenagoras of Athens. *Legatio and De resurrectione* (W. R. Schoedel, Ed. and trans.). Oxford: Clarendon, 1972.

Augustine. *City of God* (various translators). The Loeb Classical Library (7 vols.). Cambridge: Harvard University Press, 1957–1972.

Augustine. *Confessions* (W. Watts, trans.). The Loeb Classical Library (2 vols.). Cambridge: Harvard University Press, 1960–1961.

Augustine. *Enchiridion* (B. M. Peebles, trans.). The Fathers of the Church (Vol. 4). New York: Cima, 1947.

Clement of Alexandria. *Paedagogos* (C. Mondésert, trans.). Sources Chrétiennes (Vol. 108). Paris: Cerf, 1965.

Codex Theodosianus. Theodosiani Libri XVI . . . (T. Mommsen & P. Meyer, Eds.) (Vol. 1, Pt. 2). Berlin: Weidmann, 1954.

Didache. The Apostolic Fathers: A New Translation and Commentary. III. *Barnabas and the Didache* (R. A. Kraft, Ed. and trans.). New York: Nelson, 1965.

Dölger, F. J. Das Lebensrecht des ungeborenen Kindes und die Fruchtabtreibung in der Bewertung der heidnischen und christlichen Antike. *Antike und Christentum* (Vol. 4, Pt. 1). Münster: Aschendorff, 1934.

Hippocrates (W. H. S. Jones, trans.) (Vol. 1). The Loeb Classical Library. Cambridge: Harvard University Press, 1962.

Klein, I. Abortion—A Jewish View. *The Dublin Review*, Winter 1967–68, No. 514, pp. 382–390.

Minucius Felix. *Octavius* (G. H. Rendall, trans.). The Loeb Classical Library. Cambridge: Harvard University Press, 1960.

The New Oxford Annotated Bible with the Apocrypha. New York: Oxford University Press, 1973.

Noonan, J. T. *Contraception: A history of its treatment by the Catholic theologians and canonists.* Cambridge: The Belknap Press of Harvard University Press, 1965.

Noonan, J. T. The Catholic Church and abortion. *The Dublin Review*, Winter 1967–68, No. 514, pp. 300–345.

Philo. *De specialibus legibus* (F. H. Colson, trans.). The Loeb Classical Library. Cambridge: Harvard University Press, 1937.

Tertullian. *Apologeticus* (T. R. Glover, trans.). The Loeb Classical Library. Cambridge: Harvard University Press, 1960.

Tertullian. *De Anima* (*A Treatise on the Soul*). Ante-Nicene Fathers (Vol. 3). Grand Rapids, Mich.: Eerdmans, 1951.

Life Evaluations in Developing Countries

JOSEPH B. SCHUYLER, S.J.

Father Joseph B. Schuyler, S.J. is currently Professor of Sociology and Chairman of the Sociology Department of the Faculty of Social Sciences at the University of Lagos. Before going to Nigeria in 1963 Father Schuyler taught sociology at Fordham University. His higher degrees include an M.A. from Saint Louis University (1945) and a Ph.D. degree from Fordham University (1956). Besides being a return contributor to the Pastoral Psychology Series, Father Schuyler has written Current social problems *in collaboration with C. S. Mihanovich (1950) and* Conceptions of Christianity in the context of Tropical Africa *(1968). He holds memberships in the American Sociological Association, the Nigerian Economic Society, the International African Institute, and the African Studies Association.*

Whether it be the result of the new interpretation of Stonehenge, or of Inca shrines and calendars, or of Aztec artistry with gold, we have been coming to understand that our ancestors' intelligence was not evidently inferior to our own. The ancient civilization of Sumer and the Far East, the terra cottas of Nok in northern Nigeria, the geometrical land patterns of pre-Columbian Peru, to mention only what immediately comes to mind, suggest that technological sophistication was not born with the industrial revolution. We have been outgrowing earlier assumptions that illiterate peoples lacked any conception of value in matters economic, political, and legal (Evans-Pritchard, 1961). More and more we have also been coming to appreciate that such peoples possessed sophisticated ideologies. These were not limited to naïve cosmologies of pre-astronomy myth. Rather they offer a generally coherent and purposeful philosophy and evaluation of life.

Evidently every people lives by some design, more or less stable or changing. Every people experiences the opportunities and challenges of birth and death, life and environment. All receive from previous generations answers to the quest for life's meaning, and they test those answers in their own time—with more or less criticism and adaptation.

An understanding of a people's evaluation of life must be central to any attempt to understand their culture, mores, characteristics, social structures, and lifestyles. This is as true for the so-called developing as for the developed world. To achieve this understanding is inevitably difficult. Third-world cultural components are many and complex. And they are subject to change: cultural diffusions, religious conversions, veritable revolutions in urbanization, technology, and education, have produced a compounded variety of beliefs, attitudes, and behaviors which defies ready analysis. Still, depending on how one measures or plays with definitions and figures, the developing world includes some two-thirds of the human race, and their representatives now numerically dominate the United Nations Assembly. If we are concerned for human life and its evaluation implicit in national and international moralities and institutions, our interest most properly embraces the developing world.

RELEVANT FACETS OF THE DEVELOPING WORLD

One must be discriminating in talking about this world. We have come to appreciate that economic growth is not a synonym for development—particularly that economic growth the measure of which is gross national product or some other index of calculated industrial production or volume of import and export. Economics includes much more than available accounts and tabular records show. But economies themselves are but part of social systems which are more or less productively articulated and socially gratifying.

Extent of Urbanization

By 1960 the world's urban population (in localities of 20,000 and more inhabitants) had risen to 25%, a growth of 4% in a decade (Breese, 1969). Of these urbanites 64% lived in cities of 100,000 population or more. In continents of typically developing countries—Africa, Asia, and Latin America—urban population rose in the same decade from 10%,

13%, and 25% to 13%, 17%, and 32% respectively. The respective percentages of urban dwellers living in the large cities rose from 51% to 68% in Africa, 63% to 66% in Asia, and 66% to 77% in Latin America. Oceania is over 50% urbanized, with more than 80% of its urbanites living in the larger cities.

The point here is that we cannot accurately envision the developing world as merely one large forest, farmland, or sheepfold. Its cities may sometimes comprise magnificent "gold coasts" and miserable slums, and their reaches frequently extend into the hinterland. They have produced new elites, whose specific ratios of higher education and intercontinental travel must be at least comparable with their counterparts in the developed world. These cities are partially melting pots and partially conglomerations of infused scores of millions of people from a remarkable plurality of culturally variant clans, tribes, and nations. Some transform rapidly into townsmen such as may be found anywhere; others resist transformation and remain tribesmen (Mayer, 1965). It is important to recognize these changes and varieties when we try to appreciate life evaluations in the developing world.

Religious and Ideological Complexity

Another observation is pertinent and important. Great portions of the developing world have either a long tradition of, or a more or less recent conversion to, the world's great supra-national or supra-ethnic religions. One might immediately think that the adherents of these religions accept and manifest their respective life evaluations. But, of course, this is too simple. Religious or ideological purity is not a characteristic of the culturally pluralist and religiously variegated developed world; different combinations of sacred and profane are universal and commonplace. It is no different in the developing world: varieties of more or less pure religious profession are mixed with kinds of syncretism and religiocultural overlays. Often the old coexists with the new in the same persons, with now one dominant and now the other.

Just recently a news item in Lagos' *Daily Times* reported that ten bodies, unknown recent victims of hit-and-run drivers on the city's main highway, lay unclaimed in the public mortuary. At the same time, police stations have a form to be completed by unfortunate drivers who leave the scene of an accident for fear of death at the precipitous hands of aggrieved and impetuous onlookers. Can it be that the same culture produces both death-dealing recklessness and fury over sudden accidental death?

Some tribal groups, despite predilection for fertility, have a horror of twins and traditionally have killed one or both and ostracized the mother. In some places this secretly continues despite severe laws to the contrary. Yet in spite of the hue and outcry whenever such post-natal killing is reported, growing support is given to campaigns to legalize prenatal killing by abortion. In spite of the pro-life platitudes proclaimed regularly in press and pulpit, no outcry throughout the continent has countered the killings of many thousands in Uganda, Burundi, and the Sudan. This is not to point accusing fingers at Africa in particular—for Pakistan and Southeast Asia after American involvement, Northern Ireland, Argentina, and the Middle East have their own cases to answer—but to raise the question: What life evaluations underlie such behavior? The recent heavy loss of life through famine in several African countries has been more of a concern to Americans and Europeans than to fellow-Africans.

It is impossible to define any type of life evaluation uniquely peculiar to the developing world. Yet one can find certain emphases which are widespread, though with diverse manifestation. To focus on them we have to see them in their respective traditional settings. We have to prescind from the degrees of their actual integration or amalgamation with more industrialized and modernized cultures. We shall limit ourselves to certain African foci—indeed sub-Saharan Africa—which are manifold and variant enough, rather than try to encompass other major areas of the developing world.

African Scene and Its Survival Systems

I forget who first expressed it this way, but it helps to remember that we mortals are like all other humans in some respects, like some other humans in some respects, and in some other respects like no one but ourselves. This sounds somewhat banal, but peoples' response to life is basically the same everywhere: we want to survive, to develop, to succeed. Each of these objectives shows certain modalities in the experience of different life contexts, both natural and social. The Ottenbergs describe an enlightening variety of sub-Saharan socioresidential patterns, ranging along a "continuum from a small, truly nomadic band living on the simplest level of technology to a large, compact sedentary grouping possessing the industrial and scientific techniques of the Western World" (Ottenberg & Ottenberg, 1960, p. 40).

Diversity in Levels of Technology

There are the nomadic Bushmen of the Kalahari Desert, hunters and gatherers, localized around water holes in the dry season; the nomadic Pygmies, somewhat dependently related to sedentary farmers; the pastoral Fulani of West Africa, moving seasonally with their cattle, not owning, but paying for, the land which they use; the herding Masai of East Africa, who own different residential lands for use in wet and dry seasons; the more settled cattle-herding and farming Nuer along the upper Nile; the Zambian Lozi, who garden, fish, and herd around their mound residences until annual floods drive them to the plains; other more consistently agricultural peoples, like the Bemba and Lele of Zambia and the former Congo, whom poor soils periodically drive in their organized entireties to new settlements; the eastern Nigerian Igbos, settled in rural homesteads and villages; the western Nigerian Yorubas, whose agricultural life centers in large residential cities of 100,000 population or more which long antedated European arrivals; and, finally, such trading cities as Timbuctoo, the crossroads of trans-Saharan caravans and Niger River trade routes, centers of craft industries and professions, are home to groups of many different ethnic backgrounds. Added to this range are the large crop plantations of business farmers, whose provenance is native, foreign, or both, and the metropolitan cities, such as Lagos, Nairobi, and Kinshasa, which are so much a part of life in today's Africa.

Effect on Social Relationships

Types of social relationships vary too: sometimes monogamous, more often polygynous, even some polyandrous marriages; kinship-descent systems which are patrilineal, matrilineal, double, or bilateral, with varying degrees of kinship consciousness and cohesiveness; associations of age groupings, of secret societies, and of craftsmen or professionals; political structures which vary greatly in size and composition, from local acephalous autonomies to complicated interdependencies and monarchies, from relatively differentiated brotherhoods to stratified classes and specialization of labor.

For all these diversities the Ottenbergs cite several pervasive characteristics of African societies which pertain particularly to our current concern. One is that membership in African clans

> includes not only the living but the dead, for death signifies not the end of existence, but rather a change from the corporeal to the noncorporeal. As in the Chinese family, the ancestors are served through the ministrations of the ancestral cult and in many respects maintain a position of authority over the living [Ottenberg & Ottenberg, 1960, p. 30].

Speaking further of systems of marriage, they explain widow inheritance and sororate as deriving from the ideas that marriage is a relationship between lineages as much as between individuals, and that the marriage contract is not broken by death but continues through the reproductive lifetime of each partner. They refer then to "the view universally held in African societies that the goal of marriage is reproduction" (Ottenberg & Ottenberg, 1960, p. 35).

Another deep-rooted feature of African life is the individual's identification with his group—an identification which is "second nature" to both individual and group. No man is an island anywhere, but there are degrees of non-insularity. The living tradition of shared ancestry and continuing lineage, along with the intimate, mutual dependence of kinsmen and neighbors for survival and security in a relatively closed society, makes consciousness of kind a key to group inclusiveness and exclusiveness. The action of an individual toward a group outside his own inevitably involves his own group; an action directed toward an individual inevitably involves the latter's own group (Douglas, 1954/1963; Little, 1954/1963). So much is this true that an outsider's offense against a group leads the latter to demand punishment and retribution from the outsider's group more than from the outsider himself. And within the group the offenses of individuals are seen as harmful to group stability and security, and hence subject to group sanctions rather than merely deserving of personal penalties. The reason for this is, at least functionally, the safety of the group; and it is supported by the inherited, defined, and maintained attitudes of the ancestors. My reason for pointing to these vital, survival, and social motivations in African life is to make more meaningful their belief and valuation system, particularly in their individual manifestations.

AFRICAN VALUATIONS AND CONTINUITY OF LIFEWAYS

Lucy Mair (1974), recalling the changes wrought in modern Africa, answers her own question as to whether traditional lifeways are still worth studying:

> Yet when an anthropologist is able to revisit the scene of fieldwork done thirty or forty years ago, he does not find it unrecognizable; and anthropologists doing their first fieldwork today find themselves observing, with all the money, all the schooling, all the work in town, all the transistor radios, the institutions of non-mechanised societies [Mair, 1974, p. 13].

Retention of Religious Traditions

Missionaries as well as anthropologists experience that much of African life, in spite of weekly visits to mosques and churches, in spite of ad-

herence to modern laws and observances, retains a great part of its religious past. In fact, the very doubts, dilemmas, and uncertainties caused
by modern churches, schools, and cities prompt many Africans back to
the beliefs, prayers, and sacrifices of their respective traditions (Sidhom,
1969; Mbiti, 1969a). African and other scholars have sought to interpret and coordinate them. One should neither overromanticize nor over-
criticize: cultural ideals are real, though never realized. The late Professor Evans-Pritchard (1965) has noted that while Lévy-Bruhl was looking
for the pre-logical characteristics of the "primitive mentality," Vilfredo
Pareto was showing how non-logical sentimental actions were characteristic of modern society. We have advanced beyond the naïveté of the
not-too-distant past when scholars, not to mention the unlearned public,
assumed that Africans were bereft of intellectual, religious, political, economic, and cultural competence. One does not have to be a thoroughgoing functionalist to see that every myth, symbol, and ritual, however
right or wrong in itself, has a certain plausibility, given the premisses of
the total system.

These premisses and systems are not completely the same throughout
sub-Saharan Africa. The shedding of blood in circumcision and clitoridectomy is sacred to several peoples, but the Akan of Ghana prohibit
ritual shedding of life-symbolizing blood. Neighboring peoples in middle
Nigeria treat unknown visitors respectively with suspicion and utmost
hospitality. Neighboring peoples in northern Nigeria and central Sudan,
with respectively similar origins, cultures, and religions, nevertheless differ greatly in their experience and ascription of witchcraft. Some peoples
deify the greatest of their ancestors, others do not. Some admit divorce
quite casually, others almost completely ban it. Some, increasingly fewer,
insist on and sanction premarital virginity, others have no regard for it.
Some maintain preferential mating, others free choice in marriage partners; some are endogamous, others exogamous. But, whatever the variety
of these institutional patterns and cultural traits, they are always the
particular people's policy for achieving or maintaining their ultimate
value, namely: to acquire life, to live strongly, to make life stronger, or
to ensure that the life force will remain perpetually in one's posterity.

Evaluations of Life's Moments: Marriage, Childbirth

This brings us to the focal point of African evaluation. It is life; though
certainly not in the abstract, but in the concrete: living. But it is not the
life of the individual, wherever or whoever's it might be, in some individualistic sense; rather the life, the only life which is known and meaningful: namely, that of the community, inclusive of the divine Originator
of life, the living-dead ancestors, and all those living with the life in-

herited from those ancestors. This seems to be universally all-inclusive, but not quite. A typical tribal saying has it: "The things of Shilluk [the particular tribe] are good, the things of strangers are bad" (Sidhom, 1969, p. 99). There are remarkable characteristics of this life: participation in the spirit world, whose line of division from the empirical world of flesh and blood is not all that clear; its active interrelationship with all other members of the community's life universe; its inclusion of the dead who live simultaneously in their own spirit world; its limitation to past sources and present reality, with little concern for the day after tomorrow or the hereafter—a vital sense of *Urzeit*, but no sense of *Endzeit*, as John Mbiti (1969b, p. 163) puts it. Therefore, there is immediate concern with continuity; but no concern for future fulfillment, promise, or salvation in newness of life. Everything can be explained in terms of this life vision: spiritual sensitivity and material interest, fertility and witchery, High God and divinities, blood sacrifices and concern for life, assurance of immortality and fear of death.

We might view briefly some life moments in this vision. A first pregnancy, as the beginning of new life, is literally more than the life of the newly conceived: it is the sign of the arrival of the young wife to full community status.

> Unhappy the woman who fails to get children, for, whatever other qualities she may possess, her failure to bear children is worse than committing genocide: she has become the dead end of human life, not only for the genealogical line but also for herself [Mbiti, 1969a, p. 110].

Marriage is seen so much in terms of fertility function that sterility almost inevitably makes it a failure. Life must go on, and one must help it get on; if not, one is worthless to oneself and to the community. Among some peoples husband and wife do not rate as adult members of the community until they have produced more than two children. Almost universally prayers, blessings, and greetings include, often very beautifully, the themes of fertility, happiness with fruitfulness, and richness in children. A Kikuyu tradition requires that a married man drink his first beer only after his first child is born (Sidhom, 1969).

Rites connected with childbirth maintain the consciousness, not only of fertility, but also of membership in the community. The afterbirth might be thrown into the village stream to symbolize the child's belonging to all, no longer merely to the mother. The naming ceremony, in word and ritual, emphasizes that ancestors, tradition, and community are taken up in him. God is worshipped, ancestors are invoked with pride, the community rejoices. The arrival of twins or triplets occasions either additional joy or great consternation, the latter of which seems to derive from fear before the extraordinary and unexplained. Attributions of either adultery or demonic influence are accompanied by sanctions: death to one child or both, perhaps also to the mother. At the least there is sequestration, that the community be preserved from the contagion of uncleanness. In sharp contrast are the joyous welcome and special names accorded to twins in favorable communities.

Life Values in Other Rites of Passage

Names given to all children among many African peoples are meaningful and deliberately chosen. Often they recall the child's intervention in the family's or community's history; often they include an action, an attribute, a blessing of God. For example, at a recent naming ceremony in which I participated, the little girl received these names: Oluwatosin ("God is worthy of worship"), Opeyemi ("It is right for me to thank God"), Olawumi ("Honor delights me"), Ayotunde ("Joy returns"), Olugbolaromi ("God has surrounded me with honor"), and Olufemi ("God loves me"). All the names referred to or derived from some forebear and his/her experience. The new Christian baptismal rite, to which many have become accustomed since the Second Vatican Council, is quite prosaic in comparison with the apt variety of corporate involvement in these symbolic words, songs, and gestures; seeds of the earth and food attend the African child's naming. Thereafter the mother glows with the pride of achievement, her child at her breast or on her back, and the community rejoices with her.

Initiation or puberty ceremonies, next in the *rites de passage*, further express the meaning and value of life, individual but especially corporate. Many reports of third-world peoples' initiatory rites, particularly concerning sex, physical hardships, and mysterious revelations, impress the world of Christian tradition as quite shocking. Allowing for certain exaggerations in the telling and romanticism in the interpretation, we have to recognize their major contribution to personal growth and community vitality. If sex is essential to life, bravery to community defense, and knowledge of tradition to corporate continuity, it cannot be surprising that rites of graduation to young adulthood not only symbolize but demand evidence of some maturity in these matters.

Again Mbiti (1969a, chap. 12) is a helpful guide. He sees the cutting of sex organs, whether in circumcision, clitoridectomy, or otherwise, as "unlocking the issues of life." Seclusion and the physical testing of youths, whether in forests or in isolated huts, he understands as symbolizing death to childhood and selfishness. Brave victory over suffering is a kind of new birth, a resurrection, a return to community with a newness of life, adult powers, and corporate participation. The mysteries and practicalities of sex, marriage, and procreation, of community traditions and purposes, of responsibility for both the living-dead and future lives not yet born, are all revealed. It is understandable that a youth who cracks under the strain, or a girl who could not preserve her virginity, is not only a family disgrace but an offense to the whole community. Sometimes the price paid for such weakness is death on the altar of community life. Understandable, too, is the joy and pride of the community when members of a new age-group survive the initiatory tests with honor. It is also understandable that the Christian rite of confirmation, unless deeply understood and maturely received, is reckoned as quite tame in comparison.

Marriage, Procreation, and Corporate Life

From initiation we move on to full adult membership: marriage and procreation. For African peoples, marriage is not merely a normal personal fulfillment, but a normal corporate duty. Life is growth as well as continuity; marriage and procreation are normally integral to it; a non-participant is a non-starter in community life, odd, evidently subnormal. Sometimes indigent men in polygamous societies find potential wives preempted or too costly, and their bachelor existence is of mere marginal value. But women who are not wives and mothers are unnatural, or cursed, or both. Conversely, parents' blessings are in their children, not only because of the expected support in this life's old age, but because it is through their progeny that they expect to live hereafter. Having no descendants means having no future, no continuity of life: "Without children, who will remember you, who will honor you?" It is in one's children that one also pays the debt of life and obligation of immortality to one's own parents and earlier ancestors.

With this premiss we can appreciate the cultural integrality of such institutions, so often inconceivable to Western minds, as bride price, polygamy, levirate, sororate, inheritance of wives, and arranged marriages. Marriage and parenthood complete one's initiation into the community's life: everything else is subordinate to this. A barren marriage is intolerable; it must be made productive somehow—whether by divorce and remarriage, or by additional or surrogate spouse, or temporary mate, or otherwise. Preparation for this commitment to life in marriage includes a sex education generally superior to what is usually found in our modern heterogeneous societies.

Evidently the multiple African societies have a great variety of rituals and customs for celebrating marriage, but several common themes unite them: the service of future parents-in-law; moving from home and kin to new life; tokens of sacrifice in appreciation of the bride's life-producing worth and in payment for her parents' careful training; the washing of both partners in the same water, and the eating of foods symbolic of intercourse and fertility; bonds of friendship between the married couple's families; fertility, blessings, respect for ancestors, and so on.

Certain variations and modern developments make us realize, however, that African devotion to family life and fertility is often qualified. Recall the ban on twins among some peoples, mentioned earlier. In addition, many urban African families whose children are not "more arms on the farm" are less desirous of large families, and resort to abortion has become frequent—incomparably less than in "advanced" countries, but increasing nonetheless. There is need to reconcile or explain this valuation of life on the one hand, and willingness to destroy life on the other. Ultimately it is a matter of whose life is being valued; we shall return to this later.

Death and Immortality

Death is the last event in life, though life does not end. The belief in immortality seems to be almost universal among African peoples, though the understanding of it is quite varied. Idowu (1962, chap. 14) explains Yoruba belief in the normalcy of long life here and the certainty of joyous or sorrowful life hereafter depending on the character of earthly life. A short earthly life, especially when one has been barren or even when one is survived by one's parents, is tragic and open to suspicion of inimical or mysterious influences. A proverb says: "One cannot boast of having children unless one's children bury him." This is the guarantee of desired communion with earthly life in the next one.

Anomalies abound here, as in all eschatologies. But two convictions seem to be pervasive, and are expressed by many rituals for funerals and communion with deceased ancestors. First, life continues. It may be good or bad, limited to the spirit world or continuing in communion with the world of flesh, moving to a kind of divinization or return to earth in reincarnation. One might be buried quite naked as a sign of new birth in a new life, or quite enriched in clothing and food—even in human companions in earlier days—to prepare for the journey to the other world or to make a proper impression on arrival there. Frequently funerals for the elderly and successful are quite joyous celebrations; for young or unfulfilled lives, quite somber.

Secondly, as Mbiti interprets it, "Life in the hereafter inspires neither hope nor longing" (Mbiti, 1969b, p. 164). It is predicated on no belief in a resurrection, no hope in an elevation or growth or joyous, dynamic communion with God. Mbiti argues plausibly that here precisely Christianity can and does make a vital contribution to traditional African life, much as the latter could rejuvenate Christians' sensitivity to the existing spirit world of God and the living-dead and its influential closeness to our temporal world. Current Nigerian Christian death observances, particularly of the successful and elderly, contain a remarkable blend of religious and social celebration: public memorial announcements, well-attended liturgies, well-planned wakes, and lengthy social "outings." Several times recently, Nigerian priests and people alike have expressed the fervent wish that elderly missionaries remain among them, not only for an appreciated retirement, but for a deserved funeral celebration. They expressed sadness that often missionaries have gone home to lonely retirements and sparsely attended funerals. After a recent, truly inspiring funeral celebration of a well-known Nigerian priest, a prominent layman explained to me that an enthusiastic citywide public procession had been held the preceding evening so that children might realize that a celibate priest dies, not in a lonely manner, but with many hundreds or thousands of children to celebrate his passing.

A MAJOR CULTURAL ANOMALY

It cannot be surprising to the majority of people that most humans evaluate life highly. We have noted that the great moments in the lives of African persons and peoples, particularly as they are celebrated in the *rites de passage*, focus on life.

Pervasive Stress on Life and Living

We might preferably have developed a perhaps more subtle, more pervasive element in traditional African life: namely, the very language which expresses the realities of divinity and self, force and life, power and people, community of life of self, family, ancestors, and descendants. For example, as explained by Idowu (1962, pp. 60ff.; 1969, pp. 24ff.), one Yoruba word for God is *Orishe*, which, briefly, means "the source being which gives origin to all beings," and the Igbo name for God is *Chukwu* (from *Chi*, "overflowing essence of being," and *ukwu*, "immense containment"). But the very Yoruba and Igbo words for human essence, spirit, and personality are respectively *ori* and *chi*. He points to similar etymological connections in other West African languages.

Father Placide Tempels' *Bantu philosophy* (1959, p. 65 and passim) is a controversial, but much-appreciated, breakthrough which presents Bantu peoples' view of total reality, inclusive of God, man, and cosmos as "vital force." Each man, each member of a people, evidently God's own people, shares in, lives by, uses, and is used by, this vital force. God and man, man and community, life and death, corporeal and spiritual, empirical and non-empirical—all are joined in this vitality, this power, this dynamism (Mulago, 1969, pp. 149–50). Tempels makes it clear that this implies no monadic pantheism: Bantus affirm quite clearly "an essential difference between different beings, that is to say, different forces" (Tempels, 1959, p. 53). But reality is force; God is the greatest force, and man too is vitally forceful. Or, as Sawyer (1969, p. 72) puts it, life is not law but power, and power is goodness. It can be abused. Then recourse is had to High God, source of all power, that it be rectified. Thus immorality is not mere illegality but anti-life destructiveness (Adegbola, 1969, pp. 132ff.). The offering of sacrifice, for all its importance in men's relationship with God, is less to placate the divinity than to restore life's proper order, properly ordered power.

Greetings, prayers, and blessings presuppose, as well as express, this preoccupation with life. The developed world and its religions have no monopoly on essentially meaningful and truly uplifting prayer-forms. Proverbs, expressions of traditional wisdom, criteria of value derive from this centrality of life: God-life, man-life, people-life, cosmos-life. No wonder that suicide is extremely rare, and murder among a people both rare and subject to severe sanctions.

Enormous Destruction of Life

And yet, a major question remains: If human life is so highly valued, why is it so widely destroyed in Africa today? I do not refer to such events as the killing of twins, certain ritual slayings, and the former live burials of companions-designate for deceased kings. These, for all their horribleness to at least an outside world, have had a certain rationale compatible with a people's understanding of life and its due priorities. But what of today's million-plus African refugees who have fled for their lives from their respective countrymen? What of the killings in the tens and hundreds of thousands in Burundi and Ruanda, in Uganda and Ethiopia, in Sudan and Nigeria before the civil war? What of the almost minimal African concern for those dying of starvation in the recent Sahel and other droughts? Of the readiness to lynch seen or alleged thieves in a public marketplace, as happened recently in Onitsha? What of the public enthusiasm for open execution of convicted armed robbers, who have indeed come to be a veritable plague in recent years? What of the willingness of many, touched apparently by Western consumerism and social ladder-climbing, to resort to abortion in various inconvenient situations?

One should have to do much more research, be much more knowledgeable than anyone now is, to offer any kind of adequate answer to this question. We remind ourselves that many Africans, just as Asians and Americans, are at various points along the continuum of degrees of respect for various human values. However, it is most likely that an answer would be found which would derive from the kind of human life the African peoples value. The fact is that the African peoples, as others throughout human history, have identified human life with their own God and with their own people as the people of God. The names of many people—for example, the American Indian Cheyenne, the Irani, the Slavs, the Bantus, the Bachama, to mention only a few—mean humanity, or men, or noble men, or something similar. Implicitly the names seem to say: we are distinctive people; we derive from our ancestors and go back to God; we are His people. Whatever other two-legged creatures may be, we are the ones who count, and others cannot be important in comparison with us. This might be the mere rationalization of a self-survival policy. Certainly it is not unique in human past and recent history. It is subject to modification as circumstances change. In the ongoing evolution from more homogeneous to more heterogeneous social life, various national and tribal values can yield to class and personal values.

Meanwhile there has been little practical integration with supra-national religious traditions, in particular because the world which has historically housed those traditions and their values has itself violated them so frequently. Religion itself is a great part of this heterogeneity: the plurality of Christian and Muslim denominations and sects, the varieties of ideology and the degrees of secular accommodation even within them, and their diverse combinations with religions of the soil, all of which contributes to the weakening of values which were once strongly maintained.

In their place is coming that combination of consumerism and materialism so characteristic of the technologically affluent and competitive world. One must be careful to avoid exaggeration, especially during this time of transition, but it seems beyond doubt less true to say of African life today, "to be is to be religious in a religious universe."

Of course the question can be raised whether the pursuit of the better life, the life of quality rather than mere quantity, is really so much different from the past. Every people, every age, every religion, has its own gods, and the great god may always be self-survival and fulfillment; its appearance, no less than cases, being changed by circumstances. Whereas almost any human life within the community would have been traditionally valued, especially when "more arms on the farm" were so important, now it is more a matter of whether particular human lives are competitively acceptable. The same god gives different answers.

It might finally be asked whether historically and pervasively religious Africa will be absorbed in the tide of materialistic preoccupations. If so, it stands to lose that possible fulfillment of technological progress blended with religious humanization; indeed it will even lose its parallel world of the living-dead. On the other hand, if Christianity and Islam might more effectively meet, draw upon, and elevate the traditional and still continuing African religiousness, we can have an increased appreciation and direction of life more compatible with God-given human potentiality.

REFERENCES

Adegbola, E. A. The theological basis of ethics. In K. Dickson & P. Ellingworth (Eds.), *Biblical revelation and African beliefs*. London: Lutterworth, 1969. Pp. 116–136.
Breese, G. (Ed.). *The city in newly developing countries: Readings in urbanism and urbanization*. Englewood Cliffs, N.J.: Prentice-Hall, 1969.
Douglas, M. The Lele of Kasai. In D. Forde (Ed.), *African worlds: Studies in the cosmological ideas and social values of African peoples*. London: Oxford University Press, 1954. Pp. 1–26. (Repr. New York: Oxford University Press, 1963.)
Evans-Pritchard, E. E. (Ed.). *The institutions of primitive society*. Oxford: Blackwell, 1961.
Evans-Pritchard, E. E. *Theories of primitive religion*. London: Oxford University Press, 1965.
Idowu, E. B. *Olodumare: God in Yoruba belief*. London: Longmans, 1962.
Idowu, E. B. God. In K. Dickson & P. Ellingworth (Eds.), *Biblical revelation and African beliefs*. London: Lutterworth, 1969. Pp. 17–29.
Little, K. The Mende in Sierra Leone. In D. Forde (Ed.), *African worlds: Studies in the cosmological ideas and social values of African peoples*. London: Oxford University Press, 1954. Pp. 111–137. (Repr. New York: Oxford University Press, 1963.)
Mair, L. P. *African societies*. London: Cambridge University Press, 1974.
Mayer, P. Migrancy and the study of Africans in towns. In P. L. van den Berghe (Ed.), *Africa: Social problems of change and conflict*. San Francisco: Chandler, 1965. Pp. 305–324.
Mbiti, J. S. *African religions and philosophy*. London: Heinemann, 1969. (a)
Mbiti, J. S. Eschatology. In K. Dickson & P. Ellingworth (Eds.), *Biblical revelation and African beliefs*. London: Lutterworth, 1969. Pp. 159–184. (b)
Mulago, V. Vital participation. In K. Dickson & P. Ellingworth (Eds.), *Biblical revelation and African beliefs*. London: Lutterworth, 1969. Pp. 137–158.
Ottenberg, S., & Ottenberg, P. (Eds.). *Cultures and societies of Africa*. New York: Random House, 1960.
Sawyer, H. Sacrifice. In K. Dickson & P. Ellingworth (Eds.), *Biblical revelation and African beliefs*. London: Lutterworth, 1969. Pp. 57–82.
Sidhom, S. The theological estimate of man. In K. Dickson & P. Ellingworth (Eds.), *Biblical revelation and African beliefs*. London: Lutterworth, 1969. Pp. 83–115.
Tempels, P. *Bantu philosophy*. Paris: Présence Africaine, 1959.

The Value of Human Life
in Technological Society

VICTOR FERKISS

Victor Ferkiss received his A.B. from the University of California, Berkeley in 1948, his M.A. from Yale in 1950, and his Ph.D. from the University of Chicago in 1954. He was a Rockefeller Foundation Fellow in Political Philosophy, 1958–59. Before coming to Georgetown University where he is currently Professor of Government, Dr. Ferkiss taught at the University of Montana and at St. Mary's College of California. He is a member of the American Political Science Association and the author of the following three books: Africa's search for identity *(1966),* Technological man *(1969), and* The future of technological civilization *(1974).*

What is a technological society? In what ways do human beings in a technological society view life and its values differently from human beings in other societies?

SIGNIFICANCE OF TECHNOLOGY FOR MAN

Human beings are animals, and they have material needs. Other animals may occasionally use what can be called technologies to satisfy their needs. Birds build nests, beavers build dams. Various creatures use what can only be called tools for various purposes. But from his earliest days man has made and used a variety of tools for a variety of purposes.

29

Technology is not new. All societies have been based on technologies, whether the bow and arrow of the hunter, the primitive hoes and irrigation ditches of early agriculturalists, or the increasingly complex machines of modern times. Modern industrial society is distinguished from earlier societies not by its use of technologies—and it should be remembered that technologies include organizational forms and techniques as well as purely material artifacts—but by the power and ubiquitousness of these technologies and the increasingly complex nature of its dependence upon them.

Modern society is further distinguished from earlier societies by the very purpose of its technologies. In earlier societies the primary purpose of the technologies was subsistence and survival—as an old-fashioned phrase has it: "keeping body and soul together." Human beings needed food, shelter, and clothing in order to continue to live and to perform the basic physiological, social, and cultural activities which constitute human life. Technologies were not simply means toward ends, but means toward the predetermined ends of persons who derived their identity and values from sources other than their tools and techniques.

In earlier societies men and women made modest demands on technology—it was called on to sustain life. But life remained a fragile and risky business. Suspended between birth and death human beings lived in fear of forces beyond their control—the arbitrariness of nature and their fellows, the stringent limits of their powers over the world and themselves, the inevitable necessity of death. To make life bearable in such an insecure existence they turned to various cultural forms, to art and music, and, above all, to religion. Contingent events were not arbitrary because they reflected the will of supernatural beings; death could be overcome or at least given acceptable meaning through religious beliefs and practices. Finiteness, contingency, mortality: the consciousness of these things distinguished man from his fellow-animals, and their mystery haunted him.

SATISFACTIONS IN LIFE OPENED BY MODERN TECHNOLOGY

What distinguishes contemporary technological society from previous societies is that human beings are turning more and more to technology to overcome the very mysteries of finiteness and contingency which in earlier societies were dealt with in religious terms. Through science we can predict events; through technology we can control them. Proponents of cryogenics hope that eventually technology can literally overcome death itself. In such a setting all values are subtly transfigured and transformed. Self-fulfillment does not mean realizing whatever potentialities are offered by one's nature and "station in life." There is literally no limit to what we can know, the places we can visit, the sights and sounds we can hear, the experiences we can have. Where earlier technologies sought to enable human beings to perform those physical activities which they were fated to perform, modern technology holds out the hope of ever increasing activity in ever increasing variety. Earlier technologies ministered to human needs; modern technology attempts to fulfill human desires.

To state the matter thus is, of course, vastly to oversimplify. Human beings have always sought to overcome or to test the limits which fate placed upon them. Explorers, artists, conquerors, or simply the greedy are not new to human history. Most human beings even today, especially in the less developed countries, have modest aspirations for satisfaction in life, seeking only to sustain life, enjoy a few simple pleasures, see their children grow to maturity, refresh themselves for their necessary tasks. But technology has made a difference for vast millions of men and women. It has not only democratized affluence, making the life of ordinary citizens richer in experience than those of kings in the past, but in doing so it has democratized *hubris* as well. That the dreams of most will never be fulfilled is beside the point. Their non-fulfillment is more of an artifact of social factors than a limit imposed by nature. Some combinations of possibilities are inherently contradictory—no single individual is likely to be able to become both an astronaut and a great violin virtuoso, or both a prima ballerina and a major medical researcher. Skills and forms of training are often intrinsically incompatible, and time —time—time still remains an oppressive check on our multiple aspirations. But for the most part earlier notions of limits to the possible fulfillment of desires have lost most of their traditional meaning for human beings.

It is easy to see how modern science and technology with their attendant mastery over natural impediments and scarcity—for many people for a period in history at least—have opened new possibilities for the fulfillment of desire and made earlier concepts of humility, poverty, and self-denial largely meaningless. The average inhabitant of a developed society can eat almost anything he wants when he wants it, dress according to his own whims, shelter himself in a luxury denied to the richest of earlier ages, attain a longer life span, and remain active often until the moment of death. Only the wealthiest can choose anything they want anytime they want it, but most people can have almost anything they want at least some of the time. Furthermore, in a money/market economy virtually all goods are interchangeable. The most ordinary physical needs are in the same market as the most elevated cultural possibilities. This radically alters the meaning of traditional moral concepts such as greed and moderation. In a world of technologically conditioned poten-

tial affluence, the notion of need and duties appropriate to various stations in life becomes almost meaningless. To give up the fruits of technology is to give up part of one's personality.

For in technological society not only does technology provide the material basis for new experience and personal growth, it provides experience itself, sometimes directly, sometimes vicariously. Modern means of
transportation make it possible for most to travel around the world (if
they are willing to forgo something else to do so). Inexpensive books, art
reproductions, phonograph records, and the mass media make it possible
to enjoy a cultural life undreamed of in quantity and variety in other
ages. One can choose (while off the job at least or, if one has an independent income, on a fulltime basis) a wide variety of special lifestyles.
(Recently newspapers reported the case of a young man who had chosen
to live in the late-nineteenth century, dressing in Victorian clothes, living
in a house without electricity, cooking and performing all household
chores with antique devices, living completely surrounded by the books
and pictures of his chosen era.) And chosen lifestyles need not be permanent. We can change them if we find them unsatisfactory, and in a
sense we can have a variety of identities in the course of a lifetime.

One great boon to the choice of alternative means of fulfillment has
been the technologies of birth control. Sexual life, within or outside of
marriage, can be carried on without the burden of large numbers of children or any children at all. This provides opportunities for hitherto im-
practical careers for women, and allows couples not only higher dispos-
able incomes but greater flexibility in changing their place of residence
and allocating their time.

A recent study (Campbell, 1975) suggests that childless marriages—
especially now that they have lost their social stigma—are happier than
marriages with children. Obviously the individual's choice of lifestyle in
this area requires rejecting other alternatives—celibacy and marriage
and extramarital cohabitation logically exclude one another. But not entirely. The ability to control when one has children, combined with a
longer healthy life span, means that couples can have a family life for
many years and then live long and happily as "empty nesters," or, as
may increasingly be the case, decide once the children are grown to go
their separate ways to live as singles or to enter into new, childless marriages. Technology clearly makes a major contribution to the availability of alternative lifestyles.

THE BASIC VALUES IN A TECHNOLOGICAL SOCIETY

All the above-mentioned choices of lifestyle depend on one thing: the
productive mechanism of technological society must be kept in good run-

ning order. If the machine fails to deliver its affluence, the possibilities of fulfillment which it provides become problematic. When unemployment strikes, the young couple may have to move back in with their parents; the trip to Europe may be postponed during economic recession; a gasoline shortage means the use of the automobile may have to be curtailed. The price of escaping contingency and finiteness through technology is to accept the primacy of keeping the machine in running order. There is one thing about which technological society cannot be permissive: keeping the machine of the technostructure greased. There is one ideological deviation which it cannot tolerate: the questioning of the premisses of the technologically conditioned good life.

Thus the basic values implicit in technological society might be said to be the primacy of means over ends. Ends are fluid and subjective, but the means must be kept available. Technology thus becomes an end in itself. And the result is that particular individual techniques tend to become ends in themselves. Indeed, according to Ellul and others (Ellul, 1964; Habermas, 1970), in technological society the principal criterion for deciding what *will* be done is whether it *can* be done. Can we build an SST? Fine. Then we will build it. Can we send a man to the moon? Great. Let men be sent. Can we clone human beings? Possibly. Let us try. Technology knocks at the door, and human beings must answer.

Certainly there are tendencies in this direction in technological society, but the matter is not quite this simple. There are many things we can do which we do not do. We could build safer automobiles, more durable consumer goods, better insulated houses. We could provide more adequate medical care for the poor and make sure that children have better diets than those provided by junk foods. This is not done. Why? Because what is technologically feasible may be ignored for political or economic reasons. Considerations of profit and power determine what will be developed, produced, and distributed in society. Not only is man the servant of his technology; technology is the servant of the powerful in society.

Yet in spite of this, technology seems to run rampant. Why? Because there is profit to be derived from new technologies. New technologies are introduced in order to make money or to add to the power of those already in control or even, sometimes, simply to satisfy the whims of the influential. Their introduction is facilitated immensely by the basic ideology of technological society: the belief that technology is the key to human happiness. Opposition to the SST is labeled an attempt to "stop" progress; opposition to certain forms of genetic manipulation is "medieval" or obscurantist; opposition to the proliferation of dangerous nuclear power plants will prevent us from meeting our energy "needs." If an ideology, as Marx holds, serves as a rationalization for the structure of power in a society, then Herbert Marcuse (1964) and his disciples are right in arguing that technology has become the dominant ideology in our society. No values—clean air, clean water, quiet, safety, biological or psychological integrity, or privacy—can remain superordinate without a continuous struggle.

THE PROBLEM OF ALIENATION

Insofar as technology has become an end in itself in technological society, human beings are faced with the problem of alienation. We have lost our freedom in that we have become identified with something else; as Erich Fromm argues, we have become idolators in the true sense of the word, making things we have created into gods (Fromm, 1968). For traditional Marxism, alienation developed in the process of production in industrial society, and man sacrificed his identity to the goods he produced. The worker lost control of himself when he lost control over his labor and the product of his labor. For neo-Marxists such as Marcuse the process of alienation has been identified, more accurately, as occurring in the process of consumption (Marcuse, 1964). We lose ourselves not in what we produce but in what we consume. We identify with our homes, our automobiles, the kinds of places we can afford to eat in or visit. We travel not to see new things but to take pictures of our travels to show to others. We live inauthentic lives, cut off from our real selves.

A TECHNOLOGICAL SOCIETY ALTERS VALUES

Critics of technological society present a long litany of indictments along these lines. Much of it is overdrawn, but there is a core of validity. There is no question that living in a technological society presents human beings with new constraints as well as new opportunities, and alters their perceptions as well as their values.

Thus in a technological society we inevitably depend for our continued existence (as well as for the means to fulfill our aspirations) upon the activity of others and our cooperation with them. The traditional subsistence farmer needs only his ancestral land, some seed, his own labor, and the favor of God in granting good weather. Our ability to work depends on the skills we have acquired in school or through the tutelage of others, the processes of capital formation, the vagaries of personnel offices, the fiscal policies of government, the tastes of consumers or clients, and so on. We are dependent, part of a system. We are players of roles. We enforce rules not of our own making; we follow the designs and dictates of others. Only a handful of people—craftsmen and a few professionals—have much say about their own

2007460

work, and even they depend on the tolerance or desires of others. Painters without patrons starve.

Not only how we work but how we consume depends on others. However great the variety of consumer goods available, it is finite. The more important an item is, the less free our choice. We cannot buy automobiles with certain characteristics. We cannot do without an automobile and live in a certain kind of dwelling within a certain distance of our work. Things we like "go off the market." Proponents of the free-market system may argue that the structure of choice results from collective choices freely made through the market mechanism, but for us as individuals the failure of a store to continue to stock our favorite brand of coffee is a restriction of our freedom. We may have a bewildering range of choices, but they are choices structured by others.

Even our process of choice depends on the technological system in which we live. Advertising persuades us, or sets up a clamor among our children. The mass media shape our attitudes, or if not ours (surely not ours), then those of our children or neighbors, who thus influence our own behavior. And, for many of us, drugs—alcohol or marijuana, stimulants or depressants—may also affect our perceptions and our attitudes.

Not only does technological society affect us directly; it controls us indirectly as well. The automobile shapes our cities and destroys old neighborhoods. The pill changes the tone of family life whether we as individuals use it or not. Migrations of others affect the nature of our cities and states. More and more we find ourselves living in a changing world, subject to what one writer has called "future shock" (Toffler, 1971).

All these pressures affect and threaten our identity as human beings. How many of them result directly from technology or from specific technologies, and how many from increased population and the increasing bureaucratization of society, are matters of nuance and detail. Our present large population-concentrations could not exist and would not affect us in quite the way they do without technology. Bureaucracy, too, is technologically conditioned. Collectively the impact upon us is the impact of technological society.

INFLUENCE OF TECHNOLOGY ON BIRTH

How does technological society condition our values with regard to birth and death, and to life in general? I argued earlier that technology seeks to enable us to obtain the maximum fulfillment of our desires—which are assumed to be subjective—and to fulfill them by the rational use of scientific and technological power. Thus birth ideally occurs only when a child is wanted—that is, is deemed by its potential parents as enabling them to fulfill certain of their perceived desires for an object of affection, for social approval of their role as parents, or for something to occupy their time and energies. Potential children unable to fulfill these functions are considered dispensable and can be disposed of or avoided by various technological means. Since deformity and disease present challenges which most potential parents obviously do not relish, the possibility of eliminating certain abnormal children at or before birth may be entertained, and the possibility of fetal therapy to eliminate defects prior to birth is welcomed. So also is the possibility of choosing a child's sex, since this would optimize the satisfactions a child would provide the potential parents. Also approved are means to render the infertile woman capable of having a child. For some the possibility of conceiving children without intercourse or "bearing" them without the discomfort of pregnancy may also be regarded as desirable. Pregnancy as a state in itself may be welcomed by some, but this is also a matter of subjective preference. Children should be born, when possible, in hospitals rather than at home because this is the most efficient way from the point of view of the medical delivery system, optimizing both the safety of mother and child and the convenience of the staff.

The number and timing of births within a family-type unit should, of course, also be a matter of choice so that they can be related to other satisfactions sought by the potential parents, including economic and career activities, optimal sexual activity, and ability to plan the life cycle in terms of periods free from dependent children. The total number of births within the human family as a whole should ideally be regulated so as to provide only that number which can have a reasonable opportunity for the kinds of fulfillment now deemed possible and desirable for normal human beings. In a world in which misery is presumed no longer inevitable for most people, its continued proliferation through overpopulation is not only positively undesirable from the point of view of the miserable but an affront and threat to those better situated to take advantage of the new possibilities which technological society offers.

Action taken prior to birth can not only eliminate defects but produce a person who after birth will have greater opportunities for fulfillment. Genetic manipulation or *in utero* techniques such as oxygen therapy may make it possible for individuals to be stronger or more intelligent than they otherwise might be, or even to have abilities hitherto the properties of gods. The "six million dollar man" of television fame may yet walk among us if the money can be raised. Drugs and hormones are already being used to increase the strength, stamina, and ability of professional athletes to resist pain, at least temporarily. Some new technologically derived possibilities have the potential for directly affecting our perceptual systems. Drugs have always been used to heighten human consciousness; technology has simply provided new synthetic ones such as LSD. But now there is the possibility of stimulating the nervous system directly in order to produce sensations, and the possibility even of imprinting knowledge in our memories.

INFLUENCE OF TECHNOLOGY ON DEATH

Death has always been the greatest menace to human felicity. The late Ernest Becker has suggested that it, rather than sex, is the feared, repressed thing and sex—generation implying decay—simply its surrogate (Becker, 1973). We can delay death through better medical care, though we seem to have reached a plateau—a somewhat precarious one—in this respect. We can do much more to mitigate the effects of the decay which leads to death by keeping human beings functioning nearer optimum capacity later in life (though many of our efforts are mocked by the normal condition of some primitive peoples). We have not yet conquered death, though there are those who through quick-freezing techniques hope to make eventual revival possible, and organ transplants may cheat death at least temporarily. But death still remains inevitable. Most people die as they are born, in hospitals, and death can be even lonelier than birth, completely among strangers. More and more often people die while unconscious as a result of current techniques for prolonging life beyond normal functioning. Medical technology operates on the principle of maximizing efficiency in keeping people alive (in the sense of maintaining certain narrowly defined vital functions) even long after consciousness or ability to act has ceased.

There is continuing pressure in technological society to make the time of death a matter of choice as the event of birth is, one which would depend primarily on the decision of the potential "dier" (we have no good form for this predication for significant cultural reasons, since death is normally passive) as to whether continued life would represent fulfillment of desires. From birth through death and in between we see the same basic cultural drives at work. Each person within his or her ambit of decision seeks to affect events so as to fulfill his or her image of what he or she would like to be, and to fulfill it through the powers which technology gives us over nature, society, and ourselves.

THE SHIFT FROM IGNORANCE OF POSSIBILITIES TO IGNORANCE OF OUTCOMES

The same technological powers which provide new opportunities for self-expression also menace our selfhood, and not only through those often hidden compulsions which the critics of technological society stress. Technology, by freeing us from the traditional forms of our lives, threatens to alienate us from our very generic identity as human beings.

It is not so much that we are compelled to do things we do not wish to do as that we no longer have any idea of what we wish to do. It is not that we are alienated from our true selves as that we no longer have any true selves.

As I indicated earlier, the indictment of technological society as alienating and as threatening human values and identity, though powerful, is not absolutely overwhelming. Let us call as a witness—really as a "devil's advocate"—the psychologist B. F. Skinner. He has been roundly condemned for envisioning a technologically conditioned utopia in which everyone would behave properly because everyone would have been conditioned to do so by the wise (i.e., persons such as he). Critics argue that such a state of affairs would constitute a terrible infringement of human freedom. Skinner replies that everyone is conditioned anyway, by families, peers, and society. Why not do it consciously and openly? Others ask "Who will guard the guardians?" Skinner is free to reply by asking who controls the forces which control society today (Skinner, 1972).

The point, of course, is that throughout history human beings (at least since the Fall) have sought to fulfill their desires by using whatever means have been available. Why not? What else is there for them to do? Where do these desires come from? From human nature, obviously. How are they directed toward particular means of fulfillment? By stimuli from outside. Everyone seeks happiness, as Aristotle and Aquinas told us long ago. The problem is one of means.

Do not some seek happiness through the wrong means? Of course. They are blinded by ignorance and passion. But ignorance and passion antedate technological society. What technological society has done is to change the nature of ignorance. No longer are we as ignorant of possibilities as we once were, or perhaps as *a priori* in our choosing among them. As to which possibility will lead us to true happiness, that is another matter, more difficult to measure subjectively. Not only has technological society changed the nature of ignorance from ignorance of possibilities to ignorance of outcomes, it has democratized choice, making it possible for more of us to fulfill our passions, whatever they may be. And it has loosened the social bonds which often restrained us in seeking to fulfill our passions in past eras. Modern society, it can be argued, has democratized the vices of the aristocracy. So be it. But should the possibility of doing the wrong thing be limited to a few, while all others do the "right" thing through lack of effective freedom?

RESPONSES TO THE IMPACT OF TECHNOLOGY ON HUMAN VALUES

The discussion of alienation begs the question of what we are alienated from and who we are. It tends to assume that in the absence of choice we would be "ourselves." But "ourselves" is the outcome of the choices made for us by nature and by others. We are born into a certain family —save for the abandoned—in a certain class in a certain country. We go to schools run by others and read books written by others and listen to advice from others. When we are young we have little control over the stimuli which assault us. As we grow older we can have somewhat more choice of schools or stimuli or companions. But these choices are not only necessarily limited but conditioned by the previous choices which have been made for us. Who we are is the result of what our genetic inheritance and our society have made us. Is an identity somehow more authentic because we have not "chosen" it? That is the real issue.

Put another way: if human values are other than those values chosen by particular human beings, they must have another source and measure. To say that technological society destroys the "authentic" we must have some way of knowing what the authentic is. We can see this issue more clearly if we look at some of the responses which have resulted from the concern of sensitive people with the impact of technology upon values and human life generally in contemporary society. Note that these responses have been generated primarily in the United States and to a lesser extent in other highly developed and affluent societies. Most of the people of the less developed nations are still in the stage of embracing technology as a means to the alleviation of such ancient scourges as hunger and disease.

Neo-Romanticism

One response takes the form of neo-romanticism. Technology and science emphasize rationality, and rationality can be viewed as coercive, since if there is one best way of doing something—one optimum choice —the intelligent person is forced to choose it. Thus to regain freedom one must act irrationally. Following this logic one can elevate passion over reason as in classic romanticism and such derivatives as abound in the "counter culture" (Roszak, 1969, 1972).

Naturalism

As an alternative, one can choose to act arbitrarily rather than rationally as in Nietzschean nihilism and later "existentialist" philosophies. One consults one's own libido, one's own unrestrained ego, one's own inspiration or whim or blood or whatever, and makes it the source of values. The "natural" is opposed first to the conventional and then, as technological civilization succeeds bourgeois civilization, to the scientifically conditioned rational. The appeal to the natural is reflected in general terms in a veneration of the existing configuration of physical nature as in the value system which some have styled the "new naturalism" (Yankelovitch, 1972) or, specifically, in opposition to the mechanization and physical degradation of the environment found in the ecology movement. At base this involves a kind of nature worship which makes nature either the object of values or, in a more modified form, the standard of values. Nature knows best.*

Supernaturalism

Another way in which resistance to technological norms can be manifested is in various forms of fideism and religious fundamentalism. In this view the world is the province of technology, in part because it is the province of the evil one. One may make use of technology for instrumental purposes, but one's attention is focused not on human values but on supernatural ones. This world is a vale of tears which has little intrinsic value, and technology is just another form of worldly snare. Thus one can escape from the domination of man by technology and from the loss of authenticity and identity by finding these values exclusively embodied in the spiritual life. This has always been a basic orientation in Protestant fundamentalism, and recent changes within Catholicism, in which the primacy of Scripture has been emphasized, have brought Catholics closer to this outlook. It involves the incidental rejection of the natural law tradition and of the concept of the importance of philosophy and of philosophically oriented theology, and thus repeats the evolution of early Protestantism and its rejection of the Hellenic aspects of medieval civilization. Values come not from nature— in opposition to technology—but from the "outside" in a universe viewed in dualistic terms.

Return to Traditional Value Systems

Some groups and individuals have sought refuge from technological society by returning to specific traditional value systems. The new emphasis upon ethnicity—whether by blacks, Jews, Poles, or Italians—illustrates this. We will live the way we do in accordance, not with the norms of technological civilization, but with those of our own heritage. These groups say, in effect, that their ways may or may not be "natural" or "scriptural" but that they are authentically theirs. They are not generalizable norms for others but particular historically generated ways in

* Though it is sometimes not realized because of their different sociological and historical origins, traditional natural law thinking and the ecological movement have much in common.

which some people act. This group withdrawal is akin to and often associated with a "privitization" at the level of the individual or family; this "privitization" dictates that people seek the maximum of fulfillment according to some personal vision of the good life—however derived— which will enable them to pick and choose among the possibilities technological society offers but which they regard as neither a guide for others nor normative for society as a whole.

Technology Assessment

By no means have all who refuse to accept the value autonomy of technological norms, or to concede to them the position of superordinate values in our society, chosen the paths of romantic rejection, naturalism, supernaturalism, or ethnic or individual withdrawal. Many have sought to tame technology to make it instrumental to independently derived human ends. The current movement for "technology assessment"— embodied at the governmental level in both the Office of Technology Assessment and the Environmental Protection Agency—represents attempts within the framework of liberal democratic political institutions to make technological activities subordinate to externally derived human values. But what human values? The whole matter of abortion and fetal and genetic research provides an illustration of the problems involved, in spite of the fact that because of the social power of the medical profession it has not been discussed—as it logically should have been— primarily in the general context of technology assessment. In a pluralist society consensus on values is difficult to obtain. In our contemporary society the values of technological rationalization have already been accepted by a large part of the population, explicitly or implicitly, and thus are among the sets of values competing for incarnation in social policy. Technological values more and more often prevail because they are a matter of conscious choice.

CONCLUSION

Contrary to the belief of many contemporary theorists I would argue that values can be objectively derived and defended (Ferkiss, 1974). But this is not the place to choose among the various value positions currently being propounded by theorists of public policy. The point is that the choice must be made. If one objects to certain of the values which technological society imposes or permits, it is not enough to say that its norms are "unauthentic" and therefore ought to be rejected. One cannot defend the "authentic" in the abstract, or use it as a standard of comparison. One must have some reasoned definition of what the authentic human being is and some vision of the good life and the good society. Simply denouncing technology and its consequences will not do. Value choice is not automatic. To say that someone should not choose to live in a fantasy world made possible by drugs, one must be able to define reality and to defend its superiority to illusion. To say that certain lifestyles now made possible by technology are not desirable, one must have a reasoned argument as to why others are better.

Technology has become the modern equivalent of the Fall. We have eaten of the tree of good and evil and cannot return to the Garden of Eden. We cannot reject the choices made possible by technology by nostalgically returning to an era in which choices were precluded by circumstances, in which freedom was restricted by poverty and ignorance. Human values are now irretrievably a matter of choice, subject only to those constraints—however considerable—which physical nature imposes upon us and which technology cannot overcome even when it seeks to do so. What we do about birth, life, and death, and why, and how we value them are matters we must now decide for ourselves.

REFERENCES

Becker, E. *The denial of death*. New York: Free Press, 1973.
Campbell, A. The American way of mating: Marriage si, children only maybe. *Psychology Today*, May 1975, pp. 37–43.
Ellul, J. *The technological society*. New York: Knopf, 1964.
Ferkiss, V. *The future of technological civilization*. New York: Braziller, 1974.
Fromm, E. *The revolution of hope*. New York: Bantam, 1968.
Habermas, J. *Toward a rational society*. Boston: Beacon, 1970.
Marcuse, H. *One dimensional man*. Boston: Beacon, 1964.
Roszak, T. *The making of a counter culture*. Garden City, N.Y.: Doubleday, 1969.
Roszak, T. *Where the wasteland ends*. Garden City, N.Y.: Doubleday, 1972.
Skinner, B. F. *Beyond freedom and dignity*. New York: Bantam, 1972.
Toffler, A. *Future shock*. New York: Bantam, 1971.
Yankelovitch, D. *The changing values on campus*. New York: Washington Square Press, 1972.

II
PROBLEMS OF BIRTH:
POPULATION PROBLEMS

The World Population Situation: Current Trends and Issues

MARY G. POWERS

Mary G. Powers obtained her B.S. degree from Central Connecticut State College in 1955, her M.A. from the University of Massachusetts in 1957, and her Ph.D. from Brown University in 1963. From 1962 to 1965 she was a Demographer– Statistician with the Population Division of the United States Bureau of the Census. Dr. Powers came to Fordham University in 1965, where she is currently Professor of Sociology. She was Chairman of the Sociology/Anthropology Department from 1972 until 1975. She is the author, either singly or in collaboration, of somewhat over a dozen articles in scientific and professional journals, most of them dealing with population problems and urban sociology. Dr. Powers is a member of the American Sociological Association, the American Statistical Association, the Population Association of America, and the International Union for the Scientific Study of Population.

THE WORLD SETTING: PEOPLE, NATIONS, AND RESOURCES

Population issues must be defined in terms of existing people, nations, and resources. At present, planet earth has approximately 4 billion people, 163 nations, and increasingly scarce resources, as evidenced by the current food and fuel crises. Perhaps more important is the fact that, at the present growth rate of about 2% per year, world population increases by 76 million to 80 million persons annually! These figures are staggering, but all the more so when viewed in historical perspective. It took from the beginning of man's history until about 1830 for the world population to reach 1 billion. By 1930, only 100 years later, the second billion was added, and by 1960, 30 years later, the third billion was added. In 1975, only 15 years later, there were about 4 billion people unevenly distributed around the globe.

If present trends continue, there will be from 7 billion to 8 billion people on earth by the end of the century.* At this rate a doubling of food production by the year 2000 will be required merely to maintain present per capita levels of consumption. And present rates of consumption are not especially good in many parts of the world. Some agronomists maintain that food production can never be sufficient if population continues to grow at 2% per year. But more than one demographer has noted that contemporary rates of population growth could not possibly have been sustained for long periods of time in the past, and are not likely to persist for very long into the future. In other words, population growth cannot exceed the carrying capacity of the earth in the long run (Hauser, 1973).

Also of significance in defining current issues is the fact that the 163 nations of the globe may be divided into rich and poor, or have and have-not, nations, with the poorer or developing nations generally experiencing the most rapid growth rates. Recent international developments, which have resulted in astronomical increases in the price of fuel, food, and fertilizer, necessitate further distinctions among the developing nations. Some developing nations are more or less self-sufficient because they have oil or other exportable raw materials (Colombia, Tunisia, Mexico, Brazil, Malaysia) or because, by processing goods, they have access to currency and export credits and can adjust to higher living costs (Taiwan, South Korea, Singapore). Then there are the 30 or so poorest countries which lack oil, fertilizer, food, and the money to import them. Almost all these are in Southeast Asia, Africa, or the Caribbean. Together these nations have populations totaling more than 1 billion, or about one-fourth of the earth's total. They need, and will continue to need, large amounts of assistance or foreign aid from various donor nations, including the United States.

Aside from China, which is in a class by itself, the rest are "rich" nations. In addition to the industrialized nations of Europe and North America, which have traditionally been labeled developed, there are

---

* The United Nations estimated that the earth's population would not reach 4 billion until early 1975 and will not reach 5 billion until 1985, but some demographers think this is a conservative estimate.

now the 11 members of OPEC (The Organization of Petroleum Export-ing Countries), with a total population of fewer than 300 million, but with immense wealth.

The United States is one of the rich nations, perhaps the richest, and like most of the other developed countries, it has experienced low growth rates during the past decade. Final figures from the 1970 census show a population of over 204 million, an increase of 25.4 million over the previous decade. Although the numerical increase was the second largest in the nation's history, it reflected the second lowest growth rate—13.3% for the decade, or 1.3% per year as compared with the 2.0% world growth rate.

It is in this world setting that the current concern with population trends, especially fertility trends, exists. This concern was highlighted recently when the United Nations proclaimed 1974 World Population Year and hosted the World Population Conference in Bucharest in August 1974 (United Nations, 1975). The Population Conference marked the first time that all 130 member-governments came together to confront the population issue. In all, 135 nation states were represented at the conference.†

THE ISSUES

A review of the history leading up to the conference and of the views expressed by governments at the conference itself will help to define the current issues.

The idea behind World Population Year was not a new one. The United Nations is always sponsoring "years" of one sort or another to create a focal point for international cooperation around significant issues. What was new was the response of governments. The request to nations to set up national commissions to mark World Population Year resulted in nearly four times the number of commissions established for any other United Nations year. Many of these were extended beyond 1974, which is appropriate in light of the long-term nature of the problem.

It is important to remember that no government had taken serious public action to respond to the problem of rapid growth until after World War II, when Japan decided to lower its growth rate from 2% to 1%. The topic was viewed as inappropriate for open discussion by governments in international forums until the 1960s, and, even then, most attempts to do anything beyond talking were blocked by coalitions of Catholic countries, on the one hand, and socialist countries, on the

† Invitations to participate were sent to 148 nations as well as to Liberation Move-ments recognized by the Organization of African Unity and/or the Arab League.

other, who believed that with the development of resources and the redistribution of wealth population growth would take care of itself.

In the United States, there has been almost a complete reversal in attitude in this area. In the 1950s the government attitude toward growth and family planning was one of non-involvement (Hall, 1973). In 1959 President Eisenhower noted emphatically that these were matters outside the proper sphere of government activity. But in 1962 President Kennedy authorized international assistance in family-planning information; in 1968 Congress allocated funds for assistance to family-planning programs in countries requesting it; and in 1969 the Agency for International Development was asked to give "high priority" to population and family-planning assistance. It has been a high priority item in our foreign assistance programs since then and has received increasing attention on the domestic scene, especially since the passage of the Family Planning Services Act in 1970 (Powers, 1972).

As is often the case with controversial subjects, some impetus for official national and international action came from private organizations such as the International Planned Parenthood Federation. Since 1942, that organization has been supplying family-planning services, and pressuring governments to provide such services and generally to get into the population field. The United Nations established the Fund for Population Activities (UNFPA) in 1969, and the fund was largely responsible for the activities of the population year, including the Bucharest conference. The United Nations also sponsored two earlier world conferences on population, in 1954 and 1965, but these were gatherings of scholars and scientists, not of policy-makers. The 1974 conference was one of governments—and presumably of people who have the power to enact programs and policies.

WORLD POPULATION PLAN OF ACTION

Although four other substantive issues were considered (population trends; the relationship of population to development; resources and environment; and the family), the central goal of the conference was to obtain endorsement of a World Population Plan of Action. The United Nations Economic and Social Council, which had convened the conference in 1972, specified that a draft Plan of Action be placed on the agenda. The draft was prepared under the auspices of the United Nations Population Division, and included data from an advisory committee of demographers and other social scientists from around the world (United Nations, 1975).

The proposed plan *encouraged* nations to take account of population variables in all their planning, to improve data collection, especially

vital registration systems, and to give high priority to research on population matters. In line with these suggestions, it also urged improved and
increased training and education of personnel. These are matters about
which there could be little disagreement, since everyone wants more
and better data and there are generally accepted ways of obtaining
them.

The plan also made suggestions for action with respect to the basic
demographic variables: population structure and growth, morbidity and
mortality, reproduction and family formation, and population distribution and migration. As might be expected, the emphasis was on fertility.
Specifically, the plan urged all nations which had not already done so to
formulate explicit policies suited to their own needs and to set up the
mechanisms for evaluating such policies. It also proposed that the
United Nations monitor the results of such policies every five years
starting in 1979. Several specific world goals were suggested, among
which were:

(*a*) the increase of average life expectancy at birth in less developed
regions so that it would exceed 62 years by 1985;

(*b*) the reduction of infant and child mortality;

(*c*) the full integration of women into the development process, including the removal of barriers to employment and to other
social and political opportunities; and

(*d*) the dissemination, to all persons who want it, of the necessary
information about family planning, and the means to practice it,
no later than 1985.

DISCUSSION OF THE PLAN OF ACTION

There was, and is, no consensus about the desirability of all these goals
(Mauldin, Choucri, Notestein, & Teitelbaum, 1974).

During the two weeks of the conference, there was an enormous
amount of talk about the relation of population to human rights, to the
family, to resources and the environment, and to economic development.
The delegates proposed and discussed 340 amendments to the Plan of
Action. The plan which emerged from the two-week-long conference
was considerably different from the draft plan which had been presented
at the opening of the conference. The original plan had emphasized that
excessive population growth threatened worldwide development and
resources and that population limitation should be a major component
of development policies. But in the version approved by the conference
population limitation was subordinated to economic and social development. Development became the focal point and was viewed as the
primary vehicle for solving population problems.

The change in emphasis in the Plan of Action resulted from a number of factors, not the least of which is the fact that the developing nations outnumber the developed nations more than two to one in the United Nations and at the conference. The developing nations considered the original plan a product of the developed nations and drafted most of the amendment proposals with a view toward changing that document to reflect their belief that development was a paramount issue.

It is also important to note here that the World Population Conference was the first international conference to be held after the United Nations General Assembly had adopted a plan of action for a new international economic order. This new order was designed to remedy the perceived imbalance between developed and developing countries largely through setting higher prices for raw materials, exercising greater national control over multinational corporations, and effecting changes in terms of trade and aid to benefit the developing countries. In this context it is not surprising that the developing countries insisted on a shift in conference emphasis from population to economic and social development.

The basic recommendation in the draft Plan of Action was that nations work to reduce the present 2% annual increase in world population to 1.7% by 1985, with the reduction to be effected entirely within the developing nations, which have about two-thirds of the world population. The United States proposed a more specific objective—a systematic effort to achieve a replacement level of fertility, an average of two children per family, by the year 2000. The key American proposal included a measure calling on governments to set up voluntary national family-planning policies by 1985 as well as a general recommendation to reduce the average size of families. Both proposals were rejected by a majority coalition of socialist countries and Roman Catholic nations of Latin America. The proposals were replaced by Argentine amendments making no mention of target dates for setting up policies and explicitly stating that the conference "does not recommend any size norms." The conference also rejected attempts by East European nations to eliminate any mention that population growth has an impact on world resources and environment.

The trend was definitely away from specificity, and the final version set no national or international goals in terms of numbers. It merely suggested that with individually formulated national policies the world's present annual growth rate of 2% could be substantially reduced by 1985.

The plan which was finally adopted is mainly a declaration of principles and policies. It calls for the equality of women, and suggests that the affluent nations reduce their consumption of world resources. It does not confront the fact that many demographers and policy-makers think that the present world growth rate (2% per year) threatens world resources and the development of the less developed nations—a view which is seriously contested in some countries. It leaves the formulation of population policies to the individual nations, recognizing that some want to promote rather than limit growth. But it does cite the element of international responsibility in national planning and notes that international cooperation is needed in addition to economic development assistance.

THE BASIC POSITIONS ON POPULATION GROWTH

In view of the tremendous achievement involved in getting agreement merely to discuss population issues in a political forum, it should be neither surprising nor disappointing that a wide variety of ideological and professional views exist. The most common polarization of views in the past has been between the Malthusian and the Marxian interpretations of the relation of population to resources, and, by extension, to development. Although some of these same arguments persist, it would be a gross oversimplification to assume that present views are merely extensions of these earlier perspectives. Space does not permit a complete presentation of all viewpoints, however (Teitelbaum, 1974).

There are two extreme positions. One sees population growth as the major crisis facing mankind. The proponents of this view generally advocate population stabilization as soon as possible and at as low a level as possible in order to improve living standards and the environment. The low stable growth rate is operationalized in terms of fertility reduction. The opposite view perceives population growth as a good or at least as a non-problem. Proponents of this view assume that social and economic development will reduce fertility and remedy whatever adverse consequences of growth already exist. Rather than evidencing a concern with population growth, they usually emphasize a restructuring of the organization of society, calling a halt to resource depletion and/or environmental pollution, or setting a limit on the consumption patterns of developed nations.

A middle view has also emerged which maintains that although reduced population growth is not the solution to all problems, it is significant enough an issue to be part of many national policies. The proponents of this view do not suggest that reduced growth be substituted for large capital investments or assistance, but merely that it be considered a component of development.

These and other views were amply outlined at the international meeting in Bucharest in 1974. They also appear with respect to the development of internal policies in the United States.

It is easy to cite deficiencies in the outcome of international meetings or in the development of internal policies, but it is important to bear in mind that the World Population Conference and the Plan of Action represent a tremendous advance in international understanding and agreement with respect to population issues. The relationship between population and other aspects of social life is now viewed as important enough to be discussed and debated by those who make decisions as to what will be done about it.

REFERENCES

Hall, M. F. Population growth: U. S. and Latin American views. *Population Studies*, 1973, *27*, 415–429.

Hauser, P. M. Population criteria in foreign aid programs (Population Reference Bureau Selection No. 42, September 1973). Washington, D.C.: Population Reference Bureau, 1973.

Mauldin, W. P., Choucri, N., Notestein, F. W., & Teitelbaum, M. S. A report on Bucharest. *Studies in Family Planning*, 1974, *5*, 357–395.

Powers, M. G. *Population action programmes.* Background paper for United Nations Interregional Workshop on Population Action Programmes, Manila, November 1972. U.N. ESA/P/AC. 1/3 September 1972.

Teitelbaum, M. S. Population and development: Is a consensus possible? *Foreign Affairs*, 1974, *52*, 742–760.

United Nations, Department of Economic and Social Affairs. *The population debate: Dimensions and perspectives.* Papers of the World Population Conference, Bucharest, 1974. Population Series No. 57 (2 vols.). New York: United Nations, 1975.

Population Control: Methods and Morality

CHARLES E. CURRAN

Father Charles E. Curran is a priest of the Diocese of Rochester, New York, and Professor of Moral Theology at The Catholic University of America. He is a frequent contributor to periodicals and professional journals; author of the following books (among others): A new look at Christian morality *(1968),* Contemporary problems in moral theology *(1970),* New perspectives in moral theology *(1974); and co-author of* Dissent in and for the church *(1969), and* The responsibility of dissent: The Church and academic freedom *(1969). A former president of both the American Society of Christian Ethics and the Catholic Theological Society of America, in 1972 Father Curran was the first recipient of the John Courtney Murray Award of the Catholic Theological Society of America for distinguished achievement in theology.*

Population control and family planning are related but, at the same time, quite distinct. Family planning involves the decisions and activities of husbands and wives to plan the size of their families in the light of their responsibilities, obligations, needs, and desires. Reasons for family planning, such as those proposed by Pope Pius XII in 1951—medical, eugenic, economic, and social—are much broader and more inclusive than factors affecting population. Were there no need for population control, there would still be a need for family planning. Population control is implemented by family planning and many other means, and it involves various organizations, including the state, in planning the optimum pop-

53

ulation for a given area or even for the earth as a whole (Berelson, 1969;
Davis, 1967; McCormack, 1974).

Population control presupposes that there is a population problem
and that some control is necessary. As will be mentioned later, the population crisis is more complex than is often implied and might more accurately be described as population crises. There are divergent opinions
about the gravity of the population problem at the present time, but in
my judgment one must admit that a problem exists to some extent now,
is more acute in developing countries, and will become much more
serious. According to the World Population Plan of Action (n. 3)
adopted by the World Population Conference meeting in Bucharest in
August 1974 under the auspices of the United Nations (United Nations
Economic and Social Council, 1974), if the world population growth
continues at the rate of 2%, which has been the persistent rate since
1950, there will be a doubling of the world population every 35 years.
Despite disagreement about the intensity of the problem, there is need
now for some control of population. This raises questions about the
morality of the methods of population control, which in some way involves the rights of individuals, families, and nations, in the light of
broader societal and even global needs. From a theological–ethical perspective, there are four preliminary considerations which will influence
the approach taken to population control.

PRELIMINARY THEOLOGICAL–ETHICAL CONSIDERATIONS

Harmony or Chaos

Does one generally see in the world the possibility of harmony and order
among all the component aspects of human existence or is one more inclined to see these different aspects as competing forces which very often
threaten chaos and disorder? An emphasis on harmony and order has
generally characterized much of Roman Catholic moral theology. A most
fundamental question in Christian ethics concerns the proper relationship involving love of God, love of neighbor, and love of self. The
Roman Catholic tradition has tried to harmonize these three kinds of
love and sees no opposition between them if they are properly understood. Other traditions in Christian ethics have de-emphasized the love
of self, and see self-love as opposed to love of neighbor, especially the
neighbor in need. Some would even accuse the Roman Catholic approach, as exemplified in Thomas Aquinas, of a eudaemonistic ethic
which in the last analysis is seeking the ultimate happiness and fulfillment of the individual person (D'Arcy, 1956; Toner, 1968).

Pope John XXIII, in the second sentence of his encyclical *Pacem in terris*, testifies to the emphasis within the Roman Catholic tradition on order and harmony in the world:

> The progress of learning and the inventions of technology clearly show that, both in living things and in the forces of nature, an astonishing order reigns, and they also bear witness to the greatness of man who can understand that order and create suitable instruments to harness those forces of nature and use them to his benefit [John XXIII, 1963, n. 2, p. 47].

Such an approach recognizes two different aspects to this harmony: a basic order in nature itself, and the rational control of nature by human beings. It would constitute a perversion of this understanding to claim that human beings should never interfere and that a laissez faire approach will be sufficient. Nevertheless, this Roman Catholic approach acknowledges a basic order in nature and assumes that the controlling power of human reason can ensure that harmony results.

My own approach modifies and qualifies such an understanding. From a theological perspective, a greater appreciation of sin and the recognition that the fullness of the eschaton is not yet here call for the existence of stronger, opposed forces producing a greater tension in the world. From a philosophical perspective, a more historical and process understanding will also introduce more movement and change, thereby not accepting as much order and harmony as in an older, more static approach. From the perspective of human experience, the tragedy of war, the inequities existing in our world, the divisions existing within many nations, the recognition that many people have died because of famine, the pollution of the environment, and many other problems all indicate there are more tensions and possible sources of discord in our world than the first approach is willing to acknowledge.

A third approach sees nature and the world primarily in terms of antagonisms and oppositions so that individuals are opposed to one another, individuals and society are in basic opposition, and the forces at work in all of nature are often antithetical and disharmonious. These three different world views affect, not only the general understanding of our world, but also the approach to the question of population control. The third approach more easily despairs of finding any harmonious solution. The competing forces involved in the question of population control are so antagonistic that very radical solutions are necessary.

It is significant that the Roman Catholic hierarchical magisterium has at times been very reluctant to admit the existence of a population problem (Walsh, 1974; Murphy, 1975). Since the encyclical *Populorum progressio* of Pope Paul VI in 1967, there have been some indications that the stance is weakening, and yet, in his address to the World Food Congress on November 19, 1974, the pope himself failed to acknowledge the existence of any problem calling for population control. There is no doubt that this unwillingness to admit the existence of the problem or its gravity stems from the Church's condemnation of artificial contraception. Though in theory one can separate the two issues (rhythm can be used to secure a lower birth rate), in practice it is generally recognized that any effective population control on a worldwide basis in our contemporary society must include the use of artificial contraception. Nonetheless, the refusal of the hierarchical magisterium of the Roman Catholic Church to admit a population problem or the intensity of the problem is consistent with the world view which stresses the astonishing order and harmony which exist in the world.

My own position is more disposed to accept the existence of a problem such as population but it does not readily endorse drastic and radical solutions. There exists a possibility of harmonizing the different values and forces at work without having to sacrifice totally some of these values or some of the persons involved. Practical solutions will always call for some sacrifice, but radical solutions should not be that necessary. With education, motivation, some important structural changes, and the ready availability of contraception, human beings will begin to respond to reduce the number of their offspring.

The Understanding of the Concept of the State

In one Christian perspective the state owes its existence primarily to human sinfulness. Sinful human beings will tend to destroy and devour one another unless they are prevented from doing so by a superior force. The state is an order of preservation by which God, in accord with the Noachic covenant, prevents chaos and preserves some order in this sinful world. The state is understood primarily in terms of coercive power, and the individual's freedom is generally viewed as in opposition to the state and to its powers (Thielicke, 1969).

Traditional Roman Catholic theology sees the state as a natural society. Human beings are by nature not only social but political; that is, they are called by nature to join in a political society to work for the common good, which ultimately redounds to the good of the individual. Individuals by themselves cannot achieve some things which are necessary for their good, but by banding together in political society they are able to accomplish them. A harmony exists between the individual good and the common good. Coercive power is not the primary characteristic of the state because the state has the function of directing and guiding individuals to the common good, which ultimately serves for their own good. The state is not viewed as antithetical to the true freedom of the individual (Markus, 1965; Rommen, 1945).

There is no doubt that until the present century Roman Catholic theology and philosophy of the state did not give enough importance to the freedom of the individual. Strongly confident in the state's ability to discern objective truth and justice, this approach saw little or no infringement on the freedom of the individual. The freedom of the individual calls for the person to correspond to objective truth and justice (D'Arcy, 1961). Witness the teaching on religious freedom in the Roman Catholic tradition and the opposition to freedom in general in newer forms of government in the nineteenth century (Augustine, 1966). There is no doubt that the older Roman Catholic approach, in the name of objective truth and justice, did not give enough importance to the reality of human freedom.

In the light of totalitarian dictatorships in the twentieth century, Roman Catholic social ethics has come to give more importance to human freedom and to the human subject (Murray, 1965). I agree with this approach and with the fact that one cannot so readily insist on objective truth and our ability to know it. In addition, one must also recognize here the effects of the presence of sin because of which the individual will not always be willing to work for the common good and because of which the various powers existing within society might be abused by those who hold them. Such a view of the state recognizes at times the need for coercion and its proper place in the life of civil society. Free human beings by all means possible should be educated and motivated to work for the common good and the good of society which ultimately redounds to their own good. A proper functioning of society demands a high degree of consensus about the need for willing adherence to the norms of society. In the context of a discussion on population control, Rosemary Ruether (1973) makes the point that societies such as China which appear to be very coercive apparently can be perceived by the vast majority of those within them as free and liberated because of their communal élan. Society thus needs a broadbased voluntary consent to its guiding norms and principles if it is to be effective.

Applied to the question of the problem of population control, this means that heavy emphasis must be given to the education and motivation of the individuals with a great respect for their freedom to choose responsibly in the light of the total needs of the society. The report of the Commission on Population Growth and the American Future (1972, p. 91) warns that groups which feel deprived and discriminated against by current government policies will be skeptical and resistant to new governmental programs in the population field. This does not exclude at times the possibility that coercion might be necessary, but coercion can never be the first or primary means used by the state.

Another significant aspect of the theory of the state and its functions concerns the principle of subsidiarity and its application to questions

such as population control (Hellegers, 1973). Subsidiarity declares that
the larger and higher collectivity should not take over the functions
which can be performed by smaller and lesser groups. In population
matters, according to André Hellegers, it means that there be no unnecessary curtailment or abrogation of free, individual decision-making.
But a full and accurate picture must also recognize the principle of socialization which emerged in Roman Catholic social ethics in the en-
cyclicals of Pope John XXIII. Pope John (1961, nn. 59–66) points out
that one of the principal characteristics of our modern age is an increase
in social relationships. This will at times call for greater government intervention and for national and international movements, but these
increased social relationships should not reduce human beings to the
condition of mere automata. More so than Hellegers, Joseph Kiernan
(1975) rightly points out the need to recognize both subsidiarity and
socialization (solidarity–justice) in discussing population questions so
that considerations of subsidiarity are not absolutized. In practice this
means that larger communities including the state may have to intervene
in population control if this is deemed necessary.

Freedom and the Right to Procreate

One of the most important considerations concerns the freedom of the
individual couple in determining family size. Some proposals for population control call for coercion as a necessary means of achieving optimum
population. Through one means or another the state would control the
number of children whom individuals are able to procreate. The World
Population Plan of Action (United Nations Economic and Social Council, 1974, n. 13) adopted by the recent United Nations conference in
Bucharest, recommends that all countries respect and ensure, regardless
of their overall demographic goals, the rights of persons to determine in
a free, informed, and responsible manner the number and spacing of
their children. This recommendation is in keeping with a traditional emphasis in United Nations literature on the freedom of the individual
couple in questions of the size of their family.

From my theological–ethical perspective, the freedom of the couple
is very important. Through having children one responds to a very fundamental human desire and need. The freedom of the individual in this
matter is very closely associated with human dignity and the basic freedom of the human person. But freedom is not the only important moral
value to be considered here; it must be limited and influenced by other
factors.

Older Roman Catholic teaching recognized something more than just
the freedom of the individuals to do what they choose. Stressing the as-

pect of the good of the species, it asserted that the primary purpose of marriage and sexuality was the procreation and education of offspring, and that every single act of sexual intercourse had to be open to the possibility of procreation (Ford & Kelly, 1963). The prohibition of artificial contraception rests (wrongly in my judgment) on this interpretation that every act of sexual intercourse involves more than merely the couple and their freedom. Though the species aspect of human sexuality in the traditional Catholic approach has always had a pronatalist assumption, logically such an emphasis could also call for a limitation of births if this was required by the needs of the human species. By emphasizing that the procreation and education of offspring is the primary end of marriage, traditional Roman Catholic theology recognizes that the upbringing and education of the child is an important factor in the decision of the couple to have a child, and thus admits that there are limits placed on couples in terms of their right to procreate.

In keeping with traditional ethical terminology, one can assert that individual couples have the right to procreate, but that the exercise of that right is limited. In exercising their rights couples must act responsibly. If individual couples for some reason or other do not act responsibly, and if harm is being done to the public order of society, then the state can intervene to ensure that individuals act in a more responsible manner. Moreover there is a very important distinction between the right of an individual couple to have offspring and the right of an individual couple to have a particular number of children. It is much easier to recognize that the state can intervene in terms of restricting the number of children a particular couple is permitted to have, since this is not as basic and fundamental a right as the right to procreate children in general. Yet the fact that the state can intervene must not be taken for *carte blanche* authorization, for government coercion remains a last resort. There are many other questions which have to be answered before one could decide that the state should intervene and precisely how it should intervene.

If it is necessary for the state to intervene to curtail the freedom of individuals, then this must be done in accordance with justice and other relevant moral principles. This understanding of the right to procreate and its limitations seems preferable to describing it as a social right (Yale Task Force on Population Ethics, 1974, p. 105).

Proper Description of the Problem

It is obvious that any solution to the problem of population control must be based on an adequate and objective understanding of the nature of the problem itself. Judgments in moral theology are heavily dependent on empirical data, but the division between facts and values is much more complicated than might seem at first sight. Today we are more conscious of the fact that it is very difficult, if not impossible, to speak about something as being objective and value free. Very often judgments which claim to be purely objective and based on empirical data alone contain concealed value judgments about what is more important and why (Callahan, 1971, p. xii; Hauerwas, 1974, p. 240).

In attempting a proper description and understanding of the population problem, one must also honestly recognize one's own presuppositions and prejudices. In general, I eschew overly simplistic solutions to human ethical problems, basing my approach on a more relational ethical model which sees the individual ethical actor in terms of multiple relationships with God, neighbor, and the world. My insistence on complexity stems from the recognition that very often erroneous solutions are proposed not because of some error of commission but because of an error of omission—a failure to consider all the elements which must be discussed.

I am inclined to accept the analysis of Philip Hauser (1972, pp. 233–239) that human beings are complex culture-building animals, and that the population crisis is really a series of four crises or problems: (a) the population explosion maintains that, if the present trend continues, by the year 2000 the population of the developing countries will be about as great as the total population of the world in 1960; (b) the population implosion refers to the increasing concentration of people on relatively small portions of the earth's surface—a phenomenon generally known as urbanization; (c) the population displosion designates the increasing heterogeneity of people who share the same geographical space as well as the same social, political, and economic conditions, and is exemplified by the current problems in Northern Ireland and many countries in Africa, or even in Canada; (d) the technoplosion refers to the accelerated pace of technological innovation which has characterized our modern era. Hauser (1971, p. 121) acknowledges that in the developing countries much remains to be done before the control of the population explosion is ensured. But Hauser (1972, p. 236) also asserts that it is almost certain that problems created or exacerbated by implosion and displosion will create more human misery during at least the remainder of this century than the problems produced by excessive fertility and growth.

Population control cannot be limited merely to providing the means for individuals to control fertility. Under population goals and policies the World Population Plan of Action (United Nations Economic and Social Council, 1974, nn. 20–67) also cites the need for policies and goals in the following areas: reduction of morbidity and mortality; reproduction, family formation, and the status of women; population distribution and internal migration; international migration and population structure. The recommendation of the Study Commission of the Office of the Foreign Secretary of the National Academy of Sciences (National Academy of Sciences, 1971) includes these and other considerations.

Personal and national narrowness of perception as well as sinfulness may at times affect the understanding and statement of the problem as well as any proposed solutions. In general, the developed nations of the world tend to see the problem of population control and most of the problems of the developing nations in terms of the need to reduce the number of births. In the eyes of the United States government before the Bucharest meeting in 1974, population growth was a problem because it has many effects, including the retarding of economic growth and negatively affecting food resources, the environment, and governmental abilities to supply these needs. Given the causal importance of population growth, massive spending on contraceptive development in family-planning programs was the one major solution proposed (Warwick, 1974, p. 1). A more nuanced view was taken by some American scholars such as Arthur Dyck, a Christian ethicist from Harvard, who pointed out that problems such as environmental deterioration, starvation, and poverty as they exist today are not directly and mainly caused by present population growth rates (Dyck, 1972, p. 164). Neuhaus (1971) viewed the American emphasis on contraception and family planning as an unwillingness to admit many of the problems caused by the overconsumption of the developed nations and by the inequitable economic structures of modern existence. Even before the 1974 meeting in Bucharest, there was a growing realization that a more integral view of the interdependent character of population and social phenomena such as social and economic change, environmental factors, and technological developments was required. Population growth is not the only problem, or the cause of all the problems, or, indeed, the major obstacle to the solution of all problems (Henriot, 1974, p. 50).

A final caution in understanding the population problem and its solution stems from the limitations of any one science. The scientific in general is not totally identical with the human, and the perspective of one science can never be totally identical with the human perspective. One must critically examine various understandings and solutions because of the danger of distortion. Psychology is more interested in the individual whereas sociology is more concerned about society. The fact that something is genetically possible does not always mean it should be done. In general, one must be aware of solutions proposed in the name of only a partial perspective or from the viewpoint of only one science or optique.

Having discussed four important theological–ethical considerations which inform the ethical judgment about population problems, I now turn to the following specific proposals: (*a*) an holistic solution; (*b*) triage; (*c*) means used by government to control population; (*d*) means of fertility and birth control; and (*e*) the role of the Roman Catholic Church.

An Holistic Solution

Solutions for the population problem must be integral and holistic. It is morally wrong merely to propose reducing the number of births without recognizing the multifaceted nature of the problem, which must include other demographic components and social and economic changes. The danger always remains that the powerful and strong will be tempted to see the solution only in the realm of preventing births and lowering fertility, when many of the problems of the environment are caused as much by the overconsumption of the developed nations as by the birth rate in the developing nations.

There is, in fact, good evidence to support the contention that all programs aimed at lowering fertility will be unsuccessful unless they are accompanied by social and economic changes. Arthur Dyck (1971, p. 633; 1973, pp. 75–76; 1975, p. 60) relates in a number of articles the poignant story of the ghetto mother which was first told by Robert Coles. To poverty-stricken mothers in the ghettos of the United States a new child is a source of hope, joy, and fulfillment which cannot be had in any other way. The wealthier people in society may find their fulfillment in many other ways, but for the woman interviewed by Coles, child-bearing and child-raising comprised the one source of fulfillment in her life. Many other studies indicate the same result. India's programs based only on massive contraception and sterilization have been a failure (Harriott, 1974, p. 630).

Here it seems that good morality will have good results in practice— a point which Roman Catholic theology has often emphasized. Nonetheless one must also point out that narrow efficiency and ethical rightness do not necessarily coincide at all times. In the question of population control, it seems that fertility control is programmatically ineffective, not feasible, and politically and individually unacceptable if there is not the motivation which occurs when societies through socioeconomic development offer their members alternatives promising an improvement in the future quality of life (Henriot, 1974, p. 58). Thus one cannot emphasize enough the need for holistic solutions which require not only changes in the birth rate of developing nations but changes in other demographic components, changes in the consumption of developed nations, and changes in the socioeconomic structures in our world.

Triage

Even the more popular press (e.g., Greene, 1975) has been discussing triage in the light of the population problem. Triage ethics comes to the fore in disaster situations in which such a limited supply of medical personnel and/or services is available that not everyone can be cared for. Decisions must be made to care for some and not for others. The hopelessly wounded and those who need greater treatment are left to die without any treatment so that treatment can be given to a greater number of others.

In 1967 William and Paul Paddock in *Famine—1975! America's decision: Who will survive?* pointed to India as the bellwether of what will happen to other nations. It will be impossible to feed and help all the people in the world. The hungry nations of 1967 will become the starving nations of tomorrow. Some decisions must be made about giving no further help to certain nations. Garrett Hardin (1968) talked about the tragedy of the commons, which shows the fundamental error of sharing ethics. In a pasture run as a commons, each herdsman will tend to add more cattle because to do so is to his individual benefit. Before long, the common pasture will be overcrowded and will deteriorate, to the disadvantage of all. In late 1974, Hardin continued his attack on sharing ethics by invoking the metaphor of lifeboat ethics. The rich nations of this world are comparatively well-stocked lifeboats which are able to survive, but many poor nations with their people cannot survive. If we in the United States today take all or too many others aboard our lifeboat, it will sink. A world food bank and unrestricted immigration exemplify the tragedy of the commons. A sharing ethics will eventually destroy those who unwisely succumb to their humanitarian impulses and will only delay the day of reckoning for poor countries.

Both lifeboat ethics and triage have been discussed by ethicists in the past. Edmond Cahn (1955, pp. 61–71) sees in the lifeboat situation the full force of the morals of the last day. In this situation the individual, stripped of all distinguishing features and special bonds, is left a generic creature embodying the entire genus and having no moral individuality left; whoever kills another in that situation kills humankind. If no one will sacrifice himself voluntarily, they must all wait to die together.

Paul Ramsey (1962, p. 245) argues that in the lifeboat situation random selection best assures the basic moral principle of the sanctity of the individual in deciding who can be saved and who cannot. Later, Ramsey admits (1970, pp. 257–259) one describable exception to the principle: if and only if a community and its members share a single focus or purpose or goal under now quite extraordinary circumstances. Ramsey gives as two examples the lifeboat situation in which some are needed because of their special expertise in rowing in order for any to be saved and triage in disaster medicine in which priority must be given to victims who can quickly be restored to functioning. Thus even a Christian ethicist such as Paul Ramsey, who insists quite strongly on the sanctity (not just the dignity) of the individual, recognizes the moral possibility of triage and some lifeboat ethics.

Although I agree that triage and some aspects of lifeboat ethics are at times morally acceptable, in my judgment they are not moral now in the question of population control, because the problem, as real and as important as it is, is not now catastrophic or simply focused. We are not in the last days; there is still time for other solutions. But above all, the problem is not simply one of fertility control, it involves many other demographic, social and economic factors; and the rich nations of the world must share responsibiilty with the poor nations. Hardin fails to recognize that the problem is multifaceted and not simply a problem of the poor nations' producing too many offspring.

Nor do his proposals give the respect for the individual which a Christian understanding of the individual and of Christian love demands. He is too willing to sacrifice many people when it is not necessary and especially when the proper moral response might call for a more generous action on our part. It is a question not only of the dignity of the individual human being but also of the interdependence of all human beings, which Christianity as well as many rational ethics recognize. The irony is that the rich nations of the world have enriched themselves precisely through an exploitation of the poor nations. Lately the energy crisis has made many Americans much more aware of the interdependence of our own human existence. Not only is triage in this situation morally wrong because it does not give enough respect for the meaning of the individual and of the demands of Christian love for those in need, but it also goes against the basic understanding of the interdependent nature of human existence today and, therefore, even pragmatically is impossible. No one nation or group of nations will be able to go it alone because of our mutual dependencies.

Survival itself is neither an absolute nor the most important human value and imperative. The moral corollary of this statement is that there are certain things we should not do even if they aid the quest for survival. As Daniel Callahan (1973, pp. 58–59; 1974) has pointed out, the need to survive is modified by the need to realize other values such as freedom, justice, and a sense of dignity and worth. There are some means of assuring survival which are so morally wrong that it would be better not to survive than to have to survive in such a moral atmosphere.

Means Used by Governments

How should the state deal with the problem of controlling population growth? In one of the most comprehensive and synthetic articles on the question, Bernard Berelson (1969) lists and summarizes the proposals which have been advanced—extensions of voluntary fertility control, establishment of involuntary fertility control, intensified educational campaigns, incentive programs, tax and welfare benefits and penalties, shifts in social and economic institutions and in political channels and organizations. In my judgment the primary ethical considerations, in addition to the proportionality of benefits and harms, are freedom and justice, although these elements can be expanded in different ways. The Study Commission of the Office of the Foreign Secretary of the National Academy of Sciences (National Academy of Sciences, 1971, p. 81), for example, recommends the ethical criteria for fertility control policies which were first proposed by Berelson in the above-cited article.

As mentioned earlier, freedom is a most important value but it cannot be absolutized. On a scale of government interference in a continuum from freedom to coercive policies, the following general approaches can be identified—education, motivation, and propaganda for population control together with provision of acceptable means to control fertility to all who want and need them; change of social structures which affect demography; incentives offered to control population; and coercive methods employed by the government.

Questions of justice arise especially in considerations of incentives and coercion. Robert Veatch (1973) elaborates eight criteria which should be used in judging incentive proposals, but he recognizes that the principle of justice creates the gravest difficulty for incentive proposals. The ultimate reasons from justice raised against incentive proposals stem from discrimination. Discrimination exists often toward the poor who are most tempted by monetary inducements and subject to abuse in the process, whereas the wealthy are not put under that same pressure. Likewise, incentives can harm innocent children if certain penalties are inflicted on or services are reduced for the nth child born in each family. Veatch (1973, p. 220) proposes as a just incentive a progressive sliding-scale fee which might be called a child welfare fee payable every year for every child. Dyck (1971, p. 622) accepts as the least unjust of all incentive programs the provision of pensions for poor parents with fewer than n children as a social security for their old age, which takes away the insecurity which in some societies is met by the children. Edward Pohl-man (1971) argues that incentives are not ideal but they are necessary today. In somewhat the same manner Melvin Ketchel says that compulsory fertility control would seem to be the most effective and the least objectionable of any involuntary methods (Ketchel, 1971, p. 295).

In judging the morality of government policy, one must again insist on an holistic perspective. Fertility control is not acceptable if it is the only solution; it is necessary also to see the problem in the context of other demographic, economic, and social factors. All the lower effects on the scale from freedom to incentives and coercion must be employed first before one can even think about incentives and coercion. There is an intense need for education, motivation, and the provision of morally acceptable means of fertility control to all who want them as well as the need for changing social structures (e.g., the status of women) which affect demography. At the present time, except in extraordinary circumstances, it does not seem that coercion is acceptable. In some situations incentives might be morally acceptable, but here special care should be taken lest fundamental principles of justice be violated. Although perfect justice is never attainable, special concern for the rights of the poor is needed. In addition, the very important pragmatic note should be made that if incentives are employed without all the other means mentioned above, they will apparently be ineffective.

The problem of freedom and coercion does not exist only in the places where there is an attempt by government to reduce the size of populations. There are some countries in the world today (e.g., Brazil and Argentina), which are trying to increase their population; but here too the same moral question arises about the means employed by the government to bring about the desired population (Warwick, 1974). The freedom of couples and their right to determine the number of children they want should be protected. The government has the obligation of allowing couples to plan their families and of supplying the poor with the acceptable means they need to be able to achieve the legitimate goals of family planning. Here again the distinction between family planning and population control is significant. In the name of population control the government cannot take away from individuals the right to plan and limit their own families in accord with their understanding of what is right and helpful. Yet the government can through education and motivation show the need for an increase in population and appeal to the generosity of families to effect it.

Means of Fertility and Birth Control

Contraception, sterilization, and abortion are the principal means which individuals use to prevent conception and birth. What about the morality of these means? From the viewpoint of morality, there is general acceptance of the morality of artificial contraception. The official teaching of the hierarchical magisterium of the Roman Catholic Church condemns it, but dissent from such official teaching is both justifiable and widespread (Crowe, 1971). From an ethical viewpoint sterilization logically belongs to the same moral category as contraception, with the significant difference that sterilization tends to be permanent. The official hierarchical teaching of the Roman Catholic Church continues to condemn all direct sterilization, but again there is in my judgment (Curran, 1973) justifiable and growing dissent from such teaching. The primary ethical problems connected with contraception and sterilization come from government policies involving incentives or coercion, but these have already been discussed.

Abortion as a means of preventing birth and as an instrument of population control raises many more serious ethical problems and objections. The World Population Plan of Action (United Nations Economic and Social Council, 1974, n. 246) accepted at Bucharest shows the tension existing within the world community on the question of abortion. In considering morbidity and mortality, the document recommends the reduction of illegal abortions. Proposed amendments to change "illegal" to "induced" and to replace "abortion" with "miscarriage" were both defeated (n. 137). The report of the Commission on Population Growth and the American Future made the following recommendation:

> Therefore with the admonition that abortion not be considered a primary means of fertility control, the Commission recommends that present state laws restricting abortion be abridged along the line of the New York State statute . . . [Commission on Population Control and the American Future, 1972, p. 178].

The Study Commission of the Office of the Foreign Secretary of the National Academy of Sciences recommended that legal and social barriers to fertility control be promptly removed and that broad social acceptance and support of fertility control including medically safe abortions be fostered (National Academy of Sciences, Office of the Foreign Secretary, 1971, p. 84).

The Commission on Population Growth and the American Future (1972, p. 176) recognized that at the present time it is difficult to make precise quantitative statements concerning the demographic import of abortion. Arthur Dyck (1972, pp. 166–168), while reporting that permissive abortion generally facilitates a downward trend in population and that restrictive abortion policies do not prevent a downward trend in fertility, concludes that abortion is not needed to solve population problems. Abdel R. Omran (1971, p. 481) maintains that when developing countries are highly motivated to accelerate their transition from high to low fertility induced abortion becomes a popular method of fertility control. He concludes his study by emphasizing two major themes for policy formation: (*a*) there is no question that prevention of pregnancy through effective contraception is much wiser and safer than the termination of pregnancy through abortion; and (*b*) for reasons which vary from country to country, a margin of induced abortion is to be anticipated and provided for (Omran, 1971, p. 524). The primary ethical question is not whether or not abortion is an effective means of population control, although it does seem from the evidence mentioned above that Dyck (1972, p. 165) is correct in asserting that abortion is not necessary as a means of population control.

Opposition to abortion on ethical grounds cannot be based merely on its efficacy or inefficacy in terms of population control. It must be pointed out that opposition to abortion on ethical grounds is not limited to Roman Catholicism as is exemplified in Arthur Dyck's writings. It is also true that even within Roman Catholicism there is some incipient dissent from the official Church teaching, but even such dissent on the ethical teaching does not involve an acceptance of abortion as a means of population control (Ribes, 1974). Elsewhere (Curran, 1974, p. 163) I have explained my own position on the morality of abortion, which from about fourteen days after conception (the beginning of individual life) can be morally accepted only in conflict situations involving a value commensurate with human life. From the legal perspective I should prefer to avoid both abortion on demand at any time in pregnancy and restrictive laws forbidding all abortions except in extreme situations (Curran, 1975). However, I do accept the fact that in many ways the ruling of the United States Supreme Court was somewhat inevitable because of the emphasis in our jurisprudence on the freedom of the individual. I should have preferred that the time for unrestricted abortion had been limited to the first three months of pregnancy. However, my acceptance of some legal abortions does not mean that I accept abortion as a means of population control to be proposed and promoted by the government. Active promotion of abortion by governments as a means of population control in my judgment is both morally wrong and unnecessary. Above all, compulsory abortion is an ethical monstrosity which cannot be accepted.

The Role of the Roman Catholic Church

There is no doubt that the Roman Catholic teaching condemning artificial contraception puts the Catholic Church in a difficult posture in terms of population control. Though I have strongly dissented from this teaching and have urged that it be changed, I realize that it is not likely to be in the very near future. In the meantime it seems that although many Catholic couples and members of the clergy will continue to dissent, most Catholics do not have a problem with the use of artificial contraception (Hurley, 1974). In spite of the existing teaching there is thus a way around the problem in pastoral practice for individual Catholic couples. However, the present official teaching of the Roman Catholic Church continues to condemn artifical contraception as a means of family planning and population control.

Even though I personally go much farther, there is a better position which can be taken by the official teaching of the Roman Catholic Church. Couples in a pluralistic society have the right to choose the means (with the exception of abortion) by which they will plan their families and respond to the need for population control, and the government can provide them with the help necessary to carry out their decision. Such an approach is both in conformity with developing Catholic teaching on freedom in a pluralistic society and is better than mere opposition to family planning and population control. From the perspective of the official Roman Catholic teaching, one must also insist that the government provide help in the rhythm method for those who choose to use natural family-planning.

There are two interesting anomalies about the present official position of the Roman Catholic Church. First, there is evidence that, without the acceptance and provision of artificial contraception in developing countries many people in a transitional period revert to abortion (Omran, 1971, pp. 486ff.). Second, John Hayes, an Irish Catholic social ethician, has pointed out that by fostering economic development through its social teachings the Roman Catholic Church is also promoting a situation in which according to the data contraceptive practices have become more widespread (Hayes, 1974, p. 243).

It is imperative for official Catholic Church teaching to recognize the existence of the problem and to urge governments and people to take the steps necessary to deal with it, for the problem is only going to become more acute in the years ahead. However, the official Church teaching must also help to situate this problem in a broader perspective involving the sharing of food and resources, and economic development (as Catholic statements have often done) and to insist on the many ethical values which must enter into the discussion, especially considerations of freedom and justice involving the rights of the poor and the innocent.

REFERENCES

Augustine, P. *Religious freedom in church and state.* Baltimore: Helicon, 1966.
Berelson, B. Beyond family planning. *Science,* 1969, *163,* 533–543.
Cahn, E. *The moral decision.* Bloomington: Indiana University Press, 1955.

Callahan, D. J. Introduction. In D. Callahan (Ed.), *The American population debate*. New York: Doubleday, 1971. Pp. xi–xv.

Callahan, D. J. Population and human survival. In J. P. Wogaman (Ed.), *The population crisis and moral responsibility*. Washington, D.C.: Public Affairs Press, 1973. Pp. 46–61.

Callahan, D. J. Doing well by doing good. *The Hastings Center Report*, 1974, *4* (6), 1–4.

Commission on population growth and the American future. *Population and the American future*. New York: New American Library, 1972.

Crowe, F. The conscience of the theologian with reference to the encyclical. In W. C. Bier (S.J.) (Ed.), *Conscience: Its freedom and limitations*. New York: Fordham University Press, 1971. Pp. 312–332.

Curran, C. Sterilization: Roman Catholic theory and practice. *The Linacre Quarterly*, 1973, *40*, 97–108.

Curran, C. *New perspectives in moral theology*. Notre Dame, Ind.: Fides, 1974.

Curran, C. Civil law and Christian morality: Abortion and the churches. *Conversations*, Spring 1975, pp. 1–19.

D'Arcy, E. *Conscience and its right to freedom*. New York: Sheed & Ward, 1961.

D'Arcy, M. *The mind and heart of love*. New York: Meridian, 1956.

Davis, K. Population policy: Will current programs succeed? *Science*, 1967, *158*, 730–739.

Dyck, A. Population policies and ethical acceptability. In *Rapid population growth: Consequences and policy implications* (Study Committee of the Office of the Foreign Secretary, National Academy of Sciences). Baltimore: Johns Hopkins University Press, 1971. Pp. 618–638.

Dyck, A. Is abortion necessary to solve population problems? In T. Hilgers & D. Horan (Eds.), *Abortion and social justice*. New York: Sheed & Ward, 1972. Pp. 159–176.

Dyck, A. Procreative rights and population policies. *The Hastings Center Studies*, 1973, *1*, 74–82.

Dyck, A. American global population policy: An ethical analysis. *The Linacre Quarterly*, 1975, *42*, 54–63.

Ford, J., & Kelly, G. *Contemporary moral theology*. II. *Marriage questions*. Westminster, Md.: Newman, 1963.

Greene, W. Triage. *The New York Times Magazine*, December 5, 1975.

Hardin, G. The tragedy of the commons. *Science*, 1968, *162*, 1243–1248.

Hardin, G. Living on a lifeboat. *Bioscience*, 1974, *24*, 561–568.

Harriott, J. Bucharest and beyond. *The Month*, 1974, *7*, 627–631.

Hauerwas, S., The moral limits of population control. *Thought*, 1974, *49*, 237–249.

Hauser, P. World population: Retrospect and prospect. In *Rapid population growth: Consequences and policy implications* (Study Committee of the Office of the Foreign Secretary, National Academy of Sciences). Baltimore: Johns Hopkins University Press, 1971. Pp. 103–122.

Hauser, P. Population criteria in foreign aid programs. In J. P. Wogaman (Ed.), *The population crisis and moral responsibility*. Washington, D.C.: Public Affairs Press, 1972. Pp. 233–251.

Hayes, J. Aspects of the world population problem. *Social Studies*, 1974, *3*, 229–253.

Hellegers, A. Government planning and the principle of subsidiarity. In J. P. Wogaman (Ed.), *The population crisis and moral responsibility*. Washington, D.C.: Public Affairs Press, 1973. Pp. 137–144.

Henriot, P. Global population in perspective: Implications for U. S. policy response. *Theological Studies*, 1974, *35*, 48–70.

Hurley, D. Population control and the Catholic conscience: Responsibility of the magisterium. *Theological Studies*, 1974, *35*, 154–163.

John XXIII. *Mater et magistra*. Encyclical letter of May 15, 1961. *Acta Apostolicae Sedis*, 1961, *53*, 401–464. English translation: Christianity and social progress. *Catholic Mind*, 1961, *59*, 411–479.

John XXIII. *Pacem in terris*. Encyclical letter of April 11, 1963. *Acta Apostolicae Sedis*, 1963, *55*, 257–304. English translation: Peace on earth. *Catholic Mind*, 1963, *61* (September, no. 1175) 47–62; and (October, no. 1176) 45–63.

Ketchel, M. Fertility control agents as a possible solution to the world population problem. In D. Callahan (Ed.), *The American population debate*. New York: Doubleday, 1971. Pp. 279–297.

Kiernan, J. An analysis of certain population policies. *The American Ecclesiastical Review*, 1975, *169*, 118–132.

Markus, R. A. Two conceptions of political authority: Augustine, *De Civitate Dei*, XIX, 14–15, and some thirteenth century interpretations. *Journal of Theological Studies*, 1965, *16*, 69–100.

McCormack, A. The population explosion: A theologian's concern? *Theological Studies*, 1974, *35*, 3–19.

Murphy, F. X. The pope and our common future. *Worldview*, 1975, *18* (2), 23–28.

Murray, J. C. *The problem of religious freedom*. Westminster, Md.: Newman, 1965.

National Academy of Sciences, Office of the Foreign Secretary. *Rapid population growth: Consequences and policy implications*. Baltimore: Johns Hopkins University Press, 1971.

Neuhaus, R. *In defense of people: Ecology and the seduction of radicalism*. New York: Macmillan, 1971.

Omran, A. Abortion and the demographis transition. In *Rapid population growth: Consequences and policy implications* (Study Committee of the Office of the Foreign Secretary, National Academy of Sciences). Baltimore: Johns Hopkins University Press, 1971. Pp. 479–532.

Paddock, W., & Paddock, P. *Famine—1975! America's decision: Who will survive?* Boston: Little, Brown, 1967.

Paul VI. *Populorum progressio*. Encyclical letter of March 26, 1967. *Acta Apostolicae Sedis*, 1967, *59*, 257–289. English translation: On promoting the development of peoples. *The pope speaks*, 1967, *12*, 144–172.

Paul VI. Address to the world food congress, November 9, 1974. *Acta Apostolicae Sedis*, 1974, *66*, 644–652. English translation: *The pope speaks*, 1975, *19*, 208–215.

Pius XII. Address to the Italian Catholic Union of Midwives, October 28, 1951. *Acta Apostolicae Sedis*, 1951, *43*, 835–854. English translation: Apostolate of the midwife. *Catholic Mind*, 1952, *50*, 49–64.

Pohlman, E. *Incentives and compensations in birth planning* (Carolina Population Center Monograph 11). Chapel Hill: Carolina Population Center, 1971.

Ramsey, P. *Nine modern moralists*. Englewood Cliffs, N.J.: Prentice-Hall, 1962.

Ramsey, P. *The patient as person*. New Haven: Yale University Press, 1970.

Ribes, B. Pour une politique démographique mondiale. *Études*, 1974, *341*, 27–47; 199–213.

Rommen, H. *The state in Catholic thought*. St. Louis: B. Herder, 1945.

Ruether, R. Governmental coercion and one-dimensional thinking. In J. P. Wogaman (Ed.), *The population crisis and moral responsibility*. Washington, D.C.: Public Affairs Press, 1973. Pp. 167–173.

Thielicke, H. *Theological ethics*. II. *Politics*. Philadelphia: Fortress, 1969.

Toner, J. *The experience of love*. Washington, D.C.: Corpus Books, 1968.

United Nations Economic and Social Council. *World population conference*. Ocober 2, 1974, E/5585.

Veatch, R. Governmental incentives: Ethical issues at stake. In J. P. Wogaman (Ed.), *The population crisis and moral responsibility*. Washington, D.C.: Public Affairs Press, 1973. Pp. 207–224.

Walsh, M. The Holy See's population problem. *The Month*, 1974, *7*, 632–636.

Warwick, D. Ethics and population control in developing countries. *The Hastings Center Report*, 1974, *4* (3), 1–4.

Yale Task Force on Population Ethics. Moral claims, human rights, and population policies. *Theological Studies*, 1974, *35*, 83–113.

Responsible Parenthood in the Contemporary World

SIDNEY C. CALLAHAN

Sidney Cornelia Callahan received her A.B. degree from Bryn Mawr College in 1955 and an M.A. degree from Sarah Lawrence College in 1970. She has received honorary degrees from Regis College and St. Mary's College and is listed in Foremost women in communication *and* Who's who among American women. *Mrs. Callahan is the mother of six children and the author of an equal number of books:* The illusion of Eve: Modern women's search for identity *(1965)*, Beyond birth control: Christian experience of sex *(1968)*, Christian family planning and sex education *(1969)*, The working mother *(1971)*, Parenting: Principles and politics of parenthood *(1974)*, and The Prayer of Mary *(1975)*.

Discussing responsible parenthood in the contemporary world is difficult indeed, for both "responsibility" and "parenthood" are multi-dimensional realities which are complex and complicated. Perhaps a very brief discussion of responsibility should come first, followed by a discussion of parenthood and of the different ways parents can live and function responsibly. Unfortunately, "responsible parenthood" has all too often in some popular population movements meant no more than the simplistic advice "Don't have children if you can avoid it, but if you must, don't have more than two." Any such numerical quantified definition of parental responsibility is completely inadequate to the task.

73

THE MEANING OF RESPONSIBILITY

It seems clear that the meaning of responsibility can expand or contract in our usage along a continuum of imputed activity and control. The strongest use of the word implies a total responsibility in the sense that a person initiates, constructs, and controls some product, event, or situation, and is thereby responsible for it. An author is responsible for his novel, the craftsman is responsible for his product, and the puppeteer is responsible for the world of the puppets. In this understanding of responsibility, initiative and constant control are actively maintained by the responsible agent; no chance occurrences invade the arena of responsibility.

A less complete meaning of responsibility can be seen in the case of an agent's initiating an activity or situation which then proceeds beyond his full control. A pilot can be responsible for an air crash, for instance, if he mistakenly acts or fails to act in the proper way. At a particular moment a person changes the future course of events decisively, but he does not maintain control. His responsibility is for initiating an action. This indirect sense of responsibility can become even more indirect when we understand some person to have a responsibility which is ascribed through some prior connection or tie, and which is not the result of active control or recent initiation of an event. This is responsibility in the sense of an obligation to respond to a person, product, or event which one has not directly initiated and does not control. A person may be responsible for another's debts, or an owner or employer may be responsible for accidents or events taking place which he does not even know about, much less actively control.

Obviously, the varying degrees of responsibility are also differentiated by the degree of freedom, knowledge, and active intention with which the responsible agent acts or fails to act. The young, the retarded, the insane, sleepwalkers, or those under the influence of toxic substances are commonly considered not to be fully responsible for their acts. Some observers would also consider certain extreme social situations such as war or disaster as all but removing a person's responsibility for his actions. These and other aspects of personal responsibility have been discussed for generations in both law and philosophy (Gustafson & Laney, 1968). The complexities and the subtleties of theories of responsibility are immense, and it is therefore difficult to apply concepts of responsibility to parenthood.

RESPONSIBLE PARENTHOOD

Yet it does seem that a concept of total responsibility is an unacceptable model for responsible parenthood. No parent can maintain full control over a child's life in the same way a person can make a product, control private property, or handle puppets. Even the initiating act of parenthood cannot be completely controlled. In spite of amazing progress in our technical knowledge, there remains an enormous element of random chance in conception and human reproduction. It involves two persons, with all the uncertainty of two people's potentiality for fertility—to say nothing of the unknown and enormous number of variations in the particular genetic combinations of two people which no one can control. And, for that matter, each parent is a product of chance combinations and a conveyor of the genetic heritage of his own gene pool. But even if one should become a parent by legal adoption, many chance elements are still involved which keep parental initiative from being a situation of total responsibility and control.

Needless to say, from the instant of conception, more chance and random environmental factors beyond the control of the parents begin to erode the concept of parental responsibility. Once childbearing has begun, there are myriad forces outside any one person's ability to contain which will influence the parental process and the child's growth. The only total control possible where parenthood is involved is some termination of the life generated, in abortion, infanticide, or child murder. Once there is life, and while there is life, there is an unpredictability which escapes control. If moral principles forbid the killing of progeny, then a concept of totally responsible parenthood is impossible. Arguments over abortion revolve around the question of whether it is an act of killing progeny and are beside the point here.

Responsible parenthood, then, must refer to a less than total controlling sense of responsibility. But there is the responsibility of initiation and of subsequent response. If it can happen, should I, or we, attempt to initiate a new life, and how can I fulfill the obligations to respond to that life? What are the kinds of considerations which should be weighed in answering these questions? The knowledge of what a parent is and what parents do becomes pertinent here, for unless we have some idea of parental function it is impossible for us to determine what responsible parenthood might be. Is, for instance, the responsibility of initiating a new conception separate and distinct from the responsibility of child rearing? And to whom are parents responsible?

In a sense parents are triple agents with obligations and shared control going in three ways. They are responsible to and for themselves; they are responsible to and for their children individually and as a group; and they are responsible to and for the rest of the human community. Parents are given controlling power and rights from the larger human community in a temporary mandate which ends with the adulthood of the child. But the control and the rights are conditional. These powers may be removed by the larger community if the parents abuse the children or fail in their parental obligations (Katz, 1971). Parents are given rights and powers in order to protect their child from other persons, institutions, and other environmental dangers.

Protection and nurturing of a child for the child's own sake is a primary parental function (Callahan, 1973). Parents are buffers against the world, providing a specific safe situation which specific children inhabit and within which they grow. A parent is his child's advocate in the world, mediating the world to the child within various norms of protection. The many, many needs of each child must be met primarily by his parents—from physical care to social education to psychological care. Psychological cruelty and child abuse is now recognized to be as damaging as physical abuse (Gil, 1970). In fact, one of the more recent advances in all aspects of parenting is a new self-consciousness. With the development of effective contraception, and with psychological sophistication, people have begun to consider their own suitability to fulfill parental obligations.

Biological and Psychological Parenting

The rise of psychological consciousness has also brought the definition of a parent into question. Heretofore and in general the biological natural parent and the psychological nurturing parent have been one and the same. In many cases, however, the biological and social are separated, and which then is more real? In a separation of functions and in the event certain choices have to be made I would opt for psychological parenting as primary. Psychologists and lawyers have begun to wrestle with these difficult problems as the number of child-custody cases increases. To choose psychological parenting as more significant than biological parenting is to say that the development of a child is influenced more by psychosocial environmental processes than by genetic heredity.

If psychological nurturing is primary in child rearing, then the parent–child tie is created more by personal care and commitment than by blood and kinship ties. I would doubt that there is any innate parental instinct; parenting is most probably learned from one's own experiences of having been parented. As they mature children seem to learn all the roles in the family drama and that learning comes into play when they in turn become parents. Since parenting is a question of learning, it can be maintained that males can be as nurturing and as well suited for it as women. Fortunately, an androgynous ideal of parenting is being developed in our society by which the personal characteristics of the parent are deemed more important than his sexual identity. This understanding accords with the affirmation that psychosocial personal learning and development is more important than biological identity.

Another result of the affirmation that parenting can be handled equally well by men and women is the rise of single parenting. Adoptions have been granted to single men and women on the grounds that a good single parent is better than having no parent and being institutionalized. It is still recognized, of course, that having two good parents is always preferable. Even if the parenting roles are not highly differentiated by sex, there are two persons to perform protective buffering functions and two people to learn from and love. From a parent's point of view the stresses of parenting are easier when shared with a spouse. And, if possible, a big loving extended family can be most supportive to parents. When blood kinship and relatives are not available, a support system of friends and other families can be created. The concept of "fictive kin" who are bound together by love and friendship but not by blood is important.

Helping the Child to Achieve Independence

Besides nurturing and protecting a child at home, a parent must help to activate him and prepare his entry into the wider world. This is achieved in part through strategic passivity and absence. No child can be well parented if there is constant parental supervision and over-protection in his life; there must be some independence training and a gradual separation from parental protection. The difficulties which parents face in providing the right amount of independence at the right stages of development are enormous, and they experience considerable anxiety in attempting to make wise decisions about independence, especially during their children's teen-age years. An important goal of parenting is to produce adults who can achieve independence and, in turn, become parents. In a sense parents who succeed work themselves out of a job.

Another situation, which is even more politically difficult for parents, is the peer relationships of their children. Children have friends and peers who are extremely important to their development (Sullivan, 1953). Peer relationships are a case in which parents have to learn to absent themselves. If a parent tries to control his child's friendships, then the child suffers and usually rebels. Children have to make their own friends mostly on their own. Part of the value of peer relationships is that they are different from parent–child, adult–child interactions; they are more brutally honest, more playful, and more satisfying. No child can do without friends. Every child needs many different peer experiences as well as a secure parental base. Moving back and forth from the worlds of parents to peers produces maturity. Each group counters the other and frees a child from total dependence on either. Parents can safely let go, once and for all, when their children are mature enough to be self-directing and skeptical of peer pressure.

Serving as the Child's Advocate

On the way to parental success there are many political skirmishes. Parents have to be their child's advocates within the schools and other institutions necessary to a child's life and education. Parents are constantly coming into contact with professionals of all sorts who are engaged in dealing with their child. With pediatrician and principal as well as with all the other people whom parents and children encounter, a parent must provide a delicate balance of communication and advocacy. Parents are on the side of their child, but not to the extent that they cannot listen to others or manifest their rightful authority. Parents must be ready to make demands and to hold professionals accountable. Without parental advocacy there is a temptation for institutions such as schools to exploit the power differential between adults and children, or at least to become more concerned about their own self-interests.

Parenting as a Partnering Operation

In conclusion, we might say that parenting is a partnering operation in which the partnership begins with a situation of unequal power and gradually changes to one of equality. As the power becomes equalized between the partners, so do the rights and responsibilities. Although we now know that infants and children have a great deal more of an active part in the parent–child interaction than once was recognized, still there is nothing more helpless in nature than the human infant. This absolute need for long periods of care and nurturing, however, is the basis of those interactions which produce human culture. The learning of language and the emotional bonding between infants and caretakers give us as a species those distinctive features of flexible intelligence and continually transmitted culture. "The uses of immaturity" in human development is crucial.

Through parenting a sense of self is internalized, a language is learned, and an entire, complicated culture is transmitted. Moral and religious values are inculcated in many implicit as well as explicit ways. The long dependency of human children has been the basis of culture. But no child and its parents are isolated from a larger group. Most people have lived very closely within a communal structure. The village, the tribe, or the neighborhood filled with relatives and long-term family friends has also played an important part in every socialization process.

Today, in spite of the fact that many American families live in isolated private homes, the presence of television provides strong outside influence. Most children in America watch television for extended periods of time, spending far more time in front of the screen, than in school, or in conversation or activities with their families. The segregation of children from adults and their dependence upon peers and television have been blamed by many observers for the breakdown of socialization (Bronfenbrenner, 1970). But even when parents do try, they cannot keep their children isolated from many other strong forces of influence.

In other words the parenting process is one in which substantial demands are made over many years. It is an irreversible, long-term commitment to a mutual relationship, and it involves many chance factors. All a parent's resources and talents will be called upon in a unique and vitally important enterprise. Another person's life and psychological well-being are at stake. The parent's deepest emotions will be engaged in the undertaking. It is inevitable that sorrow, joy, boredom, and fascination will be a part of the process as will a constricting of some aspects of life and the opening up and widening of other vistas. Always there will be the legal and moral duty to respond to the relationship. Though parental responsibility, in the sense of the need and ability to respond, is enormous, at the same time individual parental control over the process and relationship is limited.

THE DECISION TO INITIATE PARENTHOOD

The Risk-Taking Involved

The decision to initiate parenthood, then, is the human contracting of personal responsibility, effort, and commitment without assurances of personal control. It is, in essence, a risk. A person decides to venture into an unknown future. Does anything we know about decision theory have any relevance? In the existing studies of game theory and strategies of play, there may be little which applies to decisions about initiating parenthood (Luce, 1959). At least there is no opponent in parenting except the unknown future, or, for the more superstitious, fate, or moira. There is, moreover, a limited amount of information available with which to make decisions about future play. No one even knows how much control there will be over one's own options and resources, or who the new partners will be.

One finding from studies of risk-taking and game theory does seem applicable to decisions about becoming a parent. There is often a discrepancy in risk-taking between objective probabilities and the subject's evaluation of them. While most people may generally tend to optimism about their own chances in any gamble, the range of variation is a function of individual personality. Some people know that they will win every time in every gamble. If occasionally they fail or lose out, their failure is viewed as an unusual or temporary occurrence, standing out against a background of luck and success. Other persons are just as sure that they are doomed to lose and fail in every possible way. Evidence is remembered which proves one's habitual biases of attribution.

Another variant in an individual person's perceptions of the outcomes in life situations lies in whether the individual sees success and failure as caused externally or internally. Where is an individual's "locus of control"? Many people feel that outcomes are not dependent upon their own efforts, that success and/or failure is not under their own control (external locus of control). Others feel that success and/or failure is due to their own efforts (internal locus of control). As we saw in the question of outcomes in parenting, a very mixed response to the parental situation would be most appropriate and adaptive. For a parent to have at times an external locus of control would be an objective perception of the many random chance factors which occur in parenting, but an internal locus of control is necessary to adapt to the multitude of active interventions required in nurturing and parental protection.

Importance of the Parents' own Childhood Experiences

Of greater importance, perhaps, than all the cognitive factors involved in decisions of initiating parenthood are the questions of emotional responses and unconscious motivations. In a decision which involves reproducing one's own genetic, social heritage fused with that of a partner, many heretofore unmeasurable factors play a part. How much basic self-esteem exists and how much love for the other parent? Does one respect the heritages involved? Basic to these considerations are the attitudes which each parent has for his or her own parents. If love has been given in the family of origin, then it seems psychologically possible to desire children in a family of procreation. The beloved parents of one's childhood can be imitated and identified with in a final affirmation of adulthood.

Erik Erikson has called this psychological development in adulthood generativity, and viewed it as a normal stage in the life cycle (Erikson, 1963). In a grateful reaction to having been nurtured, the mature person wishes to nurture and sustain a family for the future. If there is no personal family, this generativity will be expended upon other groups or institutions in need of sustaining. But the mark of generative maturity is the willingness to give to others, to make long-term commitments, and to assume responsibilities for those who need nurturing. For Erikson this stage of maturity is the flowering of the basic trust and hope which was engendered in a child's infancy by his caretakers. Erikson believes that caretakers of the young should be believers in the goodness of the universe so that they can induce hope as they nurture the child. As a child's demands are met and satisfied, the orderliness and goodness of the world are communicated. The future will gradually seem to be a positive and rewarding goal to which the child can progress with trust.

If things do not go well, distrust and anxiety about the disorderly future may predominate. As the child grows, there will not be much hope or trust in the future or energy left over for others. There are adults who are still engaged in giving themselves all the love and attention they missed in childhood. Having and caring for children would call upon emotional resources which are almost non-existent. Worse still, some adults may have children in the expectation that the children will provide the nurturing and satisfactions which their parents failed to give. In many cases of child abuse it seems that the parents were expecting totally unrealistic satisfactions from their own children. The children were being put in a parental role instead of a dependent one. The child was seen as "somebody to give me the love I never had" rather than as a developing human being in need of sustained care and protection.

One Extreme of Parenting: Excess of Trust

But even among those capable of giving to a child for the child's own sake, those not seeking to fulfill their own immature needs, there are other problems of attitude. Two extremes toward parenting seem unsatisfactory. At one extreme there exists a pathology of hope and an excess of trust which carries an external locus of control to the extremes of passivity and irresponsibility. Nature is simply allowed to take its course without any intervention in the processes of conception and reproduction. People are simply passive and accepting before their own potentiality of fertility. Even though the facts of reproduction and contraception are consciously understood (and, of course, if they are not understood, it is a different moral situation), no control or responsibility for one's own sexuality or fertility is assumed. No abstinence or other forms of birth control are employed because hope, trust, and passivity are absolute.

Such attitudes to human reproduction are usually part of a nature mystique as in some aspects of the counter culture. Or they may arise from a religious understanding of the world in which persons obey God through a passive acceptance of whatever happens. If children happen to come one after another, then they come, and one trusts that they will somehow be provided for. Foresight and future planning are not asked of the parents, only trust and acceptance. Child rearing is usually seen as important, but arduous or expensive efforts at education are not stressed unless the family is very wealthy. It is more important to trust and obey what is seen as God's general will than to ask what might be best for the particular people involved. Even the welfare of the children who are born is often seen as secondary to the parents' continuing obedience. There is no great concern either for the parents' welfare or the outside community's needs. The future is God's business.

Another Extreme: Complete Distrust

At the opposite extreme there is a complete distrust of nature and a refusal to accept any of the risks involved in procreation. Absolute control of life is attempted by avoiding the responsibility of childbearing and child rearing. Often such refusals arise from a couple's present-centered hedonism or, even more frequently, from a general distrust and despair over the future. The risk of bringing a child into the doomed and troubled world seems insupportable. Besides, who could measure up to the task? The burdens and responsibilities of child rearing are viewed in an exaggerated and frightening way. Moreover, a concern for the overpopulated earth is so keenly felt that no individual reproduction should contribute to the planetary danger. In addition, man's control of and responsibility for his own and the universe's fate are seen as absolute. Usually in this extreme position there is no room for any hope in God or trust in man and nature. Any and all measures which can control reproduction are seen as valid, even if potential life is destroyed.

Parenthood is a Privileged Stewardship

A more intelligent and admirable attitude toward responsible parenthood which avoids extremes would be to take the idea of stewardship seriously. Mankind has been given the world in trust, to develop and care for it as the dominant species. In the Judaeo-Christian interpretation of this stewardship, humankind is charged with subduing the world, neither destroying it, nor totally accepting it as it exists. To develop and order the world and nature while respecting it is a form of social wisdom. Persons should accept procreation and child rearing as a privileged stewardship which reproduces society and the species, but they also can make wise decisions to curtail and control fertility. Just as humankind has learned to control disease, death, and infant mortality, so the control of births is a measure of stewardship (Callahan, 1968).

Reasons for Curtailing Fertility

The reasons for curtailing fertility and the methods of control will vary with the different situations and personalities involved. In making this decision, there is an urge toward procreation as well as constraints inhibiting the moves. Many so-called accidents and contraceptive failures are ways around these stalemates; they resolve the dilemma by imposing an acceptance of a great task one might not be able to volunteer for with confidence. The responsibility involved after life begins becomes that of being responsible for and being responsive to new life. Since most of parenting is a partnering and interactive function, the acceptance of a child as "other" and as another separate human being is extremely important. A surprise pregnancy can well prepare parents for the surprise of a totally new and different personality who is in no way a simple product of the parents' desires and will. A child whose rights and dignity depend upon being "wanted" by his parents is not being granted a basic human right.

Yet when there are already children born who need parental care, the curtailment of new births can be seen as more serious and important. The welfare of the existing children and the family as a whole can be more involved. Prudent reproductive decisions are always influenced by the amount of resources available for the child-rearing task. A family's resources are physical and psychological as well as economic, and they all interact. Supremely confident, stable, competent, healthy parents leading a happily married life in relatively straitened financial circumstances can be far richer in resources than their wealthy counterparts suffering from various kinds of psychological malaise or illnesses. Wise decisions are best made by those involved who honestly assess the differing weights of the various factors involved. The future is always unknown, but the present is at least an indicator of how hopeful a couple can be, at least about their own resources.

But, as we have said before, no couple is an island. Potential parents exist as part of an extended family as well as part of a community, a nation, and the planet. How much weight should outside factors be given in responsible parenting decisions? Surely a large loyal nearby helpful extended family would be counted as a valuable resource in child rearing just as sick, dependent parents would be a deterrent. Filial and family obligations are not overthrown by marriage and parenthood. The family of procreation does not obliterate obligations to the family of origin, although in modern America procreation and the future have generally been seen to take precedence over the past. Nurturing one's children has generally been chosen as a higher duty and obligation than the duty to one's aged parents or grandparents. To this end the growth of social security and other forms of insurance has helped bring about the lessening of the economic burden of the old upon young families.

A less immediate relationship is called into question in the matter of a couple's relationship to the nation and the world. Should procreative behavior be shaped to the need of the world at large? It is a particularly confusing question if one's country needs labor and more people and so encourages birth while population experts warn of the dangers to the planet from overpopulation. Still other observers may say that because of the injustices of the present economic system of distribution, an emphasis upon population policy is premature. But individual parents do live embedded in the social matrix of their state and world. The arguments and reasoning of both one's governmental representatives and those experts speaking for the planet should be listened to with respect. If nothing else, the condition of one's children's children can be a consideration in present reproductive decisions. Private desires and private wills often have to be subordinated to the social welfare of all.

But when a reduction in a country's birth rate is sought for the common good, the results sought are overall averages. Those persons who have no children and those who have four average out to two children per family. In a nation in which many choose not to have children, others can have more children, providing those pluralistic family patterns which may have adaptive value genetically. We still know very little about what happens to a human population once contraception is available to all segments in a free and just society. It may be that those who have the most resources will also have the greatest desire for children. Those characteristics which make for social dominance may be reflected in procreative decisions to have families of more than average size. Or it may be the opposite. I should think that with the growth of self-consciousness and a realization of the responsibilities of parenting, the present trend to much smaller families would continue, except for those who feel especially favored and resourceful.

Public Assistance to Parents in their Child-Rearing Tasks

At this point in American history parents are still making reproductive and parenting decisions individually. It is considered a basic human right to procreate. I am not sure if procreation is a right or a privilege, but the discussion of the question is still in such an embryonic stage that no just public action could be taken. As long as the society at large offers so little in the way of public help and assistance to parents in their child-rearing tasks, no public intrusion seems warranted except in cases of parental failure. But even if we decide as a people that procreation should always be a private right and decision, more social assistance should be offered to parents. A society which does not invest in maternal health and child welfare is shortchanging its own future. Almost every other developed wealthy society in the Western world provides more family assistance and better health care to its people than the United States.

If we are going to promote responsible parenthood in the contemporary world, we as a society must activate more thoroughly a communal sense of parenthood. A sense of stewardship and responsibility for a new generation will be engendered in individuals if it is first a priority of the whole culture. Parents can be responsible to make responsible decisions if the larger community responds and recognizes the high value of the generative enterprise.

REFERENCES

Bronfenbrenner, U. *Two worlds of childhood: U.S. and U.S.S.R.* New York: Russell Sage Foundation, 1970.

Callahan, S. C. *Beyond birth control: The Christian experience of sex.* New York: Sheed & Ward, 1968.

Callahan, S. C. *Parenting: Principles and politics of parenthood.* New York: Doubleday, 1973.

Erikson, E. H. *Childhood and society* (2nd ed.). New York: Norton, 1963.

Gil, D. G. *Violence against children: Physical child abuse in the United States.* Cambridge: Harvard University Press, 1970.

Gustafson, J. M., & Laney, J. T. *On being responsible: Issues in personal ethics.* New York: Harper & Row, 1968.

Katz, S. N. *When parents fail: The law's response to family breakdown.* Boston: Beacon, 1971.

Luce, R. D. *Individual choice behavior.* New York: Wiley, 1959.

Sullivan, H. S. *The interpersonal theory of psychiatry.* New York: Norton, 1953.

III
PROBLEMS OF BIRTH:
EUGENIC PROBLEMS

Genetic Engineering

MARC A. LAPPÉ

Marc Alan Lappé received his A.B. degree from Connecticut Wesleyan University in 1964 and his Ph.D. from the University of Pennsylvania in 1968. From 1968 to 1970 he was an Honorary Postdoctoral Fellow at the University of California. Since 1971, he has been Associate for the Biological Sciences at the Institute of Society, Ethics and the Life Sciences at Hastings-on-Hudson, New York, and Adjunct Assistant Professor at the State University of New York at Purchase. Dr. Lappé is the author, either individually or in collaboration, of approximately 40 articles in scientific and professional journals, the more recent of which have focused on genetic engineering, genetic counseling, and the medical and, particularly, the moral problems involved.

There is a strong tendency to regard the prospect of "genetic engineering" in imagery reminiscent of the science fiction scenarios conjured up by Huxley's (1950) *Brave New World.* In Huxley's book, hatcheries were to be peopled by genetically selected embryos of greater or lesser societal potential depending upon a pre-selected functional role. The danger of this type of formulation is that it shifts the public's focus from the existing uses and misuses of genetic knowledge to more futuristic and esoteric ones. Genetic knowledge is already permeating our culture in ways which shape and distort our understanding of human potential. Genetic models of mental and physical disease, notably schizophrenia and hypertension, dislocate, for better or worse, the attention we pay to societal or environmental causal factors in favor of internal ones. No, Mr. Huxley, genetics poses more of a threat today in the way it can alter the fate of already conceived or existing persons than it does in shaping the genetic composition of future persons.

THE QUESTIONABLE USE OF GENETIC CRITERIA FOR ENSURING NORMALCY

For example, it is possible to think of "genetically engineering" human beings simply by having parents act out the biomedical options which allow them to choose children from among some of the genotypes which we can now define. The use of a test to determine the sex of a fetus *in utero*, with the option to abort the individual which does not meet parental expectations, is the archetypal example of genetic engineering. A choice of sex based on chromosome composition *already* projects expectation of gender onto a child-to-be. This option raises in starkest relief the fundamental questions which Sidney Callahan has raised in another context: Does every child not have a right to be born "unchosen," unburdened by the rigid expectations forged by his parents' own acculturation (Callahan, 1974, p. 188)? Where sex selection is exercised through amniocentesis and abortion, the mere fact that the parents are willing to use selective killing of a child-to-be of one sex eventually to assure the birth of the other almost certainly casts a pall over the life of the "desired" child. Picture, if you will, the fateful conversation in which the little girl or boy questions "Mommy, what did you do to get me?"

Genetic choice raises the specter of a world in which human deservedness is predicated on having genetic, rather than acquired, qualities. This prospect was anticipated in an article which appeared in the *New England Journal of Medicine* for May 25, 1972 (Research Group on Ethical, Social and Legal Issues in Genetic Counseling and Genetic Engineering, 1972). There a group of twenty-three signatories (including the present author) presented a set of principles to guide screening-program organizers in their attempt to anticipate the sequelae of genetic disease. In a sentence included under a section urging that screening be voluntary, these signatories stated that "It is unjustifiable to promulgate standards for normalcy based on genetic constitution." This statement has since been the subject of intensive scrutiny and review, as more and more data permitting genetic testing shortly after birth have been accumulated.

The critical moral issue in all such screening is *not* the acceptability of tests which detect markers of an underlying genetic predisposition for a disease state (a medical question), but rather the acceptability of using such tests to define the "normalcy" of the population, family, or individual surveyed (an ethical question). As a basic principle, genetic tests do not measure normalcy, merely the presence or absence of a major genetically based disease; genetic data do not indicate the adequacy of a genotype, only the presence of a critical genetic makeup which alters an individual's actuarial risks of disability. Ostensibly, then, genetic tests only refine our knowledge of a person's likelihood of experiencing the normal statistical risks of disease and disability.

As more and more such tests are applied, and as more high-risk individuals are found, the definition of "average" will shift. Initially, the public's awareness of the burden of genetically based disease will be heightened as hundreds of genetic variants are uncovered; but as more and more diseases (such as heart disease) which were previously thought to be more or less randomly distributed throughout the population are separated into categories of largely genetically or environmentally caused pathology, the public's concept of what constitutes the "normal" will change. It is conceivable that new concepts of normalcy will, in fact, be formed. No one would wish to call normal the state in which a person carries a gene for hyperbetalipoproteinemia (Type II disease) when it carries a 50% risk of a heart attack by the age of 50. Yet such a person just five years ago would have been considered "normal," albeit with increased betalipoproteins in the blood. It is the discovery that this state reflects the presence of an etiologic or causal agent *inside* the person—the gene for Type II disease—which makes all the difference. Now, for the first time, it has become possible to define a person on the basis of what he will ineluctably come to be (in this case, a young coronary patient) in a way which may shape his life and expectations radically.

THE MORAL COSTS OF SELECTIVE ABORTION FOLLOWING A
CRITICAL GENETIC DIAGNOSIS

This prospect will take on an entirely new dimension when it becomes possible for the public to exercise these new expectations through improved techniques of intrauterine diagnosis. As amniocentesis becomes more widely available and *in utero* blood tests become possible, genetic diagnosis could take on the dimension of a modern-day Spartan Lesch, in which the test for normalcy will be performed within the statutory limits of abortion, and a "defective" child could be aborted rather than thrown to the winds. Selective abortion following a critical genetic diagnosis will then pose the risk of becoming a mechanism by which we act out the criteria for acceptance into the human community. What would be the moral costs of such a program?

First, it is critical to separate the utilization of diagnostic technology for those who will be severely burdened by genetic disease from its utilization for those who are merely unwanted because of their genetic makeup. Researchers who develop prenatal diagnostic strategems may now merely wish to extend greater parental choice in the genetic makeup of their families, but the researcher will not be the one who places limits on the uses of genetic technique. In the first case for limits, there are those parents who face the birth of a child whose life prospect is cast in a pall of pain and suffering and would wish to exercise the choice to avoid this fate. To my knowledge, there are relatively few such instances where a bona fide decision can be made that it is in the child's best interest not to be born (though one possibility might be the case of a boy child with the Lesch–Nyhan syndrome, in which profound behavioral disturbances, including self-mutilation, are the normal course). More often, it is the parents' needs which dictate the choices in selective abortion.

In the second instance of parental choice, there are the options afforded by prenatal chromosomal diagnoses which permit the determination of the sex of the offspring, or, with less certainty of outcome, the presence of one or more extra (or deficient) sex chromosomes, e.g., XYY, XXY, or XO karyotypes. Because the overall frequency of these compositions at birth is so high (1 child in approximately 250 births), in comparison with other birth defects, the use of amniocentesis for other reasons may conflict strongly with the initial purposes of the testing. For example, a test to ascertain the presence of a child with Down's syndrome in a 39-year-old woman may have the same chance of uncovering an unanticipated chromosomal condition (e.g., XYY) as the presence of the extra 21–22 chromosome which heralds the likelihood of developmental retardation.

WHAT PRICE THE PERFECT BABY?

The problems which neonatal diagnostics pose for parents are thus complicated by at least two dimensions of ethical decision-making: (a) the choices needed to avoid the birth of a severely handicapped child, and (b) the exercise of choices to secure a "more desirable" outcome of pregnancy.

In my view, it is the second of these choices which poses the greatest risk to the fabric of society. Teaching prospective parents that they may exercise choices of the kinds of offspring which they may have (a possibility recognized twenty years ago through the use of artificial insemination with donor semen) brings *hubris* to the parental bond and commitment to family. It is one thing to act to avoid unimaginable suffering, another to attempt to "improve on nature."

Both the definition of "improvement" and "nature" are severely culture-bound and unrefined. Would it be an improvement over the normal prospects of birth to use selective abortion to avoid the birth of a child who carries the genetic marker which increases the risk (ever-so-slightly) of debilitating but late-onset diseases like ankylosing spondylitis or multiple sclerosis, discernible through the presence of a gene for one of the transplantation antigens (Svejgaard, *et al.*, 1975)? Our first instinct is to say, "Of course!" But what statistical gauntlet will we want to subject the next child to—and the next, and the next? As Leon Kass (1971) asked, "What price the perfect baby?"

One way to look at the options afforded parents to select their offspring on genetic grounds is to recall W. W. Jacobs' story "The monkey's paw" (Jacobs, 1969). In this story Jacobs wrote of a despondent father who, mourning the recent death of his son in a sawmill accident, wished with all his might for a way to get him back. The opportunity came in the form of the mysterious arrival of a stranger bearing a monkey's paw. With this paw, the father could make three unfettered wishes. He immediately asked to see his son alive, only to be confronted with a walking, but horribly mangled and bloody, body. He had to use his second wish to allow his son to return to the grave. With his third and last wish, he asked to have his son back the way he was before the accident. This the paw dutifully did—only to have the old man experience his son's death a second time. The old man cursed the day he received the gift. Will we come to think of amniocentesis the same way?

Every culture has its myths which deal with the question of the evil implicit in unlimited knowledge and burgeoning human control over nature. Genetic knowledge and prenatal diagnosis promise to carry their share of hope and opportunity, but also a modicum of human suffering and dismay. We already have had reports of healthy children who were mistakenly diagnosed *in utero* as having a life-threatening disease (Tay–Sachs) and aborted in ignorance of their innocent state. But even where diagnoses are perfect and prognoses omniscient, we shall still be faced with the terrible onus of having chosen to recognize the deservedness of a fellow human being on the basis of his genetic worth. The development of increasingly sophisticated genetic techniques carry with them a second-order cost: the ultimate use of genetic engineering to shape human evolution embodies the presumption that human beings have the wisdom to direct their own evolution.

REFERENCES

Callahan, S. C. *Parenting: Principles and politics of parenthood.* Baltimore: Penguin, 1974.
Huxley, A. L. *Brave new world.* New York: Harper, 1950.

Jacobs, W. W. The monkey's paw. In W. W. Jacobs, *The lady of the barge.* Short Story Index Reprint Series. Freeport, N.Y.: Books for Libraries Press, 1969. Pp. 29–53.

Kass, L. The new biology: What price relieving man's estate? *Science,* 1971, *174,* 779–788.

Research Group on Ethical, Social and Legal Issues in Genetic Counseling and Genetic Engineering. Ethical and social issues in screening for genetic disease. *New England Journal of Medicine,* 1972, *286,* 1129–1132.

Svejgaard, A., *et al.* HL–A and disease associations—A survey. *Transplantation Reviews,* 1975, *22,* 3–43.

Genetic Screening and Counseling

Andrew L. Szebenyi, s.j.

Father Andrew L. Szebenyi, S.J. was born in Hungary and studied in that country, as well as in Germany, Belgium, England, Canada, and the United States. He earned an A.B. degree in 1958, and an M.A. degree in 1961 from Oxford University. His Ph.D. degree in Behavior Genetics is from Syracuse University. Since 1963 Father Szebenyi has been on the faculty of Le Moyne College, Syracuse, where he is currently Assistant Professor in the Biology Department.

In April 1972, I attended a Symposium on Ethical and Social Problems in Human Biology at the State University of New York at Buffalo. During the morning sessions a paper was read by Dr. Verle E. Headings on "Developing the Potential of Human Genes" (Headings, 1972). In this paper, Dr. Headings described a major trend in the present state of medical genetics and counseling as the attempt to optimize the environment for the genotype and, thus, to achieve the full development of the given genetic potential. Dr. Headings' paper was like a breath of fresh air in a somewhat stifling atmosphere of bewilderment and anxiety about so-called "just around the corner" developments in human biology.

Although I firmly believe in the importance of considering the probable consequences of one's actions, I caution against establishing a preventive moral code which does not deal with realities. Consider, for instance, the following example. On the one hand, cloning in man does not exist, partly because our present knowledge and technology cannot render an artificially fertilized human ovum viable. On the other hand, medical research tries to save human lives by developing more and more efficient artificial survival systems for premature babies. The technology of the two lines of research is identical, and, thus, the more successful medical technology becomes, the more feasible it appears that cloning will one day be possible also in man. Should we say that since cloning in man is immoral we should stop the line of research on viability? The answer is obvious: cloning in man is neither moral, nor immoral; it does not exist. Medical research with its aim to save human lives is very real and is highly commendable.

Similar problems could easily arise in the context of genetic screening. A screening program is set up to sort things out, to separate one kind from another, to allow and to prevent the passage of desirables and undesirables respectively. Genetic screening could thus be conceived as a diagnostic process the aim of which is to identify genetic disorders in affected individuals (to the extent of heterozygous carriers) and to arrive at a set of decisions about those found genetically defective (Murray, 1972).

These thoughts may provoke a certain uneasiness in us, and we may begin to ask questions about the possible moral implications of genetic screening: Who should initiate a screening program? What should the criteria be for defects to be screened? To what extent (if ever) should screening be confined to ethnic groups sharing a "common" gene pool? Should it be voluntary, or compulsory? How will the screening be done? Will it necessarily entail abortion? Who will have access to the information? What controls should be placed on its dissemination or use? Do the persons screened have the right to know all the data? What moral, social, medical, and legal obligations do we accept when we screen populations (Lappé, 1971a, pp. 13–14)?

There is just one little problem with all these questions. Apart from some rather restricted and minor ventures (sickle cell anemia, PKU), genetic screening, especially in the form of an extensive mass-screening project, does not exist at present. Whether it will exist at some time in the future, I do not know. I could make some guesses, or I could express my desire for a fairly widespread, intensive mass-screening project by saying "I wish there were one" if for no other reason than for the sake of a better understanding of human genetics. It simply does not make sense to talk about the morality of a nonexistent mass-screening program. If we review the present state of diagnostic procedures, we may easily get the impression that we do not need to worry about such moral implications for a long time to come. It would be completely wrong, because of the possibility of future moral problems, to hinder the greatly needed accumulation of actual skills and knowledge in matters of human genetics.

Some minor screening programs for sickle cell anemia were instituted by law in several states in 1971 and 1972. Compulsory diagnosis of the newborn for PKU (phenylketonuria) has been in effect in many states for as long as twelve years. Most recently, Tay–Sachs disease has been considered for screening. In all these programs, the nature of the tests used, the efficacy of treatments prescribed, and the recognition of the possibility of many variants of the disorders, demand constant updating. Such legalized attempts at screening for genetic disorders are but sporadic and hasty responses to situations labeled as urgent (Powledge, 1973). In view of the large number of inherited disorders, these attempts certainly do not constitute extensive mass-screening programs.

Incidentally, the sickle cell law was repealed in Maryland, and a more general genetics law substituted in 1973. This new law does not demand compulsory testing but directs that free testing and counseling be provided to marriage license applicants, ensuring strict confidentiality of information. Since then, this legislation has been considered model legislation in genetic matters (Powledge, 1973).

There are indications that legislative compulsion may not be needed. In Canada, the provinces of Quebec and Ontario screen their newborns for PKU in voluntary programs, and get more than 90% and almost 95% participation respectively. These results approximate what we obtain by legislative coercion (Powledge, 1973).

In the real world of genetic screening the decision-making remains the responsibility of the individuals concerned. It is true that they often need guidance and advice, and in this way genetic counseling becomes a much needed part of the process. It should be emphasized, however, that both diagnosis and counseling center in and are supportive of decision-making. Let us briefly consider what is actually involved in testing, counseling, and decision-making.

DIAGNOSIS

The diagnosis of genetic disorders is a highly complex procedure which requires specialized knowledge, help, and equipment. In addition to the descriptive identification of major phenotypic manifestations of the diseases, much laboratory work may be needed, including such features as chromosome analyses, tissue culture techniques, histological and biochemical studies, and the like. In other words, the diagnosis of genetic disorders is not a simple affair (Yunis, 1974). Further difficulties may arise because of the limits of the reliability of the tests and because of the often numerous atypical variants of disorders. Take, for instance, one of the better known autosomal chromosome anomalies, the 21-Trisomy (also known as Down's syndrome and G-Trisomy, and formerly called Mongolism). Even if the presence of chromosome anomaly has been identified beyond any practical doubt by careful analysis of the karyotype, if the baby is not yet born, it is never predictably certain how much and to what extent the features of the 21-Trisomy will actually be manifested. Mental retardation, for instance, may manifest itself through a fairly wide range of IQ values in different individuals, and congenital heart disease may or may not be present (Nora & Fraser, 1974).

Since some genetic disorders, including Down's syndrome, can be diagnosed quite early in development, long before the baby is born, considerations like these should caution us against too hasty decisions about abortion.

One of the currently used diagnostic techniques is amniocentesis. The abdominal wall of the pregnant mother and the fetal membranes are punctured by a syringe, and a small amount of amniotic fluid containing cast-off cells of the developing fetus is removed. These cells are then cultured and can be subjected to microscopic examination and chemical tests. The major usefulness of amniocentesis is in such cases as Rh disease, possible sex-linked disorders of a more serious nature, and chromosome aberrations (Friedman, 1971).

Certain popularizations may try to give the rather uncritical impression that antenatal diagnosis of genetic disorders through amniocentesis is some sort of miracle technique with practically unlimited possibilities. The impression is given that, in this day of enlightenment and technology, all we have to do is to test the fetus for genetic defects as early as possible and abort it if it is abnormal. This whole idea is incredibly naïve and irresponsible.

Amniocentesis as an early diagnostic procedure has many limitations. Of some 40 candidates, there are only 16 mutant gene disorders in which amniocentesis is of diagnostic value (Nora & Fraser, 1974). This may be a partial but a practical estimate. Amniotic fluid may be obtained for diagnosis between the 14th and the 20th weeks of gestation. The first attempt is often not successful, and a second or even a third attempt may be required. The success of the tissue culture procedures may be as good as 80%. All these mean a rather tight schedule for amniocentesis as a diagnostic aid. Then the position of the placenta, determined by sound, may be a limiting factor. There is some concern of risk to the mother and to the baby. Leakage of amniotic fluid resulting in abortion is not uncommon. Since tissue cultures are obtained by cloning out the fetal cells, there is always the possibility of establishing unrepresentative cell lines leading to false diagnosis (Nora & Fraser, 1974). In conclusion, amniocentesis is a useful diagnostic technique, but, like all such techniques, it also has many limitations.

The mere diagnosis of a genetic disorder is only part of the work to be done. What is still needed is to establish the recurrence risk of the disease in probability terms for a given actual situation. The recurrence risk depends primarily on the mode of inheritance of the disorder—whether it is caused by a single major gene (sex-linked, autosomal, recessive, dominant), several genes (epistatic, multifactorial, polygenic), interactions of major genes and polygenic modifiers altering expressivity and penetrance, chromosomal aberrations (nondisjunction, translocation, deletion), or interactions between genetic and environmental factors, as in most instances. The usual question is this: What is the probability that children to be born will be affected by a genetic disorder if one of the parents or a near relative has the disease?

COUNSELING

One of the tasks of the genetic counselor is to translate the findings of diagnostic work into, for the layman, understandable language, including the proper interpretation of the probability figures of the recurrence risk. Such counseling may be done by the family doctor or by hospital personnel, including a great variety of professional people, trained counselors, social workers, pediatricians. Some may have an advanced medical degree or a Ph.D. in genetics. At present no formal qualifications are required for a genetic counselor.

> A good counselor needs a sound grasp of genetic principles, a wide knowledge of the scientific literature on diseases of possible genetic origin, and much sympathy, tact, and good sense. Preferably he should be associated with a hospital, so that he can take advantage of the diagnostic resources and the expertise of its staff, and so that he is available to his colleagues and to patient's families [Nora & Fraser, 1974, p. 352].

DECISION-MAKING

With decision-making we come to the most crucial part of genetic screening and counseling. Both diagnostic and counseling procedures try to serve this moment of decision. It is the individuals concerned who are to make the decision and not the counselor or the hospital staff, or any institution or government. Decision-making, in practice, may range from complete readiness to accept, love, and provide for a disabled child, through the various stages of care, including or excluding extraordinary means of medical intervention, to institutionalization and abortion.

Instead of trying to cover a wide range of actual cases to illustrate the crucial importance, the agony, and the reward of making the right decision in genetic matters, it seems to be more relevant to consider but a few general guidelines. The views which are being presented here are mostly personal insights. Some may not agree with my basic principles or with my applications of these principles. Some may feel that I am not radical enough, or that I am too liberal in certain views. Nonetheless, what I want to say I try to say simply, sincerely, and with compassion for suffering and the human condition. I have no special authoritative support for these insights other than my own background and rather modest experience.

Respect for Human Life

As far as I can see it, there are two fundamental principles involved in decision-making about genetic matters. One is the respect for human life; the other, the respect for the rights of the individual. By respect I mean the acceptance of the actual, and the endeavor to actualize the potential.

Common experience clothes with specific meanings these general principles. The humanity of a person is in a constant state of development. At no point in this process can we say that humanity begins but at conception, and at no point can we say that it ends but at the moment of death. A child is not an adult, and still he is a human child. Neither the time of birth nor the time of viability is a fixed point in the process of human development. In other words, we owe respect to human life from the moment of conception until the moment of death. As to quality of life, we should endeavor to improve that quality to its optimum.

Attitudes in decision-making should differ considerably in situations before and after conception. Before conception there is considerable opportunity for preventive measures to be taken if the probability of recurrence of a serious disorder is estimated as too high by the prospective parents. Obviously, probability estimates for the recurrence risk of genetic diseases are not like odds in a game of chance. Respect for human life means that we do not gamble with it. In the case of high risk of a serious disease the answer should be adoption and not abortion.

In view of the seriousness of such matters, respect for life should not be founded on tenuous grounds, but find support in effective control over procreation. No such control can be envisaged without proper methods of contraception, even to the extent of sterilization. If these statements sound rather harsh, maybe it is because we have been misled, and are thinking in terms of rather unreal expectancies. One woman receiving a diagnosis of defect in her fetus stated: "You spend all your life looking at pictures of pretty babies and their mothers and thinking that will be you. It's pretty gruesome when you are the one who is different" (Lappé, 1973, p. 8). It takes considerable love and maturity to be able to handle this kind of disappointment.*

Genetic counselors can do a tremendous amount of good by giving psychologically and factually positive support to parents of defective children. It should be emphasized that there are no "optimal" babies, and that everyone is the carrier of at least a few genetic disorders. Such a relatively high genetic load (the average number of lethal equivalents per individual in a population, i.e., the average number of recessive deleterious genes in the heterozygous condition per individual times the mean probability that each gene will cause premature death when homozygous) is the result of our outbreeding system of mating and not the shortcoming of individuals; we all share this load. On the average, 1 in 40 live births will result in some form of genetic disorder (Lappé, 1973).

Incidentally, the tolerance of a population for its genetic load could be increased in an outbreeding situation by assortative mating, which brings outbreeding to its maximum by avoiding matings between carriers of the same genetic defect. Such a mating system would avoid a new kind of "incest," by preventing the union of genes which are not identical by descent but by default.

Another positive approach to handling genetic defects is the observation that often there are considerable variations in the manifestations of disorders, and proper care can alleviate many or at least some of the symptoms. In case of mongoloid children much can be done through love and care. Karen Lebacqz at Harvard University writes: "Some of the attributes formerly considered part of the *nature* of the syndrome may now be seen instead to be a function of the *nurture* given to the person with the syndrome" (Lebacqz, 1972, p. 12).

Certain inherited metabolic disorders respond well to early treatment. In modern medicine we attempt to provide an environment in which a genetic disorder cannot be expressed. The classical example is the treatment for galactosemia caused by a recessive mutant gene in the homozygous condition. The symptoms of the disease are quite severe, but they are not manifested if a galactose-free diet is followed from the time of birth. There are some 18 other metabolic diseases which respond well to similar treatments (Nora & Fraser, 1974).

The attempt to optimize the environment for proper development

---

* For an excellent review of the actual problems of dealing with a severely handicapped child, see Reich (1973).

can be extended to all genotypes, and it is becoming a trend today not only in medical genetics but also in education and genetic engineering (Headings, 1972).

Respect for the Rights of the Individual

The other general principle, i.e., the fundamental respect for the rights of the individual, has equally important implications within the framework of genetic screening and counseling. The question of confidentiality is of importance. The subject of a genetic test has the right to know the results and to reveal that information if he or she so wishes. The diagnostician and the genetic counselor have the obligation to treat the results as privileged information (Veatch, 1972).

The genetic counselor's task is to inform and to give support to the counseled, but not to make the decisions for them unless they ask what he would do under similar circumstances. It is an infringement of the rights of individuals to restrict their choice by presenting them with only some of the facts or some of the alternatives.

Should decision-making be influenced by eugenic ideas such as maintaining that by aborting affected individuals we actually lessen the frequency of deleterious genes, and thus lessen genetic load? The answer is no. There simply are no effective eugenic methods. To reduce, for instance, the frequency of a deleterious recessive gene from 0.02 to 0.01 by sterilization of all affected individuals would take about 1500 years. This is very little return for a tremendous lot of hardship. Similar considerations exclude the effectiveness of eugenic methods against dominants and polygenes (Li, 1955). To try to sterilize the carriers of genetic defects would mean to sterilize everyone. The right of the individual should certainly prevail over an imaginary "common good."

"The best we can do . . . in the face of the inevitability of genetic defects is to minimize the impact (not necessarily the occurrence) of these defects" (Lappé, 1971b, p. 7). And, we might add, we should also try to maximize the beneficial effects of the developmental as well as the social environment.

REFERENCES

Friedmann, T. Prenatal diagnosis of genetic disease. *Scientific American*, 1971, *225* (5), 34–42.

Headings, V. E. *Developing the potential of human genes.* Paper presented at the Symposium on Ethical and Social Problems in Human Biology, at the State University of New York at Buffalo, April 1972.

Lappé, M. Genetic counseling and genetic engineering. *The Hastings Center Report*, 1971, *1* (3), 13–14. (a)

Lappé, M. The genetic counselor: Responsible to whom? *The Hastings Center Report*, 1971, *1* (2), 6–8. (b)

Lappé, M. How much do we want to know about the unborn? *The Hastings Center Report*, 1973, *3* (1), 8–9.

Lebacqz, K. Self-fulfilling prophecy. (Editorial correspondence). *The Hastings Center Report*, 1972, *2* (1), 12–13.

Li, C. C. *Population genetics*. Chicago: The University of Chicago Press, 1955.

Murray, R. F. Problems behind the promise: Ethical issues in mass genetic screening. In R. A. Paoletti (Ed.), *Selected readings: Genetic engineering and bioethics*. New York: MSS Information Corporation, 1972. Pp. 106–111.

Nora, J. J., & Fraser, F. C. *Medical genetics: Principles and practice*. Philadelphia: Lea & Febiger, 1974.

Powledge, T. M. New trends in genetic legislation. *The Hastings Center Report*, 1973, *3* (6), 6–7.

Reich, W. T. On the birth of a severely handicapped infant. *The Hastings Center Report*, 1973, *3* (4), 10–11.

Veatch, R. M. Codes of medical ethics. In R. M. Veatch *et al.* (Eds.), *The teaching of medical ethics*. Hastings-on-Hudson, N.Y.: Hastings Center, 1972. Pp. 142–147.

Yunis, J. J. *Human chromosome methodology*. New York: Academic Press, 1974.

Eugenic Abortion

JOHN R. CONNERY, S.J.

Father John R. Connery, S.J. received an
M.A. degree from Loyola University (Chicago) in
1942, and an S.T.D. from the Gregorian University
(Rome) in 1948. For the whole of his professional
life, Father Connery has been a seminary professor, lecturer, and writer, with the exception of a
period of six years in the 1960s when he served as
Provincial Superior of the Chicago Province of the
Society of Jesus. He has been a regular contributor
to such journals as Theological Studies, The
American Ecclesiastical Review, The Homiletic
and Pastoral Review, and America. Currently,
Father Connery is Professor of Moral Theology
at the Jesuit School of Theology in Chicago.

In his moral essay on anger (De Ira) Seneca says that

> [Romans] drown children if they are born weak or abnormal; nor is
> this the result of anger, since it is perfectly reasonable to separate the
> healthy from the useless [Seneca, De Ira, 1.15].

He was referring, of course, to the Roman practice of infanticide in
disposing of undesirable children. As in many pagan countries, it was
the right of the father (Godefroy, 1922) to accept or reject newborn
children. Those who could not bring themselves to engage in the cruder
forms of infanticide, such as drowning or burning, would simply abandon them. This could be done in one of two ways. If they wanted the
child to die, they would abandon him (or, more likely, her) in a place
where he would not be found or where he might be devoured by wild

animals. If they simply did not want, or could not afford, to raise the child, they would abandon him in some place where he might easily be found. The familiar story of the foundation of Rome tells of an abandoned pair, Romulus and Remus, who were nurtured by a she-wolf. But there is no reason to believe that in reality abandoned children received any more humane treatment from animals than they did from their Roman parents.

The Roman practice went far beyond the goals of eugenics, but one can presume that it included children born with hereditary diseases—at least if the symptoms were apparent at birth or shortly after. Still the motivation behind the Roman practice was often enough the same as that of eugenics: to rid society of defective or unhealthy children. But little was known in those times of hereditary diseases, and there was consequently no effort to sort out hereditary defects from those of other origin. Also, there is little or no reason to believe that the desire to be rid of weak or defective children led to abortion. Two reasons may be assigned for this: (*a*) there was no way of predicting that a child would be weak or abnormal; and (*b*) even if this had been possible, abortion was too dangerous a procedure for the mother to solve problems which could be solved by infanticide. When abortion was practiced, it was for other reasons, e.g., to cover up adultery or fornication. Infanticide would be too late to solve these problems.

TRADITIONAL OPPOSITION TO ABORTION

The Church condemned both abortion and infanticide right from the beginning, whatever the reasons for them might have been. In fact, the Apologists of the second century were able to charge the pagans publicly with these crimes and to indicate as one of the things which made the Christians different the fact that they did not engage either in abortion or in infanticide. Christians of later centuries were not all of the caliber of the early Christians, but the Church always attached the severest of penalties to both crimes. It is historically clear that the Church was the chief factor in stamping out these practices not only among the Romans but also among the various tribes it encountered as it spread over the European continent.

In the eugenic movement the desire to rid society of defective members is reappearing but in a modern and much more sophisticated dress. At present, no suggestion, at least of an overt nature, is being made to reintroduce infanticide to rid society of children born with hereditary defects. What is being discussed is, rather, the obligation to prolong the life of seriously defective children. And what is being practiced, at least when it transcends moral limits, comes closer to the Roman practice of abandoning unwanted children. Nor is there any focus on hereditary diseases as such. The aim is rather to let children die who because of some serious physical or mental defects, or both, will not be able to meet minimal standards of living. Whether the defect is hereditary is immaterial.

AMNIOCENTESIS AND EUGENIC ABORTION

The issue of eugenic abortion has been raised largely because of the discovery of a method of detecting certain hereditary diseases during pregnancy. The facts are these (Hilton, 1972). The technique being used, amniocentesis, is not new. For many decades doctors have been withdrawing amniotic fluids from the fetal sacs in order to relieve pressure in polyhydramnios. But it was not until 1955 that researchers reported success in identifying the sex chromosomes of the fetal cells floating in the fluid and, thus, the ability to predict the gender of the fetus. And it was not until 1966 that the first karyotyping—photographing and systematically ordering the chromosomes on the basis of physical characteristics—occurred. After this, researchers began identifying chromosomal-based abnormalities. For example, a fetus whose cells had three of the twenty-first chromosome rather than two would have Down's syndrome or, as it was once called, Mongolism.

While substantial progress has been made, the possibilities currently available of detecting abnormalities through amniocentesis should not be exaggerated. Even in the presumption that one knows what normality is, it is still not possible through amniocentesis to respond completely to the question whether the fetus will be a normal baby. But an accurate diagnosis of certain genetic diseases, such as Down's syndrome or Tay–Sachs disease, is possible. Before amniocentesis, even if it were known that the parents had an hereditary disease, it was not possible to predict with certainty whether a particular child would be affected, or even be a carrier. With prenatal diagnosis it is now possible to have certain information, at least in some chromosomal disorders.

POSITIVE AND NEGATIVE EUGENICS

Of what value is this kind of knowledge? Were prenatal therapy of chromosomal disorders possible, having knowledge of the presence of any such disorder as soon as possible would undoubtedly be of the greatest importance. Unfortunately, little is currently known about the treatment of chromosomal disorders. For all practical purposes, then, the prenatal diagnosis of hereditary disease through amniocentesis is useful chiefly in reference to an abortion decision. If the woman is prepared to make such a decision, the use of amniocentesis will prevent the abortion of a healthy fetus. Without amniocentesis an abortion resorted to by a person with an hereditary disease would run the risk of destroying a perfectly healthy fetus.

Eugenists usually distinguish between positive and negative eugenics. Positive eugenics has as its goal the breeding-in of desirable traits to improve the human race. A program of positive eugenics presumes, of course, that one knows what kind of qualities one would like to see in the future human race, knowledge not at all easy to come by. But even if such knowledge were easily obtainable, abortion could hardly make a contribution to such a program. Positive eugenics would call, rather, for technological and scientific reproduction, carried on in the laboratory rather than in the home. What this would do to human society, or even to the human individual, as we know them, is impossible to fathom. At the least it would seem to involve a type of manipulation of human beings deeply prejudicial to human freedom and autonomy.

THE MORALITY OF EUGENIC ABORTION

It would be more in the area of negative eugenics, the breeding-out of undesirable traits, that eugenic abortion would be of service. But there is little evidence that abortions after amniocentesis are currently all that concerned with the good of society, i.e., with preventing the deterioration of the genetic pool. It is rather the good of the child, or, even more, the good of the parents themselves, which is largely in focus. The parent cannot face the prospect of a Mongoloid child, or at least that kind of life not worth living. There is little attention given to the good of society as such. Nor is any pressure being put on individual couples currently either by the state or by public opinion to abort children with hereditary diseases. But one may have to foresee the time when public opinion first, and then public authority, will begin to frown on couples who give birth to children with hereditary diseases, knowing with certainty from amniocentesis that this was going to happen.

The question for the moral theologian is whether prenatal knowledge of hereditary disease justifies an abortion decision or, perhaps, even makes it obligatory. I do not know of anyone at present who would want to impose an obligation to have an abortion on a woman bearing a child with some hereditary disease; we can therefore focus on the question regarding the liceity of such a decision. Certainly, if the whole problem with abortion were simply the danger of wasting normal fetuses, an abortion decision where this was clearly ruled out by prenatal diagnosis could not be faulted. But an honest estimate of the tradition which

condemned infanticide without qualification would have to admit that
the aim was to protect precisely the defective and the abnormal, the
most likely victims of this crime. Nor would the fact that the life of the
fetus was taken before birth make any difference in a tradition which
condemned both abortion and infanticide. Moreover, even though there
was no opportunity to give explicit attention to this type of case in the
early Church, there is no reason to believe that it would have escaped
the absolute condemnation of abortion.

The Welfare of the Fetus

It must be admitted that the Christian tradition never considered the
case of eugenic abortion, at least as it is presented today. It might also
have to be conceded that an abortion decision based on certain knowledge of abnormality would be a lesser evil than one which would run
the risk of aborting a perfectly healthy fetus. But it would still have to
be considered an immoral decision from the standpoint of tradition. In
the presumption that such an abortion was performed for the good of
the fetus (which may not be a valid presumption at all), the only analogy one would have from the past which was actually discussed by moral
theologians was abortion to baptize the fetus. Even though the eternal
welfare of the fetus was at stake, theologians argued that abortion could
not be justified since one was not permitted to do evil even for a good
end. With this judgment in the background, it would be difficult to make
a case for something as ambiguous as eugenic abortion where the welfare of the fetus is concerned.

Whether aborting a defective fetus can be considered a benefit to the
fetus itself may be seriously questioned. St. Thomas Aquinas once said:
Melius est esse sic quam penitus non esse * (*Summa theologica*, III,
Suppl. q. 64, a. 1 ad 4). This statement may need some nuancing, but
even today those who are trying to analyze abortion after prenatal diagnosis of hereditary disease seem to realize that the primary concern is
not for the fetus itself.

The Good of the Parents

What seems to be more at stake is the good of the parents. It is with this
in mind that John Fletcher (1972), who has written much on this question, discusses the issue in an article in *Theological Studies*. For Fletcher
the discovery of a defective fetus is not and should not be for the
parents a clearcut indication for abortion. Only in circumstances in
which they simply could not cope with the presence of a defective child

* It is better to be this way, than simply not to be at all.

in the family should an abortion decision be considered. In taking this stand he is influenced chiefly by his concern for the parent–child bond— that is, the bond between the parent and other children in the family, present or future. He argues that an unwarranted abortion decision would really weaken or even destroy the bond which should exist between parents and children. But he does not feel that this bond will be affected if the parents simply do not have the psychological strength to handle a defective child in the family, and it becomes clear, consequently, to the other children that the parents had no realistic alternative. Estimating psychological strength is not an easy thing to do, of course, and it is perhaps even more difficult to judge whether parents who do not have the psychological strength to cope with a defective child have the psychological strength to cope with abortion.

THE ANIMATED AND UNANIMATED FETUS

The traditional teachings of theologians, as well as that of the Church, has condemned abortion at any stage of fetal development. It is quite true that for many centuries a distinction was made between the animated and the unanimated fetus, that is, the fetus before and after the infusion of the rational soul. But this distinction served only as a basis of classification and a dividing line for ecclesiastical penalties. It was never used as a moral dividing line (as is sometimes implied or even stated in modern writings on this subject), separating licit from illicit abortions. The only exception which was made in the past was for the abortion of an unanimated fetus to save the life of the mother. A number of respected theologians held this opinion as long as the theory of delayed animation prevailed. From the beginning of the seventeenth century, however, the theory of delayed animation (Aristotelian) came under attack, and by the middle of the nineteenth century it was largely discredited in the eyes of moral theologians. It gave way at that time to theories of immediate animation.†

With this shift in thinking, the opinion regarding the abortion of the unanimated fetus to save the mother ceased to have any practical meaning and, as such, was no longer given consideration by theologians. In the latter half of the nineteenth century some theologians argued in favor of what was called medical abortion (of the animated fetus) and even craniotomy. But the Church, which never explicitly condemned abortion of the unanimated fetus to save the mother, soon condemned both craniotomy and medical abortion. Since that time, at least up to the recent past, Catholic moral theologians have argued against abortion

† It should be remarked here that the Church itself has never made any official pronouncement on the time of the infusion of the human soul.

without exception. Fortunately, progress in medical science has reduced the problem of therapeutic abortion, which was the only case in question, to a purely theoretical issue.

ABORTION OF DEFECTIVE FETUS MORALLY UNACCEPTABLE

On the level of Church teaching abortion of defective fetuses would have to be considered unacceptable, at least in the context of its general teaching on abortion. The same would have to be said in reference to the traditional opinion of theologians. There are theologians (Fuchs, 1971) today who hold that all norms dealing with finite values or goods, are open to exceptions: namely, where a greater good is at stake, or a proportionate reason present. They would also interpret Church teaching regarding moral norms in this context. This is a theoretical stance, of course. How such a theologian would apply this principle to a practical case of abortion would be difficult to say. In other words, it would be difficult to say what he would consider a greater good or a proportionate reason. It is conceivable that he might even take the stance that his general principle could be applied only negatively here. He might admit that even though a proportionate reason would justify abortion, he cannot think of a reason which would be proportionate. In practice, then, he would not depart from the norm, even though he might consider it theoretically limited. On the other hand, he might be willing to accept some reason for abortion as proportionate; but unless he does this explicitly or sets down some exception-making principle, one could not make an inference from his general stance regarding proportionate reasons.

Even if one were to take the position that Church teaching in the area of moral norms does not rule out exceptions for proportionate reasons, it would have to be admitted that in regard to abortion several popes have *de facto* ruled out even saving the life of the mother (with other reasons) as a proportionate reason, even when the fetus would die anyway. If one were to accept this teaching, one would have to show that a good greater even than saving the life of the mother was at stake in aborting a defective fetus.

A PASTORAL CONSIDERATION

Since this is an Institute in pastoral psychology, it would not be appropriate to deal with the problem of eugenic abortion solely from the viewpoint of morality or moral theology. Something should be said, even though briefly, about the proper pastoral handling of this problem. Apart from the many other pastoral questions he will have to face, the pastoral counselor may have to confront a situation in which a counselee or penitent is swayed by a doctor toward, or is even morally comfortable with, a decision to abort which goes against the moral judgment of the counselor himself. What stance should a confessor or counselor take in such a conflict? Back in the nineteenth century when the issue of medical abortion and craniotomy was being hotly contended (Kenrick, 1860), and even after it was settled by Church authority, the theologians who opposed these procedures were well aware of the difficulties which practical decisions might involve. When the life of the mother was at stake, it was easy to see how difficult a decision not to have an abortion (or craniotomy) might be, especially when the fetus would not be saved. They were perfectly willing to apply the principles for leaving a person in good faith to this difficult situation. Although an abortion decision for eugenic purposes would not ordinarily be rooted in the same degree of paralyzing anxiety, the case of which John Fletcher spoke is not beyond the imagination. Even though a confessor or counselor could not in conscience validate an abortion decision even in this case, prudence may dictate against any effort to disturb the good faith which may be present in the penitent or counselee.

REFERENCES

Fletcher, J. The parent–child bond. *Theological Studies*, 1972, *33*, 457–485.
Fuchs, J. The absoluteness of moral norms. *Gregorianum*, 1971, *52*, 415–458.
Godefroy, L. Infanticide. In A. Vacant, E. Mangenot, & E. Amann (Eds.), *Dictionnaire de théologie catholique* (Vol. 7). Paris: Letouzey et Ane, 1922. Coll. 1717–1726.
Hilton, B. Will the baby be normal? . . . And what is the cost of knowing? *The Hastings Center Report*, 1972, *2* (3), 8–9.
Kenrick, F. *Theologia moralis*. Malines: Dessain, 1860.
Seneca. De Ira. In Seneca, *Moral Essays* (J. W. Basore, trans.) (Vol. 1). The Leob Classical Library. London: Heinemann, 1928. Pp. 106–356.

IV
PROBLEMS OF LIVING: LEGITIMATE EXPECTANCIES FOR *HUMAN* LIFE

Basic Human Freedoms

ROBERT O. JOHANN

*Robert O. Johann received his A.B. and M.A.
degrees from Saint Louis University, and his
Ph.D. from the University of Louvain. Since 1956,
Dr. Johann has been a member of the Philosophy
Department at Fordham University, where he is
currently Professor. He has been Visiting Professor
at Yale University, at Union Theological Seminary,
and at the College of the Holy Cross. He is the
author of* The meaning of love *(1954),* The pragmatic meaning of God *(1966), and* Building the
human *(1968); and editor of* Freedom and Value
*(1976). In addition, he has contributed some 30
articles to philosophical and theological journals
and compilations. Dr. Johann is a member of the
American Philosophical Association, the American Metaphysical Society, the Catholic Commission
on Intellectual and Cultural Affairs, and the
American Theological Society.*

This Institute is concerned with the problematic character of human life.
To speak of human life as problematic is to say that it proceeds, not as a
matter of course, but as a matter of decision. Its shape, at any particular
time and precisely to the extent that it is human, is never simply the
result of reacting to stimuli. Human life has its shape from the rules
by which it is structured—rules which, at least as formulated, are of
human institution and have whatever power they enjoy solely from the
allegiance given to them. What is the rule appropriate for these circumstances? Shall I conform to it? These are questions which I cannot evade

if I am to act humanly at all. An act, therefore, is human only to the
extent that it is informed by a rule with which the agent identifies and
to which he gives his allegiance.

To say that human life is problematic is thus to say that it is a matter
of self-regulation. It is because we ourselves *can* determine the shape of
our lives that *questions* arise about how we *ought* to. On the other hand,
since being able to determine the shape of one's own life is at least one
of the things we mean by "freedom," the problematic character of human
life, and so too this Institute dealing with that character, presuppose
freedom as one of life's essential dimensions.

THE MEANING OF BASIC HUMAN FREEDOMS

That, however, raises a question about my own paper. I have been
invited to deal with "basic human freedoms," and this topic, in the
organization of the Institute, fits in under Problems of Living. It would
seem from this that, instead of being presupposed by all our problems,
freedom itself is one of them. Or, at least, it is insofar as freedom *is* one
of our problems that I am supposed to address myself to it. The first
question to be resolved, therefore, is: How is freedom as itself a problem
related to that freedom which underlies, and is presupposed by, our
having problems? In answering this question, I shall not only advance
my own paper, but, I hope, shed some light on its connection with all
those which have preceded it and those which will follow it.

When we talk about "basic human freedoms," in the sense of the title
of my paper, we are talking not about that capacity for self-regulation
which underlies our problems, but rather about a product of that
capacity, i.e., a set of regulative meanings which, if they are not already
in force, it would be rational for us to adopt. Whereas the capacity for
self-regulation pertains to the very nature of the individual person, these
"basic freedoms" pertain rather to what, in the light of his interpretation
of it, a person judges to be the appropriate exercise of that capacity. As
regulative meanings, they are not unlike all the other principles of right
action which we have been seeking in this Institute: namely, principles
governing population control, abortion, euthanasia, capital punishment,
and so on.

The difference between the basic freedoms and these latter rules,
however, is that the basic freedoms are, in a sense, second-order rules.
Instead of being directly concerned with the regulation of external
affairs, these meanings have to do with regulating our very capacity for
self-regulation, with determining, that is, its range and scope and specifying its limitations. Thus, for example, in connection with freedom of

conscience John Courtney Murray once wrote about the "problem of preserving about the human person in society a certain zone or sphere . . . within which man must be immune from coercive constraints and restraints in the pursuit of the highest values of the person as such" (Murray, 1965, p. 14).

This business of "preserving" an inviolable zone of self-regulation is accomplished by a rule limiting society's right to make rules for its members in certain areas—in the area of religious belief and practice, for instance. Again, a rule specifying that the condition under which certain decisions are to be made shall be set by all those whose lives will be shaped by those decisions—a rough formulation of the idea of participatory democracy—is another example. These second-order rules are grounded in an interpretation of the proper exercise of man's capacity to shape his own life and, according to the interpretation, they allow it wider or narrower scope. Since this capacity for self-determination is at the heart of what it means to be human, it is the very humanity of our lives which is thus being extended or restricted. How this has been the case with the chief interpretations of man's essential capacity, I shall now proceed to develop. As these interpretations vary, so also will the conception of our basic freedoms.

THE OBJECTIVIST VIEW

The first conception I should like to explore is what may be called the *objectivist* one. This view understands man primarily as one kind of being among others, occupying a specific place within the cosmic order. Like everything else in the universe, a man is an individual substance, possessed of a determinate nature, in terms of which he is inserted into the overall scheme of things, and the full actuation of which is his foreordained goal. He is, for all his freedom, simply a part of the natural order and called to conform to its pattern. This is the crucial point. Man's constitutive freedom, according to this interpretation, is simply the freedom to conform or not to the determinate law of his own nature. Fulfilling this nature is not something which, given an appropriate environment, is automatic. Man, even in the best of circumstances, can fail as man. He can refuse the rule of nature and substitute the rule of whim, in which case he ends up less than human. Man's freedom, therefore, his capacity to regulate himself, looks to objective nature as its ground. This is what I mean by calling this view objectivist. If we identify his freedom with his being as subject, then, according to this interpretation, man as subject is relative to the objective order. It is only as conformed to this order that his choices are grounded and justified.

Any departure from it is wrong by definition. An eloquent formulation of this standpoint can be found in Jacques Maritain's *Man and the state*:

> Since I have not space here to discuss nonsense . . . I am taking it for granted that you admit that there is a human nature, and that this human nature is the same in all men. I am taking it for granted that you also admit that man is a being gifted with intelligence, and who, as such, acts with an understanding of what he is doing, and therefore with the power to determine for himself the ends which he pursues. On the other hand, possessed of a nature, being constituted in a given, determinate fashion, man obviously possesses ends which correspond to his natural constitution and which are the same for all—as all pianos, for instance, whatever their particular type and in whatever spot they may be, have as their end the production of certain attuned sounds. If they don't produce these sounds, they must be tuned, or discarded as worthless. But since man is endowed with intelligence and determines his own ends, it is up to him to put himself in tune with the ends necessarily demanded by his nature. This means that there is, by the very virtue of human nature, an order or a disposition which human reason can discover and according to which the human will must act in order to attune itself to the necessary ends of the human being. The unwritten law, or natural law, is nothing more than that [Maritain, 1951, pp. 85–86].

Besides forcefully illustrating the point of view I am here describing, this long quotation makes another point it may be well to emphasize. This is the largely passive role of reason in this interpretation. The function of reason in the process of self-regulation, if we are to accept this explanation, is to discover just what man's nature is, to lay bare the pattern of needs and drives by which he is constituted, and to propose this to the will as the plan to be followed. Reason adds nothing of its own to nature except consciousness—consciousness of an order already constituted. Acting reasonably and rightly thus comes to mean determining oneself in accord with the known patterns of nature.

Now, the logical strength of this view lies in the clear recognition that our capacity for self-regulation—to choose the shape of our life—needs to be grounded if it is not to be arbitrary. Unless we are confronted by exigencies antecedent to choice, so that in a true sense it can be said that we ought to do one thing rather than another, then it will make no objective difference what we do, and whatever our choice, it will be without rational foundation. But to be confronted by exigencies antecedent to choice is precisely to have some task set by nature for us to accomplish. The idea of nature is the idea of a good to be reached, something to the attainment of which our choices can be meaningfully directed. Without it, it becomes impossible to distinguish alternative claims and, so, impossible too to choose.

Another strength of this conception is more psychological in character. It is a conception the acceptance of which takes the anxiety out of freedom and thus caters to our need for security. The idea of having to decide for oneself what one is to do is, as Dostoevski's Grand Inquisitor suggested, just too much of a burden for most people. Better to have it all mapped out beforehand so that, if anyone has any doubts, he need only consult some competent authority. The fact that it thus takes the onus out of choosing is perhaps the chief reason why this view has flourished for so long. Indeed, with a few changes—e.g., the substitution of an evolutionary theory of nature for a more static one—it is the conception inherent in Marxism.

But if this view has strengths, it also has weaknesses (weaknesses which, interestingly enough, are closely related to its strengths). First of all, although it rightly recognizes the need for a ground of choice and rightly too identifies that ground with man's nature, it nonetheless radically misinterprets that nature insofar as it can serve as ground. For it is not man's nature as a determinate object in the world, that specific complex of needs, tendencies, and drives, which can provide a final basis for choice. On the contrary. Choice is the act of a being who transcends the whole realm of the determinate and who, instead of being called to conform to the determinate, exists rather as its judge and reshaper. But a judge cannot borrow his norms from what falls under his judgment. They belong to his very capacity to judge. In other words, it is man's nature, not as object, but as subject, i.e., as inquirer, judge, critic, lover—a being able to say yes or no, to give consent or withhold it, a unique and irreplaceable initiative—it is this, to which the whole order of objects (including man as object) is relative, which alone can serve as ground for choice. To make man's nature as object the ground, instead, is to subordinate the transcendent to what it transcends, the infinite in man to the finite.

Secondly, by interpreting man's freedom as basically a freedom to conform, this first view takes the anxiety out of choice only by suppressing its genuine creativity. It achieves order and wholeness, a synthesis between man and the rest of reality, only by smothering selfhood. On the other hand, a reawakening of this sense of self (with a concomitant rejection of this first interpretation of man's freedom) has been a dominant feature of the last decades. What was the excitement of the 'sixties if not the awakened appetite for new selfhood? There was an irrepressible need for the human self to throw off all the limitations it has saddled itself with and to reject every structure forcing it to accept this or that single role as the whole truth of its being. It was indeed a wholesale rejection of the objective order as normative and the substitution of a second conception of man's freedom, which I shall now take up.

If the first conception was *objectivist*, this second conception, representing the triumph of subjectivity, can only be called *subjectivist*. Its philosophic formulation, the expression of an emergent sense of personal transcendence such as I was just describing, has actually been developing since the beginning of modern philosophy in Descartes' *cogito* and it finds its culmination in the extreme existentialism of Sartre. Without getting unnecessarily technical, I may say that according to this view man in his proper reality is pure subjectivity, pure capacity to choose. Instead of being a determinate nature and part of a larger world, he exists over against the determinate world as its negation and as a continual movement beyond it. Whatever determination he has *as man*, he gives to himself by his own choices. This is Sartre's well-known idea that man is a being in whom existence precedes essence, a being whose vocation is precisely to choose what he will be (Sartre, 1946, pp. 17–18). Hence man's determinate nature, far from being normative for him, is rather a work of his own creation. Man is not called to conform to a given order; he creates his own order. But on what basis? On no basis other than his choice to do so. For the important thing is not *what* you choose, but *that* you choose, and that you stay with your choice, and stay with it, indeed, without any pretense that it has, or can have, any basis or justification outside itself.

This is a doctrine of freedom with a vengeance, a doctrine in which it is not inappropriate to say that man is *condemned* to freedom. For, if it enlarges the scope of man's freedom, it does so only by utterly isolating him, by making him a kind of lonely and despairing god. This is what Paul Tillich meant by his criticism of this viewpoint. He saw it as the second phase in the development of man's consciousness, and, though an inevitable one, still one which is ultimately no more adequate than the first (Tillich, 1952, pp. 113–154). If in the first interpretation there is a kind of suppression of self, here there is a suppression of the world as rational ground. We are really free only if our acts are groundless, that is to say, only if they and we are absurd.

Yet, although this doctrine too falls short, we should not overlook its strengths. The position's failure is its inability to synthesize man with the rest of reality. But its strength is that it shows clearly and irrefutably just what it is which has to be synthesized. If man seeks to belong to something larger than himself, it is henceforth only as a self, a creative source and not just a conforming cipher, that he seeks to belong. He is no longer willing to sacrifice his unique significance as a person for the sake of fitting in. He can no longer look to specific roles and functions in society to provide him with his identity. If, for the time being, he finds himself lost between two worlds, one dead and past, the other not yet born, he also knows that there is no going back.

As Erich Fromm has pointed out, the situation of mankind today is very much like that of the adolescent who has emerged from the security of being simply a part of the family to a new sense of selfhood, but who has not yet learned how to integrate his independence into the larger world (Fromm, 1960, pp. 256–265). He knows that growth means moving ahead, that somehow it must be possible both to be genuinely oneself and, at the same time, to have one's roots in a wider reality, but right now he does not know how, and so he flounders. This is where we are today. The significance of this second view is to have destroyed forever the acceptability of interpreting freedom as the freedom to conform. Henceforth, freedom means creativity. But the question remains: Is it possible to view man as creative without utterly uprooting him and leaving him something absurd? The attempt to answer this question brings us now to a third interpretation of man's constitutive freedom— one which, for want of a better term, we shall call the *relational* view.

THE RELATIONAL VIEW

As we have seen, the exercise of our capacity for self-regulation, for choosing the sort of person we want to be, is inevitably arbitrary unless we are ordered by nature to a goal to the attainment of which our choices can be meaningfully directed. This nature, however, cannot be our nature as objects in the world, nor the goal in question some determinate modification of that nature. For the whole realm of determinate nature, as objective, is relative to and dependent on our reality as subjects, which reality is identical with our capacity to choose. But what is relative to that capacity cannot ground it. The nature and goal in question, therefore, must be our nature and goal precisely as subjects. Subjectivity, therefore, cannot be viewed simply as a negation of determinacy, in Sartrean fashion. It must be something positive. Our capacity to choose must be a capacity for a positive state of affairs to the attainment of which choice, precisely as the actuality of ourselves as subjects, is relevant. It must be a state of affairs, that is, which includes us precisely as subjects and which only choice makes possible.

Just what this state of affairs could be is so obvious that its very neglect for so long by philosophers poses something of a problem. At least part of the reason for this neglect has to do with the standpoint from which philosophers have traditionally done their reflecting—which is the standpoint of man the thinker. For anyone adopting that standpoint, the other is never present in person, but only in idea. The primacy of the communicative relation thus gets overlooked. Yet the communicative relation, which involves a kind of conspiracy of subjects, is just that positive reality for which we are looking.

What I am saying is that man, precisely as transcending determinacy and endowed with the capacity for self-regulation—i.e., precisely as subject—is nonetheless an interest structure. In his very subjectivity, he has by nature a capacity for, and an interest in, a genuinely common life. This is the larger reality in which a person can participate and still be himself. Man the subject, therefore, to whom the whole order of determinate nature including his own determinate nature, is relative, is nonetheless himself rooted in and relative to the wider world of personal relationship. It is this ordination to relationship, identical with his nature as subject, which provides the regulative ground for choice. This is the context in which the sort of person he chooses to be, a matter of indifference in the presence of the impersonal, makes all the difference in the world. This is the context which, because it alone makes choosing finally meaningful, is that which makes subjectivity, i.e., the very capacity to choose, first of all possible. Man emerges as subject only in the context of personal relationship. And the maintenance and development of personal relationship is what his life is all about.

MAN'S FREEDOM TO BE HUMAN

Here then we get another picture of man's basic freedom, his freedom to be human. Man's freedom to be human is not a freedom simply to conform and to fit into a determinate world already fully constituted. Neither is it the freedom to be absurd in the name of creativity à la Jean Paul Sartre. Man's freedom to be human is indeed a freedom to create, but the creativity in question is a responsive and responsible creativity. Man as "I," as subject, exists only in a responsive and responsible relation with the other as "You." This relation, which is not some kind of object in the world but a transobjective reality, exists only by a continuous act of co-creation. It exists only because and to the extent that each party to it continually takes the other into account in his choosing, continually makes his actions to be affirmations, not of himself merely, but of the other as well, continually shapes the world, not as something private, but as something shared, the body of a common life. This, after all, is what communication, the process in which we as subjects are involved, really means. As John Dewey has reminded us, communication is not primarily a matter of expression, and even less the expression of something antecedent. To communicate means to make something common, to institute the grounds of a common life, to create a shared world (Dewey, 1958, pp. 138–170). From this standpoint, our choices are valid to the extent that they effect communication, create community. Indeed, we have here a test for the validity of all our meanings. Since all meanings are, in the last analysis, the ways and means to a shared life—generalized instruments of maintaining cooperation in action and of coordinating our relationships to one another and to the environment—they will be valid only insofar as they contribute to the maintenance and deepening of this communal quality.

This stress on the communal character of freedom should not be misunderstood, however. It is not my intention to be reintroducing a conformist conception of freedom under the guise of community. The common world and the common life we are talking about is not some determinate pattern, even if co-authored, which will restrict the initiatives of the parties subscribing to it. Think of it rather after the model of a friendship, which is an inclusive, transobjective affair within which the friends, far from having to act out prescribed parts, are able to be fully and spontaneously themselves. The common world we mean is not a world *between* persons but *inclusive* of them, a world which is hospitable to diversity and welcomes plural initiatives.

The freedom to be human is precisely the freedom to participate unrestrictedly in this transobjective world, to participate precisely in terms of *who* one uniquely is, both historically and creatively. Needless to say, this presupposes that one has had the opportunity to appropriate these dimensions of oneself, one's history as well as one's creativity. A person cannot participate personally unless he knows who he is and what he believes. All this, of course, means educative access to cultural resources.

But more important than these objective conditions of creativity are our individual and collective commitments to its transcendent ground. For these responsive commitments to the ground of creativity are what first gives rise to that zone of freedom, that supra-personal space, within which we can function as selves and in relation to which the external conditions of freedom have meaning and stability. Unless I am responsive to the creative source, disclosed in every subject but transcending them all, and unless I prize such responsiveness more than any determinate accomplishments, my freedom to create is meaningless. (It is meaningless precisely because it remains ungrounded.) By the same token, unless society at large is more committed to creativity than to any determinate goals, the conditions for the effective exercise of man's freedom to be human will not be maintained. That is why the decline of religion in the Western democracies is cause for alarm. For the commitment to the ground of creativity is basically a religious commitment. What we have in its place, however, is the wholehearted search for individual satisfaction. Freedom ceases to be the meaningful exercise of my being as subject and becomes instead the non-interference by others in my pursuit of myself as object. My objective fulfillment becomes the goal. My own creativity is valued and that of others is respected only insofar as they both may be necessary for *my* realization. In other words, freedom is actually of secondary importance. What really counts is "success." Small wonder, then, that genuine freedom is on the wane.

CONCLUSION

Our freedom to be human is thus a complex affair, dependent on others as well as on ourselves for its attainment. Its realization, however, which is the realization of the Infinite itself in time, is what our life is about. If we sometimes seem to be moving more in the other direction, let us at least hope that our growing sense of futility and alienation will ultimately give us pause and provide the motive for getting ourselves back on the track.

REFERENCES

Dewey, J. *Experience and nature.* New York: Open Court, 1958.
Fromm, E. *Escape from freedom.* New York: Rinehart, 1960.
Maritain, J. *Man and the state.* Chicago: The University of Chicago Press, 1951.
Murray, J. C. (s.j.) Foreword. In J. C. Murray (s.j.) (Ed.), *Freedom and man.* New York: Kenedy, 1965.
Sartre, J. P. *L'Existentialisme est un humanisme.* Paris: Nagel, 1946.
Tillich, P. *The courage to be.* New Haven: Yale University Press, 1952.

Personal Human Development

WILLIAM J. RICHARDSON, S.J.

> *Father William J. Richardson, S.J., after gradu-*
> *ating from the College of the Holy Cross (A.B.,*
> *1941), entered the Society of Jesus. From 1950*
> *to 1954 he studied theology in Belgium. In 1955*
> *he began research on the philosophy of Martin*
> *Heidegger, a project which involved a three-year*
> *sojourn in Freiburg and provided the opportunity*
> *for personal contact with Professor Heidegger.*
> *Father Richardson received his Ph.D. in 1960 from*
> *the Institut Superieur de Philosophie, Louvain,*
> *and, in 1962, as a Bollingen Fellow, he was named*
> *Maître agrégé of the same Institut. He is the*
> *author of* Heidegger: Through phenomenology to
> thought *(1963), to which Martin Heidegger con-*
> *tributed a preface, and of many articles in journals*
> *in this country and in Europe. In 1963 Father*
> *Richardson joined the faculty of Fordham Uni-*
> *versity, where he is Professor of Philosophy. In*
> *1974, he concluded psychoanalytic training at*
> *the William Alanson White Institute, and at pres-*
> *ent is on partial leave from Fordham University*
> *to serve as staff therapist and Director of Research*
> *at the Austen Riggs Center, Stockbridge, Massa-*
> *chusetts.*

A recent report tells of a mother concerned about her son's going to school. He always went reluctantly, but usually he at least went. This particular day, however, she heard the alarm go off and then not a sound. As it got later and later, she became more and more distressed.

Finally, she went to the door and knocked, saying: "Johnny, it's time to get up—you're going to be late for school." From under the covers came the familiar voice: "I won't get up—don't want to go to school." She said: "Why not?" He replied, "Two reasons: (*a*) the kids all hate me; (*b*) the teachers all hate me." She thought for a moment: "But you've got to get up—you can't stay home from school." He said: "Why not?" She answered, "Two reasons: (*a*) you are 40 years old; (*b*) you are the principal."

This vignette may not prove very much, but it suggests one problem in living which we all have to face: namely, that there is a little boy or little girl in each one of us which can still be tempted to resort to childish solutions to adult problems, and that one of the tasks of our development is to learn how to deal with that perennial child in us—in other words to reconcile development with a penchant for regression. It suggests, too, that the personal human development which is available to us is not such that it can leave our past behind, the way a snake can shed its skin, but must somehow incorporate our past into our present so that the future is somehow defined, i.e., limited, by the past. Finally, it suggests that age is not automatically a sign of growth. A person does not unfold the way a flower unfolds according to some simplistic teleology, and, therefore, the development which is possible for us is not necessarily unilinear, a steady forward march toward human fulfillment.

If we are to discuss personal human development in a contemporary context, however, we should no doubt do so in terms of contemporary thinkers who deal explicitly with the problem in a fashion which can have some relevance for the concerns of pastoral psychology. On the American scene at present, there are, generally speaking, three major orientations in psychology which we could examine in this regard if we so wished: (*a*) the behavioral, (*b*) the psychoanalytic, (*c*) the humanistic. I suggest that in the limited space at our disposal we pass quickly over the first two and concentrate on the third, since, for those concerned with the pastoral ministry, the first two will not prove very satisfying anyway.

THE BEHAVIORAL APPROACH

Behaviorism, for example, sees the human person, a product of evolution, as essentially no different from the environment in which he finds himself. According to B. F. Skinner (1971/1972, pp. 189–190), for example, "the picture [of man] which emerges from a scientific analysis is not of a body with a person inside, but of a body which *is* a person in the sense that it displays a complex repertoire of behavior" "appropriate to a given set of contingencies"—physical, social, and cultural. If such a person is credited with any privacy, it is only because it is enclosed within a human skin and to that extent is less accessible than external nature to the scientific investigator, not because it enjoys any interior autonomy as the traditional literature of freedom and dignity maintained (Skinner, 1971/1972, pp. 181–182). The human person thus conceived is shaped by his environment, and the only development possible to him is in terms of his growing capacity, potentially as limitless as the evolutionary process itself, to control the environment which controls him (Skinner, 1971/1972, p. 205).

THE PSYCHOANALYTIC APPROACH

The Freudian view of personal development is hardly more satisfying. To be sure, Freud is a clinician, not a philosopher—more concerned with the cure of illness than with exploring the possibilities of health. If we attempt to disengage a philosophical conception of man from his work, however, we may say that the human person, at least for the later Freud, is basically an energy system organized into complementary functional structures of id, ego, and superego, where the development possible to the person is a certain equilibrium ("homeostasis") between these systems which permits him *lieben und arbeiten*—"to love," i.e., to engage in satisfactory interpersonal relationships with their normal sexual complement, and "to work," i.e., to respond to the demands of the ordinary responsibilities of life. The prospects, however, are rather lugubrious. Freud (Freud & Breuer, 1893–1895/1955, p. 305) tells his hysterical patient that the best she can hope for is to transform her "hysterical misery into common unhappiness." For

> what we call happiness in the strictest sense comes from the (preferably sudden) satisfaction of needs which have been dammed up to a high degree, and it is from its nature only possible as an episodic phenomenon. . . . Unhappiness is much less difficult to experience. We are threatened with suffering from three directions: from our body, which is doomed to decay and dissolution and which cannot even do without pain and anxiety as warning signals; from the external world, which may rage against us with overwhelming and merciless forces of destruction; and finally from our relations with other men. The suffering which comes from this last source is perhaps more painful to us than any other . . . [Freud, 1930/1961, pp. 76–77].

It is all somewhat grim, but at least Freud takes seriously the tragic aspect of life—what one college freshman has called "the dark side of the moon."

THE HUMANISTIC APPROACH

The humanistic psychologists, however—they sometimes call themselves "existential" as well—offer something better: a so-called "third
force" in American psychology, i.e., a third option opposed to behaviorism on the one hand and to Freudian psychoanalysis on the
other. Why "humanistic"? Because they emphasize the positive in man
rather than the negative; they focus on his potential for growth rather
than on his debilities. Where Freud, for example, sees the best achievement of human life to be an equilibrium of psychic energies distributed
among the systems of id, ego, and superego through appropriate release
of tension, the humanists, following the terminology of Goldstein
(1939), speak of a person's best achievement as "self-actualization."
Though this orientation has many spokesmen, the high priests among
them are Abraham Maslow, Erich Fromm, and, in a certain qualified
sense, Rollo May.

Abraham Maslow

Maslow's (1954) major contribution came through the study of the
allegedly healthy personality, in which he discovered that the main
interest of such people was to be creatively active in the world. This
active creativity is easy to recognize in the ingenious production of the
great artists, scientists, or world leaders, but as Charlotte Bühler has
observed, it can also be quite modest—say, in the imaginative handling
of everyday life, such as:

> a housewife's inventive cooking, the loving understanding with which
> parents raise their family, the well-planned development of a business,
> the communicative skill of a salesman, the handiwork of a craftsman,
> or the new rose created by the gardener. Creativity can also mean the
> painting of a child or the poem of a teenager [Bühler, 1973, p. 32].

At its best it culminates in a quasi-ecstatic emotional climax which
Maslow calls "peak experiences" (Maslow, 1968, pp. 71–114).

In terms of a general theory of motivation, Maslow distinguishes between "deficiency" needs and "growth" needs. Deficiency needs are
those which supply for "deficits in the organism, empty holes, so to
speak, which must be filled up for health's sake, and furthermore must
be filled from without by human beings *other* than the subject" (Maslow,
1968, pp. 22–23). Such are the needs for safety, belongingness, love,
respect, self-esteem, etc. "Growth" needs are those the satisfaction of
which helps to fulfill one's potential as an individual. Gratifying these
needs leads to self-actualization, i.e., the "ongoing actualization of

potentials, capacities and talents; the fulfillment of a mission (or call, fate, destiny, vocation); the fuller knowledge of, and acquaintance with, the person's own intrinsic nature; [and finally] the unceasing trend toward unity, integration, or synergy of the person" (Maslow, 1968, p. 25). The healthy person is more concerned with satisfying "growth" needs than "deficiency" needs.

Implicit here, of course, is a conception of the nature of man which permits an undiluted optimism. Human nature is basically good, and human malice (destructiveness, sadism, cruelty, etc.) is merely accidental—a violent reaction to the frustration of our needs, emotions, and capacities (Maslow, 1968, p. 3). To be sure, there are negative aspects of man, e.g., the "gap between human aspirations and human limitations" (Maslow, 1968, p. 10), and the inevitability of pain and tragedy, which in their own way can contribute to human growth (Maslow, 1968, p. 4). But how all this fits in with Maslow's unabashed optimism is not clear at all. Indeed, he admits his need for a philosophical anthropology which he hopes the European existentialists will supply. In particular, he would like them to give him a way to conceive of future time in psychology. "Self-actualization," he says, "is meaningless without reference to a currently active future" (Maslow, 1968, p. 15). He would like all this if he could have it without compromising his optimism. He will have none of their "harping on dread, anguish, despair, and the like"—a sort of "high IQ whimpering on the cosmic scale" (Maslow, 1968, p. 16). But can he live with a supermarket electicism of this kind? More to the point: can we? The question is intended to suggest that Maslow's proposals are as titillating and ingratiating as the man himself but cry out for a philosophical foundation which would make them intellectually satisfying.

Erich Fromm

Erich Fromm attempts to supply just such a philosophical foundation, reproaching Maslow for his failure to find the origin of man's basic needs in the nature of man himself (Fromm, 1973, p. 222). How does Fromm himself conceive this "nature of man"?

He is no less an evolutionist than Skinner; but where for Skinner evolution leads to a denial of any true freedom, for Fromm it leads to the affirmation of it. "We have to arrive at an understanding of man's nature," he writes, "on the basis of the blend of the two fundamental biological conditions that mark the emergence of man. One was the ever-decreasing determination of behavior by instincts" (Fromm, 1973, p. 223). By this he means that the higher an animal has risen in the stages of evolution, the less is the weight of stereotyped behavior patterns which are strictly determined and phylogenetically programed. The second biological condition was "the growth of the brain, and particularly of the neocortex" (Fromm, 1973, p. 223). A consequence of the former condition is that, aside from elementary reactions such as those to danger and to sexual stimuli, man is less directed by instinct than all other animals. In this sense he is the most helpless of all animals. A consequence of this is that he is *aware* of himself as no other animal is—aware of his powerlessness, his ignorance, and his eventual end: death.

Hence man both is part of nature (i.e., as subject to physical laws) and transcends it (i.e., must assume responsibility for his own life). Fromm sees this situation as a fundamental disequilibrium in man which is inescapable—identified with human existence itself—hence, an "existential disequilibrium" which can be stabilized only with the help of his culture. He writes:

> Man's existential conflict produces certain psychic needs common to all men. He is forced to overcome the horror of separateness, of power-lessness, and of lostness, and find new forms of relating himself to the world to enable him to feel at home. . . . But each of these needs can be satisfied in different ways, which vary according to the differences of his social condition. These different ways of satisfying the existential needs manifest themselves as passions, such as love, tenderness, striving for justice, independence, truth, hate, sadism, masochism, destructiveness, narcissism, etc. [Fromm, 1973, p. 226].

What is cited here is the latest Fromm of the *Anatomy of human destructiveness* (1973). But it is essentially the same perspective as that of the early Fromm of *Escape from freedom* (1941). There the freedom he speaks of is the ambiguous freedom which characterizes man's emergence as man out of the evolutionary process—freedom *from* the control of the evolutionary forces of nature and freedom *for/to* life of his own which by reason of his self-awareness he may shape for himself. The remainder of that early book examines the different ways in which man deals with this freedom, i.e., the existential disequilibrium which is part and parcel of his nature. Negatively speaking: there are some unhappy compromises by which man seeks to escape the burden of his freedom—these are the mechanisms of escape (hence, the title of the book). One of these mechanisms is to surrender one's freedom to some irrational authority; Fromm sees sadism and masochism as covert forms of this (Fromm, 1969, pp. 163–201). Another is destructiveness (Fromm, 1969, pp. 202–208). A third is an automaton-like conformity, where the individual ceases to be himself and adopts entirely the kind of personality offered to him by cultural patterns, thus becoming exactly as all others are and as they expect him to be (Fromm, 1969, pp. 208–230).

More positively, man can *use* his freedom to unite himself actively with the evolutionary process and collaborate with it in solidarity with other men. This is possible through the spontaneous action of love and of productive work (Fromm, 1969, pp. 37–38). Love he describes as a "passionate affirmation" of another human being. It is not just another "affect" but an "active striving and inner relatedness," the aim of which is the "happiness, growth and freedom" of the beloved. Moreover, "the basic affirmation contained in love is directed towards the beloved person as an incarnation of essentially human qualities. Love for one person implies, then, love for man as such" (Fromm, 1969, pp. 134–135)—and this includes man as such when incarnate in one's self.

"Productive work," on the other hand, is another form of the spontaneity of genuine freedom.

> The "productive orientation" of personality refers to a fundamental attitude, *a mode of relatedness* in all realms of human experience. It covers mental, emotional and sensory responses to others, to one's self and to things. Productiveness is man's ability to use his powers and to realize the potentialities inherent in him [Fromm, 1967, p. 91].

In a word, then, productiveness is man's realization of what he is and can be in himself. Hence, Fromm adds, "while it is true that man's productiveness can create material things, works of art, and systems of thought, *by far the most important object of productiveness is man himself*" (Fromm, 1967, p. 97).

Obviously this is a humanism of a genuine sort—"existential" in Fromm's sense of that word. There is much which is appealing in it, for it guarantees a central place to freedom in human development and to the importance of love in the exercise of that freedom. Moreover, Fromm incorporates Maslow's "active creativity" into a broader and deeper framework in terms of philosophy and social history. But what of the dark side of the moon—the negative, the tragic elements in life? As already indicated, Fromm sees these as consequences of man's effort to shirk the burden of his freedom—as mechanisms of escape, one obvious form of which is his destructiveness. But here man's destructiveness (if we except the case where he reacts defensively to an attack) is no more than the perversion of the life force within him. "The degree of destructiveness is proportionate to the degree to which the unfolding of a person's capacities is blocked. . . . Destructiveness is the outcome of an unlived life" (Fromm, 1967, p. 218). But can we dispose of the problem of evil

in man that handily? As for the problem of death, Fromm at least faces
it as Maslow apparently did not. But for Fromm death is essentially outside of life and therefore does not enter into its meaning.

> Death remains the very opposite of life and is extraneous to, and in-
> compatible with, the experience of living. All knowledge *about* death
> does not alter the fact that death is not a meaningful part of life and
> that there is nothing for us to do but accept the fact of death; hence, as
> far as our life is concerned, defeat [Fromm, 1967, p. 50].

Is the end of all human love and productiveness, then, simply an inevitable, ultimate defeat?

Rollo May

Rollo May, I say, belongs to this orientation only in a certain qualified
sense. No less than Maslow and Fromm, he is interested in releasing
man's dammed-up potentialities so that he may achieve a genuine actualization of himself, but more than either of them he is aware of the
difficulty of doing so in an "age of anxiety" and in what he calls our
"schizoid world." In a word, he has a deeper awareness of the dark side
of the moon than do the other two. If he is called an "existentialist," it
is because he has gone to the European phenomenologists and existentialists for his conceptual framework. In *Existence* (May, 1958/1967),
he sketches that framework. In its essentials it derives from the Swiss
psychiatrist Ludwig Binswanger whose thought in turn is based on the
work of the German philosopher Martin Heidegger. If we go to May's
roots, then, we arrive at another conception of personal human development which may be more comprehensive and, therefore, more fruitful
than what we have seen so far.

THE VIEWPOINT OF MARTIN HEIDEGGER

To be sure, Heidegger (1927/1963) himself is neither a psychologist
nor a psychoanalyst. For that matter, he is not even a philosopher of
man. His question is about the meaning of Being ("what does Being
mean"), where Being is that mysterious process which lets all beings be
what they are, including man himself. Heidegger is interested in man
only insofar as man has a privileged access to Being (as evidenced by the
very fact that he can question it), and if Heidegger can examine man's
comprehension of Being, perhaps that will help him answer his own
question. This privileged openness to Being Heidegger calls "existence"
(he sometimes writes it "ek-sistence" to suggest that man "stands"

[-*sistit*] "outside" [*ek-*] of himself and toward Being), or more often *Dasein* to signify this intimacy with Being (*Sein*). He will analyze this ek-sistence, and his method will be "phenomenological," i.e., he will analyze man by letting him appear as he is. He starts with man in his most ordinary, everyday condition, as "Being-in-the-World." Let us sketch the analysis only insofar as it offers some help in understanding the nature of human development. What does the analysis yield? That man is a transcendence (i.e., passes beyond beings—including himself—to their Being) which is finite, whose ultimate meaning is time.

Man is a Transcendence

Dasein is transcendence. This appears from the close analysis of what it means to-be-in-the-World. First Heidegger examines the World and discovers it to be, not simply an horizon within which beings are encountered, but a matrix of relationships within which they have meaning. Then he examines what it means to-be-in such a World. Fundamentally it means to disclose the World, and by reason of this disclosure, beings in the World are disclosed to *Dasein*. Heidegger finds three components of this disclosure of the World through *Dasein*'s In-being. The first he calls "com-prehension," not in any intellectual sense, but as a seizure (-*prehendere*) by *Dasein* in and as itself (*cum-*) of the pattern of meaningfulness which the World supplies. The second he calls "the ontological disposition" (*Befindlichkeit*), that component of *Dasein*'s structure by which it is affectively disposed to other beings, responds to them, reverberates with them in all its various moods. Finally, the third component of *Dasein*'s In-being in the World Heidegger calls "logos." By this he understands that element in *Dasein* by reason of which *Dasein* can articulate its presence in and to the World through language.

This Transcendence Is Finite

This complex structure by which *Dasein* is in-the-World is what the phenomenological analysis discovers in transcendence. We should add here perhaps that Heidegger insists that *Dasein* is never a solitary in the World. It ek-sists with other *Dasein*s (*Dasein* is *Mitdasein*), and this interlacing structure permeated by *Befindlichkeit* (the "ontological disposition") is the basis of all empathy and, indeed, all love. Be that as it may, transcendence is finite, i.e., it is limited by many different kinds of "not." To begin with, *Dasein* is not its own master—it does not create itself but finds itself as a matter of fact in the World. Heidegger calls this *Dasein*'s "thrownness." Furthermore, *Dasein* is not independent of other beings but related to them, and in this reference depends on them to be what it is. Again, this referential dependence goes so deep that *Dasein* tends to become absorbed in other beings, becomes fallen among them ("fallenness") to such an extent that it tends to be oblivious of its openness to Being, to forget its true self. In its everyday condition, *Dasein* is normally victim of this fallenness, caught up in the throes of what everybody else says and does. Heidegger discerns this condition graphically as a subservience to "everybody else" (*das Man*), and we recognize easily here Fromm's "automaton conformity."

Another kind of "not" which marks the finitude of *Dasein*'s transcendence is the fact that Being itself, when considered in terms of beings, can only be experienced as not-a-being, Non-being (*Nichts*). But the deepest "not" of all is the fact that *Dasein* cannot be forever; it is destined to die. So deep is this negativity of death that its sign is upon *Dasein* from the beginning—not as an event still to come but as already circumscribing the finite *Dasein*. As soon as it begins to be, it begins to be finite, and the supreme finitude which circumscribes it from the beginning is death. From the first moment of ek-sistence, then, *Dasein* is Being-into-death. The sum total of all these different types of finitude Heidegger calls "guilt." Because it is finite, and inasmuch as it is finite, *Dasein* is ineluctably guilty.

Anxiety Makes Authentic Self Possible

Such, then, are the ingredients of the self—finite transcendence. Thrown among beings it is open to their Being, yet trammeled with finitude, i.e., guilt. But how are these elements experienced in their unity, as pertaining to a single self? It is here that Heidegger describes the phenomenon of anxiety as revealing the true nature of the self. Anxiety is a special mode of the "ontological disposition," an affective, nonrational attunement within us. It is different from fear, because fear is always an apprehensive response to something—like a dentist's drill—a being. But in anxiety the self is not anxious about any one thing but about no-thing in particular, about Nothing! Yet not about absolutely nothing, rather about "something" quite "real" which is still not a thing like other things; nor is it situated here, there, or anywhere. Anxiety reveals *Dasein* as exposed to "something" which is no-thing and no-where. At this moment, the things which have a "where" around us seem to slip out of our grasp, lose their meaningfulness. We are no longer at home among them. We are alienated from them, as we say—we are alienated, too, from "everybody else," from "people" (*das Man*) with all that they do and say. We discover that there is another dimension in life besides the everyday one, a new horizon of which we are ordinarily unaware, yet within which and toward which we truly ek-sist, whether we call this horizon simply the No-thing (*Nichts*), the World, or even Being itself. Through the phenomenon of anxiety, then, the self becomes aware of itself as a unified whole: open to the World (i.e., Being) but "thrown" into ek-sistence, even "fallen" upon the beings among which it finds itself within the World. This unified structure is what Heidegger calls *Sorge* (i.e., "Care"). At the same time, anxiety makes *Dasein* as "Care" aware of the possibility of accepting the fact that this is what it is (finite transcendence) or of running away from the truth, refusing to know anything except what the *das Man* knows. In other words, the phenomenon of anxiety reveals to *Dasein* the possibility of choosing to be authentic or not.

Conscience Achieves Authenticity

But anxiety as such goes no farther. It reveals *Dasein* to itself, but as such it does not call upon *Dasein* to make the choice to be true to itself. Yet, there is such a voice which calls to *Dasein* out of its very depths— a voice which invites *Dasein* to be liberated from the thralldom of other "people" (*das Man*) and to accept itself as finite transcendence, as openness to Being, permeated, as it is, with ontological guilt. This, for Heidegger, is the voice of conscience. To heed this voice means to say yes: yes to its own transcendence, i.e., to the fact that it will always be alienated from "people" (*das Man*) to the extent that its true abode is not simply the level of beings alone but the domain of Being itself; yes to its own finitude, not as if this meant blind surrender to a tragic fate, but simply a tranquil resignation to the fact that it is no more than it is. *Dasein* says yes to itself by what Heidegger calls the act of "resolve" (*Entschlossenheit*), the moment when it achieves authenticity. It is essentially an act of freedom, for by it man liberates himself unto himself, accepts himself with all his limitations, lets himself be what he is.

Man Finds His Unity in Time

Finally, *Dasein* is a finite transcendence whose ultimate meaning—i.e., the ultimate source of its unity—is time. As transcending ek-sistence, *Dasein* is always coming to *Being*, i.e., Being is coming to it. This coming is *Dasein*'s future. But Being comes to a *Dasein* which already is, for *Dasein* discovers itself as "thrown." This condition of already-having-been is *Dasein*'s past. Furthermore, Being as it comes to *Dasein* renders all beings present as meaningful to *Dasein*. This presence is *Dasein*'s present. Future–past–present: these are the components of time. What gives unity to *Dasein*, then, is the unity of time.

CONCLUSION

What does all this add to our understanding of personal human development? For one thing, it situates the problem on a deeper level than man's relationship to the evolutionary process—we deal here with man's relationship to Being itself. For another, it abstains from talking about human development in terms of human fulfillment or self-actualization, and settles for the notion of authenticity as the highest level of human achievement. This seems to me both more modest and more realistic. For, although it honors everything which the humanists want to say about self-actualizing creativity and human productiveness, it takes a more sober view of human weakness and human limitation. Given the fact that the guilt that Heidegger talks about is an "ontological" guilt, identical with human finitude, there is in his conception of finitude, especially in the notion of "fallenness," a ground for human contrariness—even of human perversity—which lets us see how failure can be integrated with authenticity as well as success, like shadows in a Rembrandt painting. Likewise, death for Heidegger is more than just an anomaly extrinsic to the meaningfulness of life (Fromm). For Heidegger it is ingredient to life and de-fines the limits within which life can have its meaning. Just as for the Greeks, the limits of a being (like a lily or a rose) were the boundaries within which it began to be what it was, so for Heidegger, death—the ultimate limit—is the boundary within which man can be what he is and be free to be himself.

Again, time in this conception is not just a unilinear succession of "nows," where the past is a "now" which was, the present a "now" which is, and the future a "now" which will be, and we carry the "nows" of our past like a heavy burden which we can never shake off. For Heidegger, time comes through the past but out of the future. We are what we have been, to be sure, but we continue to be what we are because Being is in constant advent toward us with all its mystery and all its liberating power. It makes available to us ever new possibilities which are indeed filtered through our past and conditioned by it, but always fresh, exhilarating, and "creative." Thus a much-badgered school principal—to return to the original vignette—is challenged to achieve authenticity in the present by fidelity to the future, even though it be colored by the past of his perennial childhood.

Finally, in this mysterious advent of Being, the religious man can find hope. To be sure, Being for Heidegger is not God (God cannot be discovered by phenomenology)—but it does not exclude God for those who have experienced Him in some other way. Docility to the voice of conscience is docility to whatever can be uttered to man through that voice which wells up from his innermost self. If this voice calls man to become authentic, i.e., fully alive, it can be an invitation to achieve what the experience of faith in an Irenaeus calls the "glory of God"—*gloria Dei est vivens homo*—"the glory of God is a man fully alive." If the experience of religious faith introduces a new language to man's conception of his own finitude, such as the language of "sin," it also introduces the language of "forgiveness" and a new meaning of the word "love." In short, it introduces the notion of "redemption," according to which "the Word became flesh and dwelt amongst us" (Jn 1:14)—living in the confines of human limitation, dying in failure, but rising again to share with us the "fullness" (if not fulfillment) "we have all received." This, presumably, is a humanism of a higher sort.

REFERENCES

Bühler, C. Responses to contemporary challenges. In T. C. Greening (Ed.), *Existential humanistic psychology.* Belmont, Cal.: Brooks/Cole, 1973. Pp. 15–42.

Freud, S. Civilization and its discontents (1930). In J. Strachey (Ed.), *Standard edition of the complete works of Sigmund Freud* (Vol. 21). London: Hogarth, 1961. Pp. 57–145.

Freud, S., & Breuer, J. Studies on hysteria (1893–1895). In J. Strachey (Ed.), *Standard edition of the complete works of Sigmund Freud* (Vol. 2). London: Hogarth, 1955.

Fromm, E. *Man for himself.* New York: Fawcett, 1967. Original edition, 1947.

Fromm, E. *Escape from freedom.* New York: Avon, 1969. Original edition, 1941.

Fromm, E. *The anatomy of human destructiveness.* New York: Holt, Rinehart & Winston, 1973.

Goldstein, K. *The organism.* New York: American Book, 1939.

Heidegger, M. *Being and time* (J. Macquarrie & E. Robinson, trans.). New York: Harper & Row, 1963. Original German edition, 1927.

Maslow, A. H. *Motivation and personality.* New York: Harper & Row, 1954. Revised edition, 1970.

Maslow, A. H. *Toward a psychology of being* (Rev. ed.). Princeton, N.J.: Van Nostrand, 1968. Original edition, 1962.

May, R. Contributions of existential psychotherapy. In R. May, A. Angel, & H. Ellenberger (Eds.), *Existence.* New York: Simon & Schuster, 1967. Pp. 37–91. Original edition, 1958.

Skinner, B. F. *Beyond freedom and dignity.* New York: Bantam/Vintage, 1972. Original edition, 1971.

V
PROBLEMS OF LIVING: SEVERE LIMITATIONS OF HUMAN EXPECTANCIES

The Physically Handicapped

LEONARD DILLER

Leonard Diller received his B.S. degree from City College of The City University of New York in 1947, and his M.A. (1950) and Ph.D. from New York University. Dr. Diller has devoted his entire professional life to work with the physically disabled. He has been associated with the Institute of Rehabilitation Medicine at the New York University Medical Center since 1951, where he currently is Chief of Behavioral Science. He has served as consultant for numerous organizations devoted to work with the physically handicapped, among them United Cerebral Palsy of New York City, Goldwater Memorial Hospital, the Department of Neurosurgery of St. Barnabas Hospital, and the Blythedale Home for Crippled Children.

What are the problems in living for the severely disabled? One is tempted to paraphrase the reply of William James to a similar question: "It depends on the liver." But society has a more normative answer in the rehabilitation movement. This movement comprises a variety of services designed to meet the needs of the disabled in daily living. The rehabilitation enterprise recognizes that handicapped people always have more than one thing wrong with them and that no one with a severe handicap has only a single problem. For example, in the case of a patient with a spinal cord injury we typically will find that, in addition to a host of biological problems including respiration and metabolic functions, there are the problems of the paralysis and its reversibility, changes in sensation, loss of bowel, bladder, and sex functions, loss of self-care skills such as walking and grooming, loss of ability to perform a job, and potential changes in the individual's role as worker, sex partner, spouse, and parent.

How does one treat all this? Where does one begin? Is there any lawfulness to the treatments? We approached these questions from several directions: (a) we asked people entering a physical medicine and rehabilitation program what they wanted from the program; (b) we studied the records of the way in which people spend their time in the program; and (c) we asked whether people with different rehabilitation goals have distinguishing characteristics.

EXPECTANCIES IN REHABILITATION

When asked "What would you like to achieve in rehabilitation or why did you come here?" patients' responses are found to follow a generally consistent pattern. Almost every patient (95%) said that he would like some type of physical recovery. People wanted to be able to move their limbs and to recover their sensations. A second set of goals included a variety of statements which may be grouped under the development of self-care skills. "I want to take care of myself. . . . I want to be able to walk and get around. . . ." This occurred in approximately 80% of the patients. A third set of goal statements involved solving problems in the vocation and/or social environment. "I want to be able to go back to my old job. . . ." "I won't be able to manage in my apartment. . . ." Here we find a precipitous drop in goal statements to 40%. Finally, there is a fourth set of goal statements: "I want help because I'm unhappy. . . . I'm no good. . . ." This occurred even less frequently—5% to 10% of the time. The sample was taken at the Institute of Rehabilitation Medicine at a point when the patients were close to entry in a rehabilitation program. All patients were orthopedically handicapped adults; most were males with spinal cord injuries, although there were some stroke victims, amputees, and referred patients complaining of chronic low back pain.

What can we learn from this? Goal statements appear to be organized in a hierarchic way. Not all goals are seen as equally relevant or equally pressing. The hierarchy tends to operate in a one-way direction, i.e., if one wants help for a psychological problem, then it is safe to assume that one wants help in the other areas. If one wants help in mastering skills in Activities of Daily Living, then one wants help in physical restoration. The converse is not true. A patient who wants physical restoration does not necessarily want help in other areas. A person seeking help in self-care does not necessarily want help with social, vocational, or psychological problems.

This type of hierarchy may be seen as analogous to the well-known hierarchy of Maslow (1970) who speaks of levels of needs in which more basic biological needs preempt culturally imposed needs. A similar hierarchic model has been used to explain reactions to crisis situations (Fink, 1967; Shontz, 1975).

Some support for the model is gained from an examination of the program cards of patients in rehabilitation settings. In such settings, treatments are usually scheduled hourly. If one examines rehabilitation as an individually prescribed education program for living with a disability, one finds a stratification of time and effort remarkably parallel to the pattern of goal statements. More time is spent in physical therapy than in other areas. The least amount of time is spent with a psychologist. One might argue that a patient's goals are subtly shaped to meet the services, but one could also put it the other way and maintain that the services are congruent with what people really want.

While the findings form a coherent picture, they also present a puzzle. It does not make clinical sense to say that only 10% of the people have psychological problems. I should assume rather that every patient has a problem in every area. All the patients have psychological problems just as all the patients want total recovery. Why is there such a disparity between what people say and what one senses they need?

I should suspect that there are different level task demands associated with different goals. It is easier to fix on recovery and increasingly more difficult to focus on developing skills for independence in self-care, coping with social and vocational realities, and psychological problems. Indeed working through "psychological" problems may be the most difficult of all the tasks in rehabilitation. It is not that patients do not have such problems, but that work on these problems is deferred. Some evidence for this may be seen in a number of studies we conducted.

In one study, we used the Rorschach Test,* but not in the usual clinical psychiatric sense. Rather we viewed the test as a particularly difficult task. Because of the ambiguous nature of inkblots, there are no right or wrong answers. The patient is thrown on his own resources. We were interested in how well the patient would be able to meet the task demands of the test rather than in using it as a personality test. Would the person fail to respond? Would he respond in stereotyped ways? Would he show responses in which his own internal needs and frustrations get in the way? Or would the patient respond to the requirements of the task in spite of evidence of anxiety or psychopathology?

We found indeed that those patients who offered few responses, re-

---

* A test developed in 1942 by the Swiss psychiatrist Hermann Rorschach utilizing a series of 10 bilaterally symmetrical inkblots and employing the responses of an individual to these blots as a means to the diagnostic investigation of personality.—Ed.

peated the same response, and grossly distorted the blot tended to offer goals focused on the lower end of the continuum of needs. From this I deduce that those patients who have difficulty maintaining task-relevant behavior when faced with complex demands will not be able to cope with the more complex and demanding tasks in rehabilitation, while those who can meet the minimal requirements of a difficult test can also meet the more complex task demands of rehabilitation. I would argue on several grounds that for a physically disabled person the demands of psychotherapy are more difficult than are the demands of physical therapy.

Let me offer some comments on the model lest the picture seem overly simple. We can ask two basic questions: (*a*) Does this picture change over time or is it invariant? (*b*) Does this picture apply to other kinds of handicapping conditions and other kinds of settings, or is it specific to the population and the setting I have described?

LIVING WITH A DISABILITY OVER A PERIOD OF TIME

The problems of living with a disability over a period of time have surfaced on two levels—a clinical or individual level, and a public or community level.

The Clinical or Individual Level

On a clinical level Davis (1963) has described the recovery from polio as a passage through crisis. A typical longitudinal paradigm to fit the course of response to severe illness proceeds as follows. There is an initial disbelief that tragedy has struck, which is accompanied by the worst possible fear that death will take place. The two alternate. When it is clear that death will not strike, the individual still feels that (*a*) nothing terrible has happened, and that (*b*) the thing which has happened is only temporary and will go away in a very brief time. In this state the individual thinks about the appointments he cannot keep and the way in which his life can be rearranged to take care of the fact that he is temporarily out of commission. He also begins to set up a type of internal deadline. "By Monday, I will be walking out of here," or "Wait until the weekend, I'll be all better." Or, sometimes, "I'll give myself until the weekend, if I am not better by then I'll really let fly." When the weekend arrives and nothing much has happened, the individual may experience disappointment or may again postpone recovery and attach it to another magical date.

This process is repeated throughout the first year of an acquired, permanent disability. The patient may alternate between denying the fact of the disability or its consequences and severe depression when he begins to think about the losses imposed by his new condition. At first these losses are overwhelming and appear to know no bounds (Dembo, Leviton, & Wright, 1956; Garrett & Levine, 1973). Gradually both the denial and the depression associated with loss tend to lose their force although they may be reawakened. This process is similar to the mourning which is common after the loss or death of a love object. Individuals who go through it are then said to "accept" their disabilities. Individuals whose major energy is tied up in denying their disability or in mourning it tend to focus on the more simple task demands in life. They are concerned with recovery and perhaps with self-care, but they are not ready to come to grips with more complex role demands and planning for a realistic future. Such individuals cope only with day-to-day demands. It is typical for counseling in this situation to cover only day-to-day concerns. Indeed, counseling sessions are oriented toward the present, almost as if the person had no past and no future.

There are individual differences in undergoing this process. Some people do it more quickly than others. For some the process extends interminably to the point of limiting the effectiveness of intervention efforts. The factors which account for these differences—e.g., premorbid personality, age, social class, ego strength, family support, and environmental opportunity—may be interrelated. Their values as measured by their correlations with actual outcomes suggest that it is difficult to pinpoint one at the expense of others.

If we track people in a rehabilitation setting over time, there is a shift in concerns (Powell, Diller & Grynbaum, 1976). Nonetheless, in a follow-up study of stroke victims who were left with permanent paralysis (hemiplegics), we found that half of those who gave permanent cure of paralysis as a goal a month after admission to a rehabilitation setting wanted a permanent cure a year to a year and a half later. While most stroke victims want cures, they also come to grips with other problems in their daily environment. Those who focus only on cure do not. They deny the disability or, to put it more accurately, they deny the consequences of the disability.

The Public or Community Level

On the community level, one of the weakest areas in rehabilitation is the absence of follow-up and follow-along services. This weakness has been acknowledged in the new rehabilitation legislation which mandates a follow-up study of people who have been through our state systems. It has also been brought to our attention in the growth of self-help groups among the disabled (Wright, 1971). Taking a cue from the civil rights movement of a decade ago and the women's liberation movement which is also more than a decade old, the handicapped have become conscious of how poorly a society designed by and for non-handicapped people serves the needs of the handicapped. Various consortia of groups of the handicapped are beginnning to serve as their own most effective lobbyists at the local and the national levels. The major exclusionary barriers in our society in this regard are found in architecture and transportation. Handicapped people are just stuck at home. Environmental inaccessibility is often such a problem that it does not pay for the individual to work. Job discrimination, sometimes falsely rationalized with the excuse that insurance rates rise when a disabled person is hired, is a major factor in the immediate lives of the disabled. The growth of the consumer movement among handicapped people is beginning to be felt not only in legislation but also in the adaptations made in resort areas, businesses, and hotels. Guides to restaurants which are wheelchair-accessible and published descriptions of barriers in public buildings are growing in popularity.

From the standpoint of public responsiveness, the physically disabled have been likened to a minority group. Although the similarities and differences in physical condition, skin color, sex, and ethnic identity as bases for minority-group status is an intriguing one, there appears to be a growing attempt to include the handicapped with other minorities. If this is indeed the case, then the fate of handicapped people on a public policy level will be similar to the fate of other minority groups. For example, in a period of economic recession, it is more difficult to sell the slogan "Hire the handicapped" (Wright, 1960).

A brief aside. The growth of consumerism and the analogy to minority-group status give rise to a major question: How well do institutions designed to serve handicapped people do their job? Serious doubt has been raised as to whether our vocational rehabilitation system adequately meets the needs of the severely handicapped. Is the criterion of placement on a job a good indication of successful rehabilitation? Most people would agree that such an approach is overly simple. One might also question the national priority in special education which calls for an attempt to eliminate special education by mainstreaming and integrating handicapped children with non-handicapped children. The data at this point are too limited to warrant comment. One could note only the wide variety of contingencies involved here: (a) some children are excluded from regular class because of physical conditions totally irrelevant to education, e.g., inability to travel, lack of training in bladder or bowel control; (b) others are excluded because they have difficulties in learning, e.g., mental retardation, learning disabilities; (c) still others are excluded because as a result of emotional problems they are difficult to manage in the classroom. With such a complex array of conditions, mainstreaming for all will not be possible; indeed I wonder whether it is even desirable. Should we not try to create special environments for children with special needs?

My point is that rehabilitation as a system of delivering services to physically handicapped people works well during the post-immediate period of the onset of a disability. Yet there are many problems which surface in the post-treatment efforts. These can be illustrated through a closer look at the different settings and situations of various disabled people.

THE SITUATION WITH SELECTED GROUPS OF THE DISABLED

How well does the model derived from observations on an in-patient physical medicine and rehabilitation program apply to other settings or to other disabilities? I should suspect that some kind of hierarchy of needs exists for different populations of disabled in different settings and that the specific form of this hierarchy varies with populations and circumstances. A measure of whether a situation is adequate is whether it meets the needs of the people it serves. Let me cite three instances to illustrate the complexities. They include populations of (*a*) those suffering low back pain; (*b*) those afflicted with cerebral palsy; and (*c*) the physically handicapped elderly.

Low Back Pain

In the case of people with presenting pain, whether psychogenic or physical in origin, we have found that relief from the pain captures all the individual's energy. It is almost as if one major worry eliminates all minor ones. Indeed, patients in pain have generally fared least well in traditional rehabilitation. I have always suspected that this results from the fact that the treatment is not tuned to expectancy. Recent years have seen attempts to correct this.

In one approach using behavior modification, Fordyce and his colleagues (1973) report improvement in patients with long histories of medical, including surgical and psychiatric, therapy. The basic idea is that pain is treated as a verbal behavior which reinforces a state of dependency. Talking about pain, or even focusing on it, reinforces the pain. The method of treatment is twofold. The first is to prevent the patient from receiving reinforcement for his pain behavior (e.g., the staff deliberately ignores the patient's complaints about his pain) and to provide medication according to an external schedule rather than in response to patient complaint. The second is to reward substitute behaviors (e.g., recording the amount of physical exercise, or walking, and offering praise for it create an atmosphere which will not reinforce the complaint or dependency). Sarno (1975) finds that a combination of physical therapy and psychotherapy is optimal when an attempt is made to show the connection between pain and psychological factors. Indeed, psychopathology is manifested when a patient refuses to see the connection or is involved in interpersonal relationships which reward the pain behavior, e.g., the housewife who is pain-free in a treatment program because she feels out of the clutches of a perfectionistic, demanding husband.

The case of pain is interesting. It suggests that if a person focuses on a single problem which creates or is related to his dependency condition and alters his entire lifestyle to fit this state, the hierarchy of goals and the seemingly lawful pattern which I have indicated becomes less salient. The notion of a person's being able to pick his way through a number of problems in some kind of predictable way seems less cogent. The psychology of presenting tasks with different demands to meet needs has to be modified.

Cerebral Palsy

The fact that cerebral palsy is a congenital condition throws a number of situations into immediate relief. To begin with, there is the situation of the parent. Parents must cope with the following problems: (*a*) facing the fact that one has given birth to a handicapped child; (*b*) clarifying the extent of the handicap and determining its manifestations and prognosis; and (*c*) making all the decisions in child rearing, ranging from those which exist in the case of non-handicapped children to issues of whether a handicapped should receive special treatment because of his condition to major alterations in planning, extending from placement in a special school to actual placement in an institution. The task of parenting a physically handicapped child is extraordinarily complex. Sociologists are quick to point out that such parenting occurs in a social context, and a number of observers have focused on social class, religious, and ethnic factors.

I happen to work as a consultant to the United Cerebral Palsy of New York City. In visiting the pre-school programs in different parts of the city, one can note the similarity of the children attending schools in the different boroughs, but the profiles of the parents differ considerably from borough to borough. Consider the following examples. Given the same child—perhaps one who is mildly retarded with perceptual and auditory problems, poor eye–hand skills, and difficulty in ambulation, and who is a fussy eater and sleeper—what advice would you offer in the following cases?

(*a*) In the Bronx, to a Puerto Rican mother living on welfare, deserted by her husband, with responsibility for two other young children.

(*b*) On Staten Island, to an Irish-Catholic mother, married to a policeman, feeling tied down by a handicapped child, not being able to complete a college education to advance herself.

(*c*) In Manhattan, to an upper-class Jewish mother, who is trapped by her family's wanting to take over and manage her life, and her husband's relative lack of attention to her and to the child.

(*d*) In Brooklyn, to a black mother struggling with problems of poverty and narcotics.

In connection with the above cases, I should like to make three observations. (*a*) There is a priority of concerns which differ in different contexts. (*b*) When mothers bring their children to the pre-school program and describe them, they focus first on the physical aspects of the handicapping condition, rather than on the psychological or mental aspects. (*c*) If mothers are brought together in a family camp setting, the interplay between differences in social background and similarities in concern about problems in rearing a handicapped child is complex.

The fact that cerebral palsy is a congenital condition raises another interesting problem. While children with cerebral palsy have been studied, diagnosed, and treated for a host of difficulties, including language, and intellectual, sensory, and motor capacities, there have been very few advances in the area of social development. The least understood but most common problem in the growing cerebral palsy child might be called social immaturity, for want of a better term. This is manifested in many ways: inability to grasp social nuances, inability to maintain meaningful conversations, formation of unrealistic goals, lack of close friends. Indeed loneliness is a lifelong problem. A child with cerebral palsy may suffer from an impoverished or distorted history of interpersonal feedback throughout his life span (Richardson, 1965). Consider the fact that a normal child has many more interpersonal encounters than does a cerebral palsy child every day of the year; consider the fact that people avoid interactions with others who look different; consider the fact that we have no solid ways of measuring social skills or treating their deficiencies. I submit that we have an important but neglected problem.

Paralleling and reinforcing the isolation of the cerebral palsy child is the fact that (*a*) we have not developed adequate educational programs to foster maximum independence; and (*b*) we have not created good vocational and housing conditions to maximize opportunities for this population. Follow-up studies of cerebral palsy children indicate that the vast majority remain financially dependent when they grow up, even after treatment in our finest institutions (Klapper & Birch, 1967).

Because of our lack of money, knowledge, and determination, we have been forced to create temporary conditions—e.g., workshops and activity centers, and finally institutionalization—and then to look upon these as if they were permanent solutions.

Aging and Chronic Disability

I once had occasion to study the "social adjustment" of older handicapped people in an institutional residential setting. The most striking finding was not in the responses to formal attitude scales, but in the fact that 40% of the residents literally could not name people on their own ward. Some had not seen themselves in a mirror for many years. Many had had no visitors or received any mail in a previous six-month period. This lack of human relatedness appears to be more than an exaggeration of the loneliness common to all physically disabled after they are discharged from an active treatment program. Often it is difficult, even when one asks, to assess problems and needs in such a situation. One is required to make a judicious assessment, and to act at a level where there appears to be a need.

CONCLUDING COMMENT

While the physically disabled have been considered in this Institute under the category of Severe Limitations of Human Expectancies, I am not at all sure that handicapped people would see it this way. What I have tried to show is that the expectancies of handicapped people are influenced by the same forces which influence non-handicapped people. A proper understanding of the expectancies of the handicapped person would require placing oneself in his position. Yet when one is viewing from that vantage point, one is better able to uncover patterns in expectancies—patterns which can serve as useful bases for assisting the handicapped in more appropriate ways.

REFERENCES

Davis, F. *Passage through crisis: Polio victims and their families.* Indianapolis: Bobbs-Merrill, 1963.

Dembo, T., Leviton, G., & Wright, B. Adjustment to misfortune—A problem of social–psychological rehabilitation. *Artificial Limbs*, 1956, *3*, 4–6.

Fink, S. L. Crisis and motivation: A theoretical model. *Archives of Physical Medicine and Rehabilitation*, 1967, *48*, 592–597.

Fordyce, W. E., *et al.* Operant conditioning in the treatment of chronic pain. *Archives of Physical Medicine and Rehabilitation*, 1973, *54*, 399–409.

Garrett, J. T., & Levine, S. E. *Rehabilitation practice with the physically disabled.* New York: Columbia University Press, 1973.

Klapper, Z. S., & Birch, H. G. A fourteen-year follow-up study of cerebral palsy: Intellectual change and stability. *American Journal of Orthopsychiatry*, 1967, *37*, 540–547.

Maslow, A. H. *Motivation and personality* (2nd ed.). New York: Harper & Row, 1970.

Powell, B. R., Diller, L., & Grynbaum, B. Rehabilitation performance and adjustment in stroke patients: A study of social class factors. *Genetic Psychology Monographs*, 1976, *93*, 287–352.

Richardson, S. A. Social factors related to children's accuracy in learning peer group values towards handicaps. *Human Relations*, 1965, *26* (1), 77–87.

Sarno, J. E. Pain, psychic conflict and rehabilitation. *Archives of Physical Medicine and Rehabilitation*, 1975, *56*, 560.

Shontz, F. *The psychological aspects of physical illness and disability*. New York: Macmillan, 1975.

Wright, B. A. *Physical disability: A psychological approach*. New York: Harper & Row, 1960.

Wright, M. E. Self-help groups in the rehabilitation enterprise. *Psychological Aspects of Disability*, 1971, *18*, 43–45.

The Psychologically Disabled

WILLIAM F. LYNCH, S.J.

Father William F. Lynch, S.J. earned all his degrees at Fordham University: the A.B. in 1930, the M.A. in 1939, and the Ph.D. in 1942. His principal life work has been as editor and writer. He served as editor from 1937 to 1948 of the national Jesuit monthly magazine The Messenger of the Sacred Heart, *and from 1950 to 1956 of Fordham University's quarterly,* Thought. *Father Lynch has contributed to many scholarly journals and periodicals, and is, in addition, the author of the following books:* An introduction to the metaphysics of Plato *(1959),* The image industries *(1959),* Christ and Apollo *(1960),* The integrating mind *(1962),* Images of faith *(1973), and* Images of hope *(1974). On three separate occasions, and for three of the above-mentioned books, Father Lynch has been the recipient of the most distinguished book-of-the-year award.*

My intention in this paper is to try to bring to some helpful focus that broad and very loosely knit accumulation of thoughts, images, and feelings with which the well among us approach and thereby severely limit the psychologically disabled.

I begin by looking at a few of the general and generalizing images the well have of the mentally ill, the psychologically handicapped, the retarded. I make no apology for turning so quickly to these general images and feelings because in this case the more general and vague pictures of a reality happen to be the most immediate, the most powerful, and the most operative attitudes with which human society approaches this form of sickness or handicap.

THE IMAGE THAT THE MENTALLY ILL DO NOT BELONG TO HUMAN SOCIETY

Basic to all these vague but powerful feelings about illnesses of the mind is the attitude of human society that those who are sick or substantively handicapped in mind and heart do not really belong to human society; at best they are marginal people who live on the edge of that society, just outside its golden gates; therefore we expect that they will not do, feel, or think the things which are human. Obsessed as they are with an image of the human and of human society as beautiful, the people within that society, within that city of man, fortify their position by building limiting walls about their city and casting psychic illness and substantive handicaps outside them. What is limited here is the image of man and the image of the human. This image does not contain the types of illness or handicap we are talking about in this paper. What is demanded of the sick, for example, is that they become well *before* they are entered into this city, before they can be accepted as human. But to the degree that this is a true picture of our situation, the picture helps to create a potentially terrible impasse. For if our desolate friends and cousins are healed only by discovering that what is wrong with them is altogether human, if on the other hand they are excluded from the human and from the city of the fair, the competent, the normal, the well, then where is their hope?

For the further elaboration of this situation let me take the help of a fairly well-known Austrian by the name of Sigmund Freud (1917/1935, pp. 464–465); a great American analyst, Harry Stack Sullivan (1956); and a remarkable Danish thinker, Martti Siirala. Freud himself, I am sure, would have had nothing to do with this breakdown of humanity into the two separate cities of the well and the sick. For he thought that what was wrong with the ill could always be found in degree in the well. Sullivan gave us the splendidly encapsulated sentence that what was wrong with the sick was simply human. Note the simplicity and yet the absolute centrality of the opening sentence of Sullivan's book:

> In approaching the subject of mental disorder, I must emphasize that, in my view, persons showing mental disorder do not manifest anything specifically different in kind from what is manifested by practically all human beings [Sullivan, 1956, p. 3].

But perhaps Siirala has put it best of all:

We in our modern society tend to build upon a myth of an ideal society, consisting of selected and approved individuals—of "normal" human beings, with average intelligence, average bodily health, and with a sufficient degree of psychic maturity. These selected and privileged individuals have—it is true—the obligation on their shoulders, in the name of humanity, to take care of the others who do not belong in this class of the "true" society. This kind of care does not, however, acknowledge the sick as belonging to the body, *unless* they recover. One might say that sick people do not belong (according to the dogma we enact in our shared life—without, it is true, ever becoming aware of this doctrine by practice) to the true society. The prevalence of this idea among us is obvious if we think how we speak of the sick man's "return" to society, as if he had not been in his society while sick—especially if he has been in a hospital. Racial discrimination is not in any way an isolated phenomenon among us! It is as if we thought that human defects and illness do not belong to our "proper life" and that individuals who had by an accident succumbed to the fate of being ill (or dying!) were not actual, proper members of society—unless they could be made healthy again.*

It is this image of themselves among the well (an image of normality, perfection, beauty) which defines human nature and human society and serves as a limit not to be crossed by the ill. This mode of action and reaction is probably true of human society everywhere but it is especially true of America. On this subject I particularly recommend R. W. B. Lewis' (1955) *The American Adam* or Robert Penn Warren's (1975) "Bearers of Bad Tidings," a comprehensive article on the powerful development of these American images of beauty and innocence in some *vs.* the awful presence of dirt, corruption, and commonness in the masses of mankind. Warren draws his materials † from Emerson ("Leave this hypercritical prating about the masses. Masses are rude, lame, unmade, pernicious in their demands and influence. . . . I do not wish any mass at all, but honest men only . . . and no shovel-handed, narrow-brained, gin-drinking million stockingers or lazzaroni at all"), Whitman (who thus describes what he found in the North after the Civil War: only cities "crowded with grotesques, malformations, phantoms, playing meaningless antics"), Henry James, Justice Holmes, Mark Twain (according to Twain the human race was "muck"), and Theodore Dreiser, of whose heroes we can say that they "represent the poles of the 'tragedy' of America, a land of fictive values seized, or yearned after, by fictive selves." And then there were the heroes of Faulkner and Hemingway ("Hemingway's indictment of modernity was more desperate, more radical, and more contemptuous").

* From a mimeographed paper by Martti Siirala for private circulation.
† I have taken the following texts from Warren's brilliant article.

THE AMERICAN PASSION FOR PERFECTION

One of the positive conclusions which might be drawn from this evidence is that there is a permanent passion for perfection in the American character, the American experiment, and the American dream. This is certainly true of the intellectuals and the campus culture, which is passionately opposed to the middle class. But the middle class has its own dreams, even if they are thought to be a vulgar imitation of the real thing by the more sophisticated group which bars its gates to the vulgarians. And there are those many whom the middle class in turn will not permit through its own beautiful gates. Even the very last immigrant groups will not allow into their version of beauty and the dream those who are desperately seeking entrance from our Southern border. But there is a final exclusion on which all agree—and that is the exclusion of the mentally ill. There have been giant steps forward in legislation for the handicapped. Twenty-two states, the District of Columbia, and the federal government have outlawed job discrimination (four years ago only five states had such legislation). But even in the present advanced states there are some which exclude such help for the mentally ill.

But, we may say to ourselves, or others may say to us, how can an efficient society possibly survive if it allows the physically or psychologically handicapped into its sacred presence? Now, this is just the reverse of the way we should be thinking. We start with an image of the well, and without thinking we accept their way of doing things as efficiency. We should widen the image of the human to include the physically and psychologically handicapped and then accept as efficiency the way *that* society can operate. An image is not necessarily a thing which enters our passive consciousness ready made, objective, and ready to go. Images are, much more than we think, active things, and we are the responsible actors. A civilization will therefore be judged by its images much more than by anything else.

Let me move briefly from the better known to the less well known in order to clarify the central images which rule our images of an ideal (but destructive) city of man. If I now return to the subject of the physically handicapped in human society, it will be to use it as a metaphor which might illuminate the plight of the psychologically disabled and the mentally ill.

It has been estimated that there are from 20,000,000 to 50,000,000 disabled people in the United States. In what way does our image of this enormous number of people exclude them? Let us think of this problem in its most visible forms. Let us think of the architectural structure of one of our fair cities. Our architectural imagination prevents people in wheelchairs from using buses, trains, subways. They cannot enter most buildings. Because of an infinite number of curbs they cannot cross streets. (Why must there be that many curbs?) These people cannot use most lavatories. It has been made incredibly difficult for them to take a plane. Their income is limited. Their job opportunities are limited. Their education is limited. What is behind this placing of endless limitations on the lives of the physically handicapped? Most people do not want to be frequently in the presence of the handicapped because they do not wish to be reminded of what can happen to them. Again, they are not comfortable when in the company of human beings so different from themselves. R. N. Anderson (1932) has told us there are hundreds of jobs the handicapped can perform. That is the reality. The rest is fantasy.

THE PSYCHOLOGICALLY DISABLED

If the situation is so serious in the case of physical disability, we can be sure that it is even more serious when there is question of mental handicap or mental illness. Our society is so constructed in the order of ideas and the spirit that if most people were asked which they preferred, a reputation as a great sinner or a reputation for mental illness, most, I think, would spontaneously choose the first. Since this is the way we are made, legislation is all the more necessary. There are eighteen states which have enacted such legislation.* In Pennsylvania the court prohibited the state from using any law which would postpone or in any way deny mentally retarded individuals access to a publicly supported education. And the same court included programs, tuitions, and home instruction. A District of Columbia court joined the battle for the handicapped and mentally retarded children and for children suffering from orthopedic disorders. Various courts in Maryland, New Jersey, and New York have ruled that it be the policy of their states to provide a free education to everyone between the ages of 5 and 20, and that this policy must include the mentally retarded, no matter how profound the retardation. Another court has ruled that education in a regular school class is to be preferred to segregated classes.

For myself and my earlier argument, these last few stages symbolically represent the most important areas of all for further exploration. The question of how far the disabled and the mentally ill can become partners in life and work with the rest of mankind must be explored even to an extreme point. And here I approach my ending at the point

* I have been greatly aided in these pages by an unpublished paper entitled "Invidious discrimination against the disabled," written by Thomas F. McDonnell, a student in the Fordham University School of Law.

where I began. For our mental and/or physical *segregation* of various forms of mental handicap and mental illness are the points which create our central problem. It is in the case of the mentally ill above all that our vague images and fears draw very clear limiting lines of segregation and exclusion from our image of the human. The novelist and essayist Walker Percy makes a suggestion which—even if it is only partially true—is valuable. He suggests (Percy, 1975) that since the seventeenth century—that is, since the beginning of the great age of reason, science, technology, and the Enlightenment—we have been living a double and divided life; we have been torn between the images of the Enlightenment and the images of the Judaeo-Christian tradition. We have not done well in putting the two together. And the fact that the two have not yet been humanely and adequately put together is probably the biggest reason for the occasional eruption of revolution in our culture. When Christianity is most itself it is most interested in building the kind of society which is dedicated especially to the poor, the maimed, the mentally ill, the halt, and the blind.

I return to a seemingly small fact which I mentioned earlier and which in its turn I should like to use as a metaphor. I wish to use the decree of one court (that the education of handicapped children occur in non-segregated classes) as a symbol, a symbolic plea that the life of the mentally handicapped or ill be spent as much as possible in the presence or company of all those who are classified, or who classify themselves, as well.

One of the more extreme statements of this kind of solution for handicap, and especially for mental illness, is to be found in two books by Szasz (1963, 1970). It is well known that Szasz refuses to accept the label of mental illness, and calls attention to the fact that all the hospitals or clinics for the mentally ill obviously segregate their patients from the rest of human society. There is no easy solution for this problem, especially in a culture which has such limiting views of the human. But we need to reject the more extreme form of prescription if we are to move toward more acceptable and more accepting views of illness and handicap. And the author of these books is a rational thinker with a rational case.

THE EXAMPLE OF GHEEL

But surely the finest form of the desegregation of the mentally ill we have all read or heard about is the town of Gheel in Belgium where it has been (certainly since the thirteenth century) the vocation of an entire population (in 1969 the census report was just short of 30,000) to care for the mentally ill in a desegregated way, in the midst of their own homes and families (Aring, 1974). There may be questions to what limits and within what degree of desegregation any repetitions of this experiment may go. There may be a recurring question how far mental illness has been cured in particular cases and groups. But if there will always be some doubt remaining here, there is no doubt about what has happened to the *well* of Gheel. Nurtured from their own childhood in friendly and fearless images of illness, they are not beclouded by the usual fantasies the well have of the mentally ill. It still is the most beautiful story I know of the dissolving of these fantasies and the desegregation of these altogether human people. The entrance of the sick into the world of the human, and the entry of the well into the same city (where even beautiful people can lay down their terrible burdens of being perfectly well and beautiful), has been such a preoccupying thought with me that I have spent many years of my life in reading and writing (Lynch, 1974) about that central spot of the well and the ill where both may meet in this common world of the burdens of earthly men and women.

REFERENCES

Anderson, R. N. *The disabled man and his vocational adjustment* (Department of Labor, U. S. Bureau of Labor Standards, Bulletin No. 11). Washington, D.C.: U. S. Government Printing Office, 1932.

Aring, C. D. The Gheel experience: Eternal spirit of the chainless mind! *Journal of the American Medical Association*, November 18, 1974, pp. 998–1001.

Freud, S. *A general introduction to psychoanalysis*. New York: Washington Square Press, 1935. (Original German edition, 1917.)

Lewis, R. W. B. *The American Adam: Innocence, tragedy, and tradition in the nineteenth century*. Chicago: The University of Chicago Press, 1955.

Lynch, W. F. (s.j.). *Images of hope*. Notre Dame: University of Notre Dame Press, 1974.

Percy, W. *The message in the bottle*. New York: Farrar, Straus & Giroux, 1975.

Sullivan, H. S. *Clinical studies in psychiatry*. New York: Norton, 1956.

Szasz, T. S. *Law, liberty and psychiatry*. New York: Macmillan, 1963.

Szasz, T. S. *Ideology and insanity*. Garden City, N.Y.: Doubleday, 1970.

Warren, R. P. Bearers of bad tidings: Writers of the American dream. *New York Review of Books*, March 20, 1975, pp. 12–19.

The Economically Disadvantaged: The Constricted Life of the Poor

JAMES R. KELLY

James R. Kelly received his B.S. degree from Fordham University in 1963 and his Ph.D. from Harvard University in 1969. He joined the Fordham University faculty in 1972 where he is currently Associate Professor of Sociology. Prior to coming to Fordham he served as Research Associate on Poverty and Housing for the St. Ambrose Housing Center, Baltimore. Dr. Kelly is a member of the American Sociological Association, and is a contributor to such journals and periodicals as: Sociological Analysis, Journal of Ecumenical Studies, Journal for the Scientific Study of Religion, America, *and* Commonweal.

In one of the earliest American studies of poverty, Robert Hunter (1904/1965) reported a conversation he had had with William Dean Howells about Hunter's visit with Tolstoy. In the conversation Hunter had praised the Russian novelist's voluntary sharing of the hardships of Russian peasant life. Howells himself shared this admiration, of course, but he tempered Hunter's enthusiasm with the remark that it was impossible for Tolstoy truly to share the peasants' poverty. " 'For poverty,' he said, 'is not the lack of things,' it is the fear and the dread of want. That fear Tolstoy could not know" (Hunter, 1904/1965, p. 1).

As Howells recognized, poverty is not simply a lack of economic resources. Even more, it is the horror of hopelessness and insecurity. In

159

societies which are technologically advanced and secular, the poor are economically obsolescent, socially superfluous, and spiritually unnecessary. Economic and spiritual superfluity is the invincible sin of most of the poor.

Since poverty involves economic, political, and sociological dimensions, analyses of it engage more than the dispassionate intellect. There is significant disagreement about its causes and enormous disputes about the appropriate social policies to deal with it. Conflicting judgments about poverty involve conceptions of social change, differing theories of social stratification, and, most vexing of all, differing ideas of social justice. We shall do well initially to sort these issues out and then re-gather them toward the end of the paper. For now, the following issues can be discretely discussed: How is poverty defined? Are the poor different in major cultural and personality aspects from the non-poor? If major differences are found, how are these cultural differences explained, and what social policies have been thought appropriate to the condition of the poor? Definitions, differences, and designs for policy—these three headings will serve to organize much of the contemporary knowledge about poverty.

DEFINITIONS OF POVERTY

Since "poverty" is a relative term affected by historically changing standards, the term has no univocal definition. By world standards, a poor American would be considered materially prosperous. Most poor American families own a television set and have direct access to hot water. Obviously, cultural standards and social expectations dramatically affect the way any society defines poverty.

But we must not proceed too quickly. In fact, there have been attempts to define poverty in an objective and apolitical way.

The federal government has devised what at first glance might seem to be an objective and precise definition based on the Department of Agriculture's estimate of the minimum cost of a diet ensuring physical survival. Adopting the Department of Agriculture's 1964 economy food plan, which provided for $4.60 per person per week, or 22¢ a meal, and multiplying the yearly food cost by 3, the Social Security Administration established a 1964 poverty line of $3,100 for an urban family of four. Of course, the poverty line changes as the cost of food changes. So, by 1970 a non-farm family of four with an income below $3,968 was officially poor; and in 1973 $4,250 designated the poverty line for this same family of four.

The multiplication by 3 (called the Engel coefficient) of the cost of a minimally low diet seems to generate an objective measure providing an estimate of the percentage of Americans living in poverty over a specified period of time. For example, this measurement of poverty shows that from 1959, the first year for which data on poverty are available, to 1969 there was an average annual decline of 4.9% in the number of poor persons. Still, in 1970 about 25.5 million persons, or 13% of the population, were below the poverty level. Since 1969 the number of the officially poor has increased. Obviously, the current combination of recession and inflation plays havoc with the assumption of the 1960s that continued national productivity will lessen the percentage of those below the poverty line.

The poverty statistics compiled during the 1960s are useful for showing certain generalities about the kinds of people who are poor. The poverty rate for blacks, for example, is usually 3 times that for whites. The sex of the head of the family is associated with the poverty status of families, and in 1970, persons in households headed by women constituted only 14% of all persons but about 44% of poor persons.

Obviously, the government's index of poverty provides a useful instrument for measuring a certain type of poverty over time and for determining some of the characteristics of those classified as poor. But the appearance of precision and objectivity associated with this index merely serves to highlight the complexities of definition in this area. Even within its self-defined limits, the index is arbitrary in several respects, including the size of the Engel coefficient, the actual diversity of nutritional need, and the disparity between the actual consumption patterns of the poor and the expert judgment required to determine under the condition of an exceedingly low income the ingredients of an adequate diet.

The size of the Engel coefficient, of course, affects estimates of the extent of poverty and, in fact, had the Social Security Administration used the 1960/1961 finding of the Bureau of Labor Statistics that on the average about 25% of the income of all families is spent for food, it could have multiplied minimum food costs by a factor of 4 rather than of 3, significantly increasing the number of those officially designated as poor. Moreover, the index makes no adjustments for differing nutritional needs based on levels of physical activity. And the low-cost food plan assumes that the housekeeper is efficient and knowledgeable, one who can expertly juggle a minimum food allowance—in spite of the fact that the low-income housewife is likely to be a relatively uninformed consumer and likely to pay higher-than-average prices for her food. So, even the government's subsistence measure of poverty cannot claim to rest solely on a technical or scientific definition of nutritional adequacy.

Values, preferences, and political realities influence the definition of subsistence. The arbitrariness of the government's index of poverty based on subsistence requirements does not give us much confidence that definitions of poverty encompassing more than a notion of physical subsistence can be developed with an objectivity transcending political and philosophical differences. Yet many commentators insist that an adequate measure of poverty should include more than economic indicators.

Poverty, it is argued, is not only a condition of economic insufficiency but also a state of social and political deprivation. Miller *et al.* (1970, p. 18) insist that a minimum approach by government to poverty should provide for rising levels, not only of income and basic services, but also of self-respect and political participation. Similarly, Gans suggests a measurement of poverty which includes notions of equality and social cost. He argues that large differentials in social inequality inevitably give rise to feelings of inferiority, which in turn generates a self-hatred which is costly to society:

> inequality is a major source of social instability and unrest and is even a cause of the rising rates of crime, delinquency, and social pathology —alcoholism, drug addiction, and mental illness, for example [Rainwater, 1974, p. 21].

Poverty, then, can be defined in terms of subsistence (basic physical needs), inequalities (political power and social respect), and externalities (the costs of poverty-related pathologies to the larger community). Finally, poverty can be viewed as a fact or as a problem. The transformation of the fact of poverty, however defined, into the problem of poverty requiring some public redress depends on the possibility for the poor themselves or others who champion their cause to make effective claims on the resources of the non-poor. The relativity of the notion of poverty and the variable number of dimensions associated with it need not make all critical discussion on the topic ambiguous, nor all points of view arbitrary. Historical relativity does not logically require a response of moral relativity and political quietism. The historical relativity of the notion of poverty can also suggest to each observer that he square his arguments with the most humane principles available to him. "Each generation," Titmus writes, "has to undertake anew this task of reinterpretation [of poverty] if it wishes to uphold its claim to share in the constant renewal of civilized values" (Titmus, 1962, p. 187). Before renewal, we must first intellectually appropriate our cultural history. To understand contemporary social policy and the popular attitudes underlying poverty policy, a brief historical analysis of the meaning of poverty is necessary. To renew the present the past must be understood.

For most of history poverty was a fact and not a problem. In societies characterized by scarcity, low technological development, and relatively fixed class strata stabilized by religion and tradition, poverty was assumed to be normal for most people. Nor was it generally seen as causally linked to moral failure. Low status was culturally ascribed, the result of birth not of meager talent or faulty character. The notions of God, nature, and sacred tradition harmoniously combined to provide a moral coherence to preindustrial, stratified societies and made poverty morally and intellectually unproblematic. But the society conserving themes of divine will, sacred tradition, and hereditary rights also gave the poor a measure of dignity and self-respect. In medieval Europe, for example, the rich were expected to give alms to the poor, and the religious dogmas of creation and redemption symbolized the moral connection of the poor with the larger society.

The poor could claim a spiritual equality with others, and a denial of reciprocal obligations between the poor and the rich could not in principle be legitimated by the religious conceptions which underlay personal and collective identity. Yet new theories emerged in Western society which radically changed the medieval understanding of poverty as essentially inevitable and invincible. The relationship of the non-poor to the poor became normatively unstructured and morally problematic. Since Max Weber's *The Protestant ethic and the spirit of capitalism* (1904/1930), the importance of some *unintended* economic consequences of Reformation Calvinism has dominated discussions about the modern understanding of poverty.

Calvinism and Poverty

Religious thought has always attempted to find for life an ultimate meaning and a moral coherence. Calvin attempted to resolve some of the root antinomies of life, such as the problem of freedom and necessity, through the doctrine of predestination. The rich ambiguities of the Christian narrative were narrowed to fit the requirements of theodicy. From all eternity, Calvin taught, some were saved and others doomed. Stressing divine omnipotence and transcendence, Calvinism denigrated the more Catholic notions of confession, indulgences, and good work, all of which mediated between the conceptual polarities of contingent liberty and eternal omnipotence.

Calvin's theodicy had indirect secular effects. Uncertainty about salvation, Weber argued, led to a pursuit of worldly success which, the believer hoped, might also be a sign of God's eternal favor. In its doctrine and preaching early Calvinism never glorified riches but it *indirectly* created a disciplined drive for worldly success. The economic profits accruing from such a "this-worldly" asceticism were not to be squandered on pleasure or ceremony, but were to be reinvested in the quest for ever larger successes and thus even stronger confirmations of God's eternal favor. As Weber noted, the link between Calvinism and capitalism was partial and indirect. Calvinism did not create human acquisitiveness, of course, but it molded personalities whose religious interest led them to express their acquisitiveness, not in self-indulgence, but in the systematic and rational pursuit of constantly reinvested profits. Traditional man worked to live. Calvinist man lived to work. Work became an "ethic" and worldly success a premonition of eternal salvation. Calvinism provided character types which, along with other developments, brought rational capitalism to the center of Western life.

Calvinism and capitalism radically affected the traditional meaning of poverty. The rich interpreted their worldly success as an indication of spiritual election, and both theological logic and self-interest led them to view the unsuccessful poor as the predestined spiritually damned. In the Middle Ages poverty was generally viewed as having some spiritually redeeming qualities. In fact, in religious orders voluntary poverty was honored as one of the bases of a higher religious calling, and the culture gave some plausibility to the biblical notion that only by straining camel-like through the eye of a needle could the rich achieve their salvation.

In preindustrial Europe there were no cultural themes or theories which severed the poor's sense of membership in a common polity. But in the Europe of industrial capitalism several religious and then secular theories were available which placed the poor beyond the requirements of conscience. Calvinism's indirect association of the worldly poor with the spiritually damned initiated the legitimation of the severance of poverty from national conscience. Indeed, Calvinistic theodicy soon became peripheral to the functioning of the capitalist mode of economic organization, but secular interpretations of poverty quickly took up the ideological slack.

To justify the plight of the poor to the non-poor, secular versions of predestination were available. In his *Social statics* the British sociologist Herbert Spencer (1880) toughmindedly argued that poverty purified society. In Spencer's thought, Calvin's eternal decrees of election and damnation outlived Calvin's God. Spencer was scornful toward reformers who, he said, indulged a misinformed conscience with a compassion for the poor which, actually, is an irresponsibility to the species.

> Blind to the fact that under the natural order of things society is constantly execrating its unhealthy, imbecile, slow, vacillating, faith-

less members, these unthinking, though well-meaning, men advocate an interference which not only stops the purifying process, but even increases the vitiation . . . [Will & Vatter, 1970, p. 37].

The view that the poor were evolutionary misfits and thus outside the reasoned responsibilities of the larger society was cross-cultural. In America the late-nineteenth-century sociologist William Graham Sumner also argued against a compassion toward the poor with a toughminded moral calculus of progress and efficiency.

They [reformers] do not perceive, furthermore, that if we do not like the survival of the fittest, we have only one possible alternative, and that is the survival of the unfittest. The former is the law of civilization; the latter is the law of anti-civilization [Will & Vatter, 1970, p. 39].

In their different vocabularies both the Calvinist doctrine of pre-destination and the secular ideologies of poverty equated economic productivity with social progress.

American Attitudes Toward Poverty

American society has also stressed economic expansion and, thinking the two intrinsically related, has emphasized a competitive individualism. The dark obverse of these emphases on efficiency and competition is a general lack of sympathy with those who are unproductive or functionally unnecessary, or those who do not measure up to ever higher standards of economic performance. In fact, Spencer-like arguments retain a tenacious hold on American social consciousness. In his community study of political attitudes, Lane (1963, p. 93) found among his middle- and working-class respondents little sympathy for those lower in the income scale than they. In their explanations of unemployment or low wages, his respondents made few references to external forces or circumstances such as sickness, the death of a breadwinner, senility, the relocation of factories, and so forth.

In another study of attitudes toward the poor, Feagin (1972) reports that most of his respondents adhered to an individualistic, micro-level explanation of poverty. The dominant explanations given by his respondents included loose morals, drunkenness, laziness, and improper management of personal affairs. Feagin asked his respondents to list the major reasons why there are poor people in this country. The three most frequently given reasons were: (*a*) lack of thrift and proper management of money; (*b*) lack of effort by the poor themselves; and (*c*) lack of ability and talent. Cited ninth was the "failure of private industry to provide enough jobs." Indeed, most studies of attitudes toward the poor (cf. Lineberry & Sharkansky, 1974, p. 248) show that the over-

whelming majority of Americans suspect that great numbers of able-
bodied men are deliberately receiving welfare rather than working.

Many Americans, then, explain poverty in terms of the moral failing
of the poor themselves. The poor are commonly thought to be willfully
unprepared for responsible work and unwilling to accept the employment for which their meager talents suit them. Though this is a commonly held opinion, empirical research does not corroborate it. Many
studies find among the poor a general willingness to work and a widespread actual attachment to the work force. In a study which included
welfare mothers and sons, trainees in a Work Incentive Program, and
suburban families, Goodwin (1972) researched the following question:
Do the unemployed and underemployed have basically different orientations toward work from those of the regularly employed and persons
whose parents have worked? On the basis of his research (a home-
administered questionnaire) Goodwin concluded that the plight of the
poor cannot be blamed on their having deviant goals or a deviant work
psychology:

> Evidence from this study unambiguously supports the following con-
> clusions: poor people—males and females, blacks and whites, youths
> and adults—identify their self-esteem with work as strongly as do the
> nonpoor. They express as much willingness to take job training if
> unable to earn a living and to work even if they were to have an
> adequate income. They have, moreover, as high life aspirations as do the
> nonpoor and want the same things, among them a good education and
> a nice place to live. This study reveals no differences between poor and
> nonpoor when it comes to life goals and wanting to work [Goodwin,
> 1972, p. 112].

Goodwin's study of work orientations is corroborated by several
studies which include measures of work behavior. In his study of relief
statistics, Stein (1971) reports that a remarkable proportion of the
poor work despite such employment-inhibiting characteristics as old
age, low educational levels, or the need to care for minor children. For
example, in 1966, 31.9% of the poor worked for the full year and
27.2% worked part of the year. In 1968, 35.8% of poor male family
heads were year-round, full-time workers, and 24.4% worked during
part of the year. A majority of the poor male nonworkers were disabled
or over 65 years of age. Since a majority of the poor had some attachment to the labor market and yet did not earn their way out of poverty,
Stein concludes that laziness or unwillingness to work is not a significant
cause of poverty.

Still, many citizens characterize the poor as "disreputably poor," thus
considering them as individuals willfully avoiding the discipline of regular employment (Matza, 1966, p. 289). There are many reasons for

the discrepancy between research findings and popular images of the poor, among which may be a general lack of information about the poor and an ignorance perhaps made invincible by a suspicion that empirical research is often informed by a "liberal" political point of view which colors its conclusions.

Obviously, economic rationality can also be associated with the furtherance of pejorative images of the poor. Several authors suggest that unfavorable stereotypes of the poor legitimate low welfare benefits and low minimum wage laws, and ensure a pool of workers constrained to work at extremely low wages. For example, when he was governor of Georgia, Lester Maddox complained about some proposed welfare reform measures and candidly noted, "You're not going to be able to find anyone willing to work as maids or janitors or housekeepers" (cited by Aaron, 1973, p. 49).

Besides misinformation and economic rationality, there are more subtle reasons for the persistence of images of the poor as moral failures who lack both marketable skills and a willingness to contribute to society through work. For its responsible positions a technological economy requires extensive schooling and considerable self-discipline. For average citizens, a minimum of material advancement and upward mobility often require holding two jobs or working overtime. In a culture which emphasizes success, efficiency, mobility, and competition, both workers and professionals will at times feel repressed and insecure. To some degree, success is always precarious and, for most, there is always some danger of falling behind in the race. Individuals aware of their own tense efforts to maintain status and security may find it psychologically difficult not to view the poor as moral inferiors. Baldwin suggests that black poverty in particular may serve as a status benchmark for the rest of the country:

> Now I think there is a very good reason why the Negro in this country has been treated for such a long time in such a cruel way, and some of the reasons are economic and some of them are political. . . . Some of them are social, and these reasons are somewhat more important because they have to do with our social panic, with our fear of losing status. This really amounts sometimes to a kind of social paranoia. One cannot afford to lose status on this particular kind of ladder, for the prevailing notion of American life seems to involve a kind of rung-by-rung ascension to some hideously desirable state. . . . When one slips, one slips back not a rung but back into chaos and no longer knows who he is and this reason, this fear, suggests to me one of the real reasons for the status of the Negro in this country. In a way, the Negro tells us where the bottom is: because he is there, and where he is, beneath us, we know where the limits are and how far we must not fall [Baldwin, 1963, pp. 111–115].

"Culture of Poverty," "Cycle of Poverty," and "Cultural Deprivation" are terms commonly used to describe the conditions of poverty. The near banality of these phrases is indicative of the basic agreement about the appearance of poverty. Disputes emerge, not about how the poor are to be described, but about the causes of poverty and the possible remedies, if any. The poor are commonly described as fatalistic, impulsive, present-time oriented, cynical, low skilled, especially prone to physical and mental illness, and deficient in their powers of abstraction and conceptualization.

Stressing the importance of early socialization, Banfield (1974) argues that the present-time orientation which poverty children learn from their parents and their immediate environment produces egos incapable of impulse control and gratification deferral. He argues that the likelihood that such children will acquire the disciplined habits of work required by most modern jobs, even those which pay modest salaries, is minimal.

Poor adults are especially prone to suffer mental illness (Meyers & Roberts, 1959). One observer suggests that the prevalent lifestyle of many lower-class adults can be characterized as one of constant emotional depression (Carter, 1966, p. 31). The condition of poverty, then, is commonly described as comprising more than a lack of material resources. Subcultural values, norms, and beliefs are transmitted to children and form a distinctive culture of poverty resistant to change. To varying degrees, middle- and upper-class families emphasize an active, rational, self-confident, relatively optimistic approach to society, and, in such families, the child normally expects a measure of personal success, provided he or she acquire the requisite skills and persevere in efforts toward long-range career goals. Lower-lower-class families on the other hand are observed to instill in their children attitudes which are dysfunctional in technologically advanced societies: fear of the unknown, fatalism, magical thinking, distrust of school and other institutions.

Among the poor, common law marriages, broken families, and those headed by women are common.

Judged by the standards of the larger society, the poor live in an intricate web of pathology. The daily difficulties they face make the neuroses of the middle class seem like psychic luxuries. A narrow range of experience, few marketable skills, pervasive distrust, constant insecurity, feelings of powerlessness, and, above all, the internalization of failure make psychological growth an enormously difficult achievement. More often than not, the poor internalize the majority opinion that they are morally reprehensible and without worth. Economic indicators do not adequately describe the demoralizing effects of cumulative social rejection. A constriction of spirit and the loss of self-respect are the more subtle but true indicators of persistent poverty. As Harrington (1964) suggests, if we are to see them truly, the poor need a novelist as well as a sociologist.

ARE THE POOR IRRECONCILABLY DIFFERENT?

Without excessive difficulty the determined compiler can find general agreement among scholars about how the poor are to be described. But there is no consensus about how poverty should be interpreted in terms of causality and social policy. Several authors emphasize socialization processes and early childhood experience and are correspondingly pessimistic about public policies designed to improve the lives of the poor.

Other authors stress the "value pluralism" of the poor and are more optimistic about the possibilities of social policy designed to alleviate poverty. As we have seen, several scholars note that most poor people have the same general values and aspirations as the working and lower-middle class. Like most people, the poor generally want consumer goods, economic security, good education for their children, and stable marital arrangements. To describe the value pluralism of the poor— that is, the attachment by many of them both to general cultural values and to distinctive lower-class adaptations to the stresses of poverty— Rodman (1973) suggests the notion of a "value-stretch." In conditions of persistent economic insecurity the values of impulse control, responsibility, and long-term goal commitment become difficult and perhaps impossible to maintain. In such situations casual sex, low achievement aspirations, fatalism, and a weak attachment to the world of work can be viewed as adaptive mechanisms of the poor to objective environmental conditions. Carter (1966) even suggests that in situations of low employment possibility and persistent frustration the attempt to implement working- and middle-class values might be psychologically costly to the poor. "A more goal-committed, rationalistic, involved and verbal approach," she writes, "might lead to higher rates of mental breakdown than now occurs" (Carter, 1966, p. 30). The subculture of poverty, then, interacts with larger social forces such as automation, federal employment policy, discrimination, and federal policies which favor suburban areas. In this context, much of the self-defeating and pathological behavior observed in poverty areas can be partially interpreted as adaptive responses to an insecurity and hopelessness not amenable to rational control by the poor. Liebow (1967) wryly remarks that for the most part the poor behave exactly as anybody else does when the future is radically uncertain. They embody a folk wisdom older than Horace's *carpe diem*.

POLICY ON POVERTY

Until the Depression of the 1930s, the United States had no explicit federal policy dealing with poverty. The market economy and a constantly increasing productivity were expected eventually to remove any residual pockets of poverty. Even the New Deal legislation assumed that poverty would be of minor future significance. Congress believed that the Social Security Act, which included unemployment insurance and old age insurance, had definitively resolved the issue of income security. Public assistance (or relief) was included in the act primarily to provide for the aged citizens who would not be eligible for old age insurance. Public assistance was treated as a residual category.

Indeed, the history of legislation dealing with the poor reveals striking historical continuities, and reflects the deepest cultural assumptions of an activist, expansionary, industrial economy. Indeed, since the British Poor Laws around the early 1600s, there has been no substantive *difference* in the way most political leaders viewed the problem of poverty. Levels of aid, of course, rose as national prosperity increased. But since the Poor Laws there has been an emphasis on some local responsibility (even when the causes of poverty were non-local), minimal standards of upkeep (out of fear of providing a work disincentive), and the administrative attachment of some stigma to the acceptance of relief (to reduce the number of claimants). Throughout its history, assistance to the poor has emphasized, not the right of the poor to exist humanely, but the *dangers* of public assistance: the fear of encouraging dependency, the fear of tempting people from dull jobs to the dole, the fear of supporting irresponsibility. These fears were and are expressed in public policy through minimal payments to welfare recipients * and by the public visibility of relief recipients through such programs as food stamps and public housing.

Rein (1970) is probably correct when he writes that a majority of the non-poor have always believed that dependency would disappear if only the personal inadequacies of the poor could be corrected. Social thinking and public policy have remained tied to the belief that the "improvident" poor have mostly brought their ills upon themselves. Their enemy is within. Until very recently even welfare professionals believed that they could overcome problems of economic dependency by the application of casework techniques and in-depth counseling. Until

---

* There is an enormous variation in welfare payments. Stein (1971) reports a range from an average of $55 per month in Mississippi to $332 per month in New Jersey.

recently the regnant ideal in the social work profession was small case-loads for the social workers and therapy for the clients (Stein, 1971, p. 25). Few permitted themselves the discomfiting thoughts that economic progress itself could create a disadvantaged class, that technical progress itself could increase dependency, that economic efficiency itself could lead to social diseconomies, and that economic progress might not be an unambiguous good.

Despite their long history and persistent popularity, many of the punitive aspects associated with public assistance to the poor have little empirical justification. Most empirical studies fail to corroborate the assumptions of those poverty assistance programs which emphasize the moral transformation of the poor as the solution for poverty. Most of the poor say they want work; many on relief do work as much as they can, and when job training is available the trainee positions are quickly oversubscribed. Relief payments have not been shown to reduce the incentive to earn more if recipients are not financially penalized for working.†

Recent studies conclude that the guarantee of a certain minimum of economic security does not operate as a work disincentive. Indeed, economic theory alone cannot predict the effect of income security on work incentives. With a modicum of economic security people can raise their aspirations and acquire a taste for higher incomes. Despite their surface plausibility many of the principles underlying poverty assistance programs receive no empirical corroboration. There is little empirical support for the widespread fear of providing work disincentives and the general blaming of the poor themselves for their own poverty. On the other hand, it must be admitted that reform advocates seeking to minimize the stigma attached to relief through such programs as family allowances, a negative income tax, housing subsidies, guaranteed employment, and the federal assumption of welfare programs, cannot empirically prove that these reform measures will "work." An empirical social science can with modest certainty analyze only what has existed or does exist.

IN SEARCH OF A POINT OF VIEW

Empirical studies of poverty are necessary, but for the reader interested in social policy and the values underlying it they can only be preliminary. They do not directly suggest what society might do about the problem. Usually empirical studies simply surprise the non-poor by showing that economic progress and affluence do not automatically solve the problem of poverty. Michael Harrington's 1962 study *The other America*

† Before 1967 most states reduced welfare payments $1 for each $1 earned.

(Harrington, 1964) was said to have shocked many Americans when they learned of the extent of poverty in America. But the surprise occasioned by the discovery of poverty during normal periods of general prosperity is cross-cultural. An Australian government commission recently reported that, contrary to its own expectations, even in normal times poverty in Australia is far more severe than is commonly believed.‡ Much earlier, the work of Arthur Young on the rural poor of late-eighteenth-century Britain and Charles Booth's studies of the London poor in the late 1880s (Booth, 1889–1897) caused similar astonishment among their contemporaries. Soon after, Robert Hunter's 1904 American study entitled *Poverty* caused a public controversy by his claim that of a continental population of 82 million at least 10 million, and perhaps 20 million, Americans, lived in destitution even in years of alleged prosperity. The constant rediscovery of poverty shows both a lack of insight into the attendant imbalance and dislocations caused by industrialization, and a studied reluctance to admit facts which challenge deeply held convictions about national morality.

Economic Productivity as the Solution to Poverty

In terms of social policy, then, the gathering of facts is a necessary but insufficient step; vexing questions of political and moral assumptions remain. Generally, the nation has been spared the jagged controversies which result from an examination of conflicting moral principles under conditions of perceived scarcity. Even the sometimes bloody battles of the labor union movement were resolved under the common assumption that increasing productivity would enable all participants to make ever increasing gains without causing great hardships on any distinct social strata. The shared belief in increasing productivity honeyed most economic controversies and enabled conflicting parties to search for rational ways of sharing in the rising affluence.

Throughout American economic history the notion of "zero sum" situations, in which one participant's gain had to be another's loss, was confined to game theorists. When they thought about it at all, most Americans relied on gains in productivity and a presumed constant increase in the general prosperity to solve the problem of poverty, at least in its direst forms.* Toby even suggests that much of the impetus behind the ill-fated Economic Opportunity Act of 1964 ("The War on Poverty") derived from professional economists who worried about

‡ *The New York Times*, February 17, 1975, p. 24.

* The reliance on increased productivity for the peaceful resolution of economic conflict is not singularly American. Titmus (1962) feels that British welfare reform is based on the premiss that economic growth will solve all national problems involving choice, distribution, and priorities.

economic stagnation and who feared that economic growth was increasing federal revenues faster than worthwhile programs on which to spend them could be invented! The case for the poor was argued on the basis of economic rationality:

> And if the tax bonanza was not spent, it would slow economic growth and might even cause a depression. In short, for a brief period before the Vietnam war heated up, before the cost of pollution control was assessed, before an energy crisis developed, before the United States experienced serious inflationary problems, fiscal experts believed that the health of the national economy required massive new expenditures. If the money had to be spent anyway, why not spend it on ending poverty [Toby, 1975, p. 11]?

Thus the direct intervention of government into the problem of poverty in the early 1960s did not represent a fundamental departure from the historical reliance on economic productivity to resolve the problem of poverty. But in this instance the poor were to help the affluent by absorbing economic surpluses. John Maynard Keynes had replaced Adam Smith, but the priority of economic progress remained intact. But in an economy of scarcity the problems of the allocation of resources are especially likely to involve questions of policy which cannot easily evade the political and moral assumptions underlying economic policy. Rein describes the positivistic promise that a "science of policy making" will rescue the analyst from deciding among conflicting values, interests, means, and ends as "crackpot rationality" (Rein, 1970, p. 267). Of course, at no time in history has rational management actually replaced politics, but the seductive promise of an ever increasing prosperity could, for those who ardently wish it, make politics appear to be the art of rational management.

Lowering the Expectations among the Poor

It is increasingly difficult for us to return to the faith of benign economic progress. In all likelihood, a less expansive economy will bring to the forefront the conflicting definitions of the just domestic society which an economy of abundance partially blurred. In such situations even social scientists might be expected to stray occasionally from positions of value neutrality. For example, Banfield (1974) argues that since poverty is always relative, the demands of the poor, once awakened, can never be satisfied. Poverty reform, he argues, can only feed the flames of resentment and envy. Discussing welfare, he argues that, given the attitudes of working Americans toward "reliefers," it is impossible to devise a welfare system which will deal generously with the poor and yet be tolerable from the standpoint of the non-poor voters and tax payers (Banfield, 1969, p. 100). Moreover, a welfare system which provides a humane level of support for all who are by some reasonable definition poor will, he argues, offer powerful incentives which will induce others to become poor in order to qualify for benefits. Since there is no way out of this bind, Banfield chooses to make benefits to the poor lower than "generosity, or guilt, might prompt." For Banfield, the best poverty reform would be the lowering of expectations among the poor.

Increased Benefits to the Poor

Advocates of changes in government policy toward the poor generally suggest an increase in benefits, income transfers which lessen the possibility of social stigma, and guaranteed employment. Many reform advocates also assume a general increase in economic productivity which might make these reforms possible without greatly affecting the present income structure.* Some evade the problem of income distribution by the use of sanitized "sociologese," as in the following: "Programs for job training may be paid for by 'nontarget' persons who have increased trouble staying employed because of the improved success of 'target' persons" (cited in Toby, 1975, p. 25). Some authors are more straightforward, and one simply writes that redistribution means that some of the "haves" must give up something in favor of the "have nots" (Stein, 1971, p. 159).

The Notion of Justice as Fairness

A recent major philosophical effort which, better than any other moral theory, provides a philosophical ground for poverty reforms such as guaranteed employment and income transfers is John Rawls's (1971) notion of "justice as fairness." Rawls argues that technological efficiency, meritocracy, or equality of opportunity alone cannot legitimize social institutions. Social peace can be based only on the widespread conviction that social institutions are just and that social privileges are fair.

The problem, of course, is determining the standard by which we should determine which differentials in income and power are "fair." As commonly understood, the prevailing liberal principle accepts the elimination of ascribed differences in order to ensure for all citizens an equal opportunity; yet the same principle justifies unequal results on the basis of native talent. Rawls wants to mitigate even the arbitrary effects of the genetic lottery. *In justice as fairness the primary good of self-*

---

* For example, see Committee for Economic Development, 1970, p. 9.

respect for all citizens has a central place. Only those principles of stratification are judged to be fair which would be accepted by reasonable men in a hypothetical "original position"—that is, before men knew where talent, fate, and history would place *them* in the social order they are deciding about. Thus, justice as fairness allows a claim to be called just only if it derives from a principle which the claimant would have accepted *before* knowing whether by the acceptance of the principle he or she might be the loser rather than the gainer. So the principles appealed to in the name of justice must, in Rawls's conception, be principles by which everyone would be prepared for his enemy to assign him his place. The test of inequalities from the vantage point of justice as fairness is whether they can be justified to the losers, and for the winners to be able to do this, they must be prepared, in principle, to change places.

Rawls argues that two principles of justice would be chosen in the original position by reasonable men who did not know their genetic or historical fate: (*a*) each person is to have an equal right to the most extensive basic liberty compatible with a similar liberty for others; and (*b*) social and economic inequalities are to be arranged so that they are both reasonably expected to be to everyone's advantage, and attached to positions and offices open to all.

By Rawls's principles, the distribution of wealth and income need not be equal, but the distribution must be to *everyone's* advantage. The social order is not to be so arranged as to establish and secure the more attractive prospects of the more fortunate unless doing so is to the advantage of those less fortunate. Moreover, unless there is a distribution which enriches all citizens, an equal distribution of income and power is to be preferred.

Rawls notes that, more than any other moral theory, justice as fairness maximizes the possibility of self-respect for all citizens. Rawls argues that self-respect is a primary good, for without it nothing will seem worth doing and all activity will seem empty and vain. Without self-respect, he writes, we sink into apathy and cynicism. Thus the main point in justice as fairness is that the parties in the original position would wish to avoid at almost any cost the social conditions which undermine self-respect. Rawls suggests that the fact that justice as fairness gives more support to self-esteem than other theories do is a strong reason for those in the hypothetical original condition to adopt it.

As commonly understood, social science cannot provide a social ethic. But, as Rainwater (1974) suggests, one of the contributions social science may make is to suggest alternative points of view from which the problem can be assessed, and to note that point of view which best squares with most of the variables considered important by scholarly opinion. Rawls's theory of justice as fairness is presented here because as a metasociological point of view it takes into account nearly all the variables which analysts of poverty consider essential to a serious discussion of poverty: the relationships among income, self-respect, prestige, power, and reform. Even in strictly sociological terms a philosophical contribution which gives a context to the facts of poverty and which points toward policy changes which accord with our empirical knowledge of man and society is not otiose. Bell has recently written that a technocratic society is *not* ennobling and that the lack of a rooted moral belief system is the deepest challenge to the survival of that society (Bell, 1973, p. 480). Sociology itself affirms the need for a social order perceived as generally just. The temper of the age is to give the notion of progress a new statement: one resting, not upon release from community and tradition, but upon a kind of craving for new forms of moral and social community (Nisbet, 1966, p. 9).

Religion and Poverty Reform

To be sure, philosophical principles alone do not seem to inspire most men or to mold their institutions substantially. And, of course, among philosophers there are major disagreements with Rawls's theory of justice (see Barry, 1973; Nagel, 1973; and Nozick, 1975). More likely than philosophy to be carriers of values antithetical to mere technological efficiency are religious traditions, perhaps especially those which preserve notions of collective solidarity which arose in preindustrial eras. Reflecting on historic images of human solidarity, McWilliams (1973, p. 100) remarks that at best the Judaeo-Christian religious institutions expressed a wisdom which the Enlightenment did not possess, and that they indirectly, and sometimes directly, provided an emotional and symbolic basis for the appeal to fraternity in American politics as an immediate need.

The relative decline in social and political importance of institutional religion and the separation of church and state generally make any link between religion and social reform indirect and subtle. In the churches and synagogues there is some political activism but far more conservatism and even political quietism. The relation between religion and poverty reform may be analogous to the relationship between faith and reason. It has been traditional to argue that reason does not prove faith and that faith does not contradict reason. For faith, reason is a negative norm. Faith is not derived from reason, but reason is thought to indicate that faith is not unreasonable. So too, perhaps, in matters of religion and poverty reform. No specific theory of justice or social policy is known to flow directly and logically from religious belief. But religion can be a negative norm. Some theories of justice and some social policies can be known as "incoherent" with religious beliefs. For example, all theories of justice or social policies which absolutize efficiency, techno-logical progress, and material productivity run counter to the Judaeo-Christian conviction that societies should be so arranged that each individual have the resources to maintain a self-respect enabling him to consider himself significant enough to choose or personally to appropri-ate ultimate beliefs and to nurture an inner life.

When considered in the light of *Realpolitik* and the intricate relation-ship of poverty to political power, poverty-reform proposals may appear quixotic. Symbols validated by their evocative powers rather than by their empirical accuracy are probably required to sustain the plausibility of such reforms. If a just society cannot be imagined, it cannot be striven for. If it is finally concluded that a just society is politically impossible, men will no longer be able to hide from themselves and from others the fact that the problem of social order is amenable only to predatory solutions. And if that is the case, society will require darker myths than those available in the existing religious traditions. For these reasons the poor cannot be examined either apart from the power of the non-poor or from the cultural assumptions which underlie the society in which both live out their very different lives.

REFERENCES

Aaron, H. J. *Why is welfare so hard to reform?* Washington, D.C.: The Brookings Institution, 1973.

Baldwin, J. *Nobody knows my name.* New York: Dell, 1963.

Banfield, E. C. Welfare: A crisis without "solutions." *The Public Interest,* Number 16, Summer, 1969, pp. 89–101.

Banfield, E. C. *The unheavenly city revisited.* Boston: Little, Brown, 1974.

Barry, B. *The liberal theory of justice.* Oxford: Clarendon, 1973.

Bell, D. *The coming of post-industrial society.* New York: Basic Books, 1973.

Booth, C. *Life and labour in London* (17 vols.). London: Macmillan, 1889–1897.

Carter, G. W. *Growing up poor.* (Welfare Administration Bulletin No. 13). Washington, D.C.: U. S. Government Printing Office, 1966.

Committee for Economic Development. *Improving the public welfare system.* New York: Author, 1970.

Feagin, J. R. Poverty: We still believe that God helps those who help themselves. *Psychology Today,* November 1972, pp. 101–110.

Goodwin, L. *Do the poor want to work?: A social-psychological study of work orientations.* Washington, D.C.: The Brookings Institution, 1972.

Harrington, M. *The other America.* Baltimore: Penguin Books, 1964.

Hunter, R. *Poverty.* New York: Harper Torchbooks, 1965. (Originally pub-lished, 1904.)

Lane, R. *Political ideology.* New York: Free Press, 1963.

Liebow, E. *Tally's corner.* Boston: Little, Brown, 1967.

Lineberry, R. L. & Sharkansky, I. *Urban politics and public policy* (2nd ed.). New York: Harper & Row, 1974.

Matza, D. The disreputable poor. In R. Bendix & S. M. Lipset (Eds.), *Class, status, and power* (2nd ed.). New York: Free Press, 1966.

Meyers, J. K. & Roberts, B. H. *Family and class dynamics in mental illness.* New York: Wiley, 1959.

McWilliams, W. C. *The idea of fraternity in America.* Berkeley: University of California Press, 1973.

Miller, S. M., Rein, M., Roby, P., & Gross, B. A social indicators definition. In R. E. Will & H. G. Vatter (Eds.), *Poverty in affluence.* New York: Harcourt, Brace, & World, 1970. Pp. 18–22.

Nagel, T. Rawls on justice. *Philosophical Review,* 1973, *82,* 220–234.

Nisbet, R. A. *The sociological tradition.* New York: Basic Books, 1966.

Nozick, R. *Anarchy, state and utopia.* New York: Basic Books, 1975.

Rawls, J. *A theory of justice.* Cambridge: Harvard University Press, 1971.

Rainwater, L. (Ed.). *Inequality and justice.* Chicago: Aldine, 1974.

Rein, M. *Social policy.* New York: Random House, 1970.

Rodman, H. The lower class value stretch. In J. R. Feagin (Ed.). *The urban scene.* New York: Random House, 1973. Pp. 150–165.

Spencer, H. *Social statics.* New York: Appleton, 1880.

Stein, B. *On relief: The economics of poverty and public welfare.* New York: Basic Books, 1971.

Titmus, R. M. *Income distribution and social change.* Toronto: University of Toronto Press, 1962.

Toby, J. The war on poverty: Politics of unrealistic expectations. *Contemporary Sociology,* 1975, *4,* 11–18.

Weber, M. *The Protestant ethic and the spirit of capitalism* (T. Parsons, trans.). London: Allen & Unwin, 1930. (Originally published, 1904.)

Will, R. E. & Vatter, H. G. (Eds.). *Poverty in affluence.* New York: Harcourt, Brace, & World, 1970.

VI
PROBLEMS OF DYING:
THE PROLONGATION OF LIFE

Defining Death

ROBERT C. NEVILLE

Robert Cummings Neville earned all his academic degrees at Yale University: the A.B. in 1960, the M.A. in 1962, and the Ph.D. in 1963. From 1965 to 1973 he was a member of the faculty of Fordham University; since 1974 he has been Professor of Philosophy at the State University of New York at Purchase. Dr. Neville is a frequent contributor to professional journals, principally in the fields of philosophy and theology, and is the author of God the Creator: On the transcendence and presence of God *(1968),* The cosmology of freedom *(1974), and the forthcoming* Spiritual liberation. *He is a member, among other organizations, of the American Philosophical Association, the Metaphysical Society of America, and the American Theological Society.*

DEATH: THE PROBLEM

My title, "Defining Death," contains an ambiguity. It might mean "conceiving what death is," or it might mean the way death itself defines things. In fact, how death defines things is the clue to what death is. Of course, *life* is what death chiefly defines. Since classical times people have said that life is had most abundantly when it is oriented toward its own limits, toward death. With Socrates we might believe that the cultivation proper to life is preparation for death. With Jesus we may think true life comes only after a prior death, literal or metaphorical, one's own or the Savior's, now or hereafter. With Naciketas in the *Katha*

181

Upaniṣad we may find that enlightenment is a lesson taught only by Death himself. In all these beliefs death defines life in some sense, and its own meaning is relative to the life it is said to define.

But suppose we just want to know for practical purposes what it is for a person to be dead. For instance, is it time for relatives to mourn, life insurance companies to pay, or the next-in-line to succeed to the person's office? Can the spouse remarry without being a bigamist? Can the person's property be distributed according to his will?

The definition of death in the sense of "what it is" has become an issue in recent years because of other practical questions. Medical technology has made it possible artificially to sustain a person's heartbeat and respiration when those functions have ceased spontaneous activity. Usually, of course, this is done when the patient's brain is otherwise intact, and it is hoped that the person can have a decent life with a pacemaker and respirator, or even be cured completely. But the technology makes it possible to sustain the life of much of a person's body long after his brain is dead. Now, if a person's foot dies from disease and is amputated, we would not call the person dead. But if his brain dies, it is more tempting to say that he does too. In fact, the "Report of the Ad Hoc Committee of the Harvard Medical School to Examine the Definition of Brain Death," entitled "A Definition of Irreversible Coma," says just that, and has been influential in changing legal definitions of death (Beecher *et al.*, 1968).

Traditional definitions of death emphasize heartbeat and circulation. *Black's law dictionary* (Black, 1951) defines death as "the cessation of life; the ceasing to exist; defined by physicians as total stoppage of the circulation of the blood, and a cessation of the animal and vital functions consequent thereupon, such as respiration, circulation, etc." If a person's spontaneous circulation and respiration should cease, however, and be started up again and sustained by artificial means, we do not say that he has died and come back to life; that would mean that his spouse could collect his life insurance and that he would have to remarry her to share in the benefits. We say rather that heartbeat and respiration are only conditions for life, and if those conditions are met in some other way, or restored, the person has not died.

On the other hand, the injury to the person might be such that circulation and respiration are maintained but the brain is lost, with the attendant loss of many functions such as consciousness and communicability which we ordinarily associate with the human quality of life. If we admit for the moment that the brain is a more intimate seat of human qualities than the heart, what are the arguments for moving to a brain-death definition of human death?

One is that with the existence of cardiac and respiratory life-support systems a person can be kept alive in a minimal way while his tissues and organs slowly die, one by one; at the end of the process, when only the machines are going, we would say that the person had died sometime before. But exactly when? For emotional, legal, and ritual purposes a time of death needs to be ascertained, and the time of the death of the brain, insofar as that can be fixed, seems a good candidate.

Another argument for the brain definition of death is that several of a person's organs, particularly kidneys, heart, and eyes, might be transplantable to someone else whose life they may save. But if the potential donor is called "alive" until the transplantable organs decompose, that would be impossible. Better to call him dead when his brain dies so that his organs are available; then perhaps the respirator should be kept on, not to preserve his life, but to preserve his organs as long as possible.

Another argument is that in most cases a dying person is using valuable medical resources on which other patients also have a claim. If it is the case that a person is really dead (through brain death) months before his body is completely dead and artificial life-support ineffective, then scarce medical resources ought not be spent on his corpse.

DEFINITION OF DEATH

It is important here to distinguish the question of defining death and identifying its criteria from the question of whether life is worth living. Life may in fact not be worth living for a person when he is still alive. In fact, it may not be worth living even before he is born. In these cases the questions of suicide, euthanasia, and abortion must be faced. But for these to be relevant options, it must be supposed that death itself has not occurred. It is one thing to limit life by deliberately causing death; it is another to do so by defining life to be ended. Although the effects of these two may appear the same if a new definition of death includes some who were not dead on the old definition, the warrants for the two kinds of judgment are entirely different. To say someone's life is not worth living and to take steps to end it is a prudential judgment of utmost gravity, freighted with the most profound existential dilemmas of uncertainty and personal responsibility. Someone in particular is always responsible for that kind of decision. To say that death occurs with brain death, for instance, instead of heart–lung death is a conceptual judgment about the nature of things, made with appeal to reasons and *without* regard for particular consequences such as who will be declared dead. In fact, if such a judgment is made with particular people in mind, as a doctor might do with a transplant case or when he knows families are suffering, there can be no way around the inevitable bias of *wanting* to declare someone dead because his life is not worth living—at least compared with other lives. The question of the definition of life and death must be resolved on a general level without regard to particular cases, except insofar as particular cases provide experience as to what it is to be alive.

Just what kind of conceptual judgment is a definition of death? A start can be made in answering that question by pointing out that it itself is not a scientific question. The scientific contribution to the discussion of death has to do with two main kinds of evidence. The first is that science can establish causal connections between various bodily functions. It can show, for instance, that although certain parts of the brain are dead other parts still alive are sufficient to maintain heartbeat and respiration. The second scientific contribution is to show that certain neurophysiological functions are necessary conditions for certain mental events of thought, feeling, or behavior. This kind of psychobiology has lagged far behind the other scientific contribution, mainly because of difficulties in experimenting with humans. Most evidence comes from observing the effects of brain destructions in accident victims or patients on whom brain surgery must be done for other reasons. Electrode implantation techniques are making research safer in this regard, though we still know little about the biological conditions of the mind.

In order to be relevant to a definition of death, however, the contributions of science, even if extrapolated far beyond their present development, require a higher-order understanding of the human meaning of life. We must know, for instance, what kinds of mentation are definitive of human life before science can tell us that the biological conditions for these are absent and the person is dead. For death is the end of a *human* life. Most of those who argue that brain death is equivalent to person death do so on the grounds that a person's most essential quality is consciousness; and the brain, not the heart, is the seat of consciousness. But the identification of consciousness with the essence of human life is a philosophical judgment, not a scientific one. So, although it is clear that we must turn to science for the physiological conditions for death, which might serve as death's criteria, the definition of death must come from elsewhere. I know of no thoroughly satisfactory candidate.

The most parsimonious definition of death, in light of our previous discussion, is derived by analogy from a sense of death which we have used several times: namely, the death of an organ in the body such as the brain. Death there means that the organ is no longer able to carry on its functions with respect to the rest of the system, that its internal metabolism breaks down, and that in time it decomposes. What death puts an end to is an harmonious process which is both internally harmonious and externally harmonious with respect to a larger system. But what is the analogy with a human life? Because human beings are indeed conscious some of the time, they enter into symbolic connections with things far beyond their biological connections. Their internal harmonies are also more complex than biological models illustrate. Are we to say that a person is dead because he contradicts himself or has unharmonious family relationships? If so, only in metaphorical senses. Harmony with the sociophysical environment and with the depths of one's own being may be good metaphors for being *ideally* alive, but if they are taken literally as defining life in the practical sense meant here, we would nearly all be dead.

The mention of *ideal* life, which was really unavoidable, raises a deeper question as to the meaning of defining death. Suppose we admit that death is a peculiar limit of life, and that the basic task is to define life with reference to that limit. What is it to define something like life?

Plato pointed out that there are two very different cases of definition. One is the definition of abstract forms, which is relatively easy: one must simply postulate adherence to certain imagined conceptual structures and keep a logical eye out for consistency. The other is the definition of concrete things in the changing world, which Plato said is literally impossible because such a thing never *is* its definition but is on its way to *becoming* something else. There is something unreal about a thing which is changing because it has no definition. Aristotle later suggested that one could define a changing thing by its essential trajectory; but this requires a universe in which things maintain rather tight continuity with themselves through time, in rather great isolation from the rest of the world, and in rather remarkable similarity from case to case. This seems not to be our world, and anyway that is too special an hypothesis to be good metaphysics.

Plato's own solution to the problem of defining changing things was to say that a thing's identity consists, not only in its actual and potential states, but also in an ideal which bears upon the change. The real "what" of a thing is a mixture of its "ought to be" and its fictional "stages of process." The stages of process, as Plato pointed out, are not natures fixed in concrete actuality but rather abstract forms hypothesized as useful fictions for locating changing things.

Of course, for Plato, as well as for us, the interesting intellectual problem is to discover what ideal is *relevant* for giving identity to the process at hand. This *ideal* must be an abstract form, to be sure, but not one postulated freely. Rather, it must be a form which harmonizes just the components given in the process. So the definitions of piety, justice, or virtue are neither free speculations nor a reading off of descriptive characters, but constructs justified as giving the greatest harmony to the components we feel ought to be harmonized in those definitions. And, of course, this pushes us back to the prior problem of determining what ought to be included in such definitions. Plato usually pushed far enough to find a generally accepted value in having just those components together.

Our own situation is similar. We want to define life with reference to one of its defining limits, death. This means we must construct an ideal of all the things we would agree are worth going together in life. Put this way, the task is circular, since we would have to know what life contains to know what fits into it well. But the circularity can be put aside for the moment because the task is still misstated.

Death is not a limitation of life at its best; disappointment, immorality, and rejection are limits of the ideal life. Death is a limitation of life at its least. When a person dies, he does not suffer less life; he ceases to have life at all. The task, therefore, is to establish a minimal realization of ideal life, less than which does not count as an embodiment to any degree of the ideal of life.

The limit death puts on life is similar to the limit of coming-to-life. Together, the two define those conditions within time sufficient for the ideal of human life to be relevant. That is, between coming-to-life and death the sufficient conditions exist for the human ideal to be relevant. But there is something intrinsically intelligible about coming-to-life because it can be understood in terms of approaching an ideal. Death is intrinsically unintelligible because it marks the end of the applicability of the ideal of human life. At death the body can be understood only as moving toward a variety of non-human ideals depicting biological processes. There are so many ways by which an ideal can cease to be applicable!

Suppose we say then that the sufficient condition for the human ideal to be applicable is consciousness, and all the biological mechanisms necessary for that. This is the usual suggestion in the debate about brain death. But suppose someone is in a dreamless sleep, totally unconscious; suppose also that, since he is dreamless, even his unconscious in the Freudian sense is non-functioning. Is this person dead? If consciousness alone were the desideratum of life, we would have to say yes; but few of us would.

Most of us would distinguish between the unconsciousness of deep sleep and that of death by saying that in the former there is the possibility of reawakening guaranteed by biological conditions (barring violent intervention). But this is to move beyond consciousness alone as a minimum mark of the relevance of human ideal to a conception of some kind of rhythm of consciousness and unconsciousness based upon biological factors and, probably, social factors as well. It is not just being conscious, but being conscious in a human way which makes the crucial difference, and this way can include periods of unconsciousness.

Human consciousness is consciousness to which the human ideal is relevant, the ideal which defines its embodiments as human. After some 3,000 years of philosophy it ought to be possible to state that ideal simply, but it is not.* Yet, we function with that ideal, and each of us knows in some way what it is. Let us consider the ideal for three components of consciousness.

With regard to perception, the human ideal is to *live in the truth*. That is, to comport oneself in such a way that perceived things can be what they are in being perceived by oneself, can be acknowledged in their nature and worth without having to be distorted by one's own needs. Heidegger's philosophy is the great thematic treatment of this aspect of the ideal in the twentieth century.

With regard to action, the human ideal is to act purely, to accomplish one's ends with the greatest economy and respect for the things affected. The internal or intentional side of this was best expressed by Kierkegaard in his phrase "the Purity of Heart is to Will One Thing." The overt side is best recognized in the Taoist conception of non-action, without force or competition.

With regard to the subjective integration of these things, the human ideal is to be creative: that is, to harmonize the given components in the best way possible, imagining new patterns of integration where necessary, minimizing the exclusion of things from experience, and maximizing the production of value. From the subjective side, the success of harmony is beauty; from the objective side, justice. The philosophies of Plato and Whitehead emphasize these themes.

Most of us would agree that the ideals for the three elements of consciousness are relevant for guiding both private and public life. Regarding the private side, what it means to live in the truth, to act purely, and to exist creatively implies the perfection of certain capacities: to act well in a physical sense, to be free to choose between live options, to do so on the basis of standards one has approved, and to be inventive and critical. It also implies the perfection of certain character traits: to develop psychic integrity or will to heroic proportions, to develop sagacity or wisdom about the world, and to transform the desires of one's heart to love in the proper senses.

* I tried carefully to define a small part of this ideal approached from the standpoint of freedom, in a book of over 400 pages (Neville, 1974).

Regarding the public side, what it means to live in the truth, to act purely, and to exist creatively implies the development of participation in society on all levels relevant to a person's historical situation, particularly participation in the media of communication, production, and government. This also implies the development of social structures which allow ideal participation without negation of people's private integrity.

Finally, the human ideal requires throughout all these dimensions that attention be paid to the difference between relative and absolute aspects of things. The relative aspect of an event includes the way in which it is the culmination of processes and the initiation of consequences, and the way in which it is appreciated from particular perspectives. The absolute aspect is the way in which the event stands with respect to its own existence. The relative aspect is a secular dimension to the human ideal; the absolute, a religious or spiritual.

The human ideal, I believe, is not an ideal type but a norm for making the best harmony of a variety of things deemed important for human life. The list of its components sketched above is doubtless too brief; but it indicates something of the range of the human ideal. The task now is to ask: Under what conditions is the ideal applicable or relevant and how might those conditions cease?

Any extensive realization of the human ideal requires many things besides living humans. Because the ideal guides human life in its dealing with whatever is around, a whole world is needed for the ideal to be relevant. So the question must be reformulated as follows: What must a thing be in order to occupy a human place in a world governed by the human ideal? A thing is a living human being if it has this character *even if the world does not provide the arena in which it might realize its ideal.* A person without society on a desert island, or one raised in the woods by wolves, is still a human being even though the extra-human conditions for realizing his or her ideal are absent.

We are now in a position to consider a definition of human life. *A thing is a living human being if it has the biological capacity to behave according to the human ideal when the conditions for such behavior are present.* The life of a human being is a biological process with a history and dates. It begins with conception and ends with death. Death is the alteration of conditions such that the biological organism ceases to have the possibility of behaving humanly even if the conditions are right.

Consider a person whose body is damaged by disease or trauma in such a way that he cannot communicate, act, or perceive external sensations. Whether this person is still alive depends on whether there are intact parts of the brain such that the person's living experience is what it would be normally except for the absence of outer contact. The contents of thought would be memories and feelings not dependent on outer stimuli; the process of thinking would lack the organization which comes from an orientation to a stable external environment, and intentions would be frustrated and confused. Like any organism which needs to sleep such a person would sometimes lapse into unconsciousness; because of lack of external orientation this might happen irregularly or even nearly always. It may well be that such a state is so emotionally painful, worse than any psychosis we know, that a life like that would not be worth living, and should be ended. But the person would still be alive until the biological conditions for the truncated experience were stopped.

Does this not suppose that there is some core of mental–biological activity which is central to human life? A person's personality is significantly formed by the way he hears; but if he is made deaf, we do not say that he is destroyed, only that he is denied a part of his personality. The same with the other senses which involve mediation from outside the brain to inside. What is the inner core of mental life which *would* mean the death of a person if it were destroyed? We might almost be safe in saying that he is alive as long as there is some residual consciousness there, when he is not asleep, however confused the consciousness by its isolation. But the isolation might indeed be such that the person is permanently asleep. Is he still alive as long as his brain *could* become conscious if neural connection with the outside world were to be re-established?

It would be tempting to say that a living organism is human if it once exercised human capacities, or could be expected to do so someday in the absence of preventing causes. Very senile people, for instance, are clearly alive and human even though they no longer exercise human capacities even when conditions are right. Shall we say that they have sunk to a less than human level of life, and are called live human beings only out of respect for their past? No, because senility seems to be the natural human condition of many old people; babies, too, are incompetent. The problem here is that people with damaged brains can be alive in the sense that some of their organ systems keep on going with the aid of artificial life-support systems, but the parts of the brain which deal with consciousness or human organization in any sense are dead. In this case the organism is living, and although it once exercised human faculties the part which exercised the human faculties is now dead. Would we want to say that the human life is ended because what was ever human about that person is not just incapacitated but dead? Its biological conditions are gone. Or would we say rather that the person has slipped to a subhuman (e.g., "vegetable") state but still lives on?

Part of the confusion here is that we know so little about the brain and its connections which make up mental life. If we knew more, it might be easier to say what parts of the brain are necessary for minimal mental capacities. But we would have to depend on our philosophy to define minimal mental capacities. I know of no sure philosophic way to distinguish between cessation of human life and degeneration to a sub-human but still living state. This is the problem when technology allows an organism to die.

CONCLUSION

Certain practical consequences seem to me to follow from basic uncertainty here.

First, because many faculties, particularly those having to do with sense memory and emotional feelings, are associated with organs deep within the brain, it is not enough to certify a person dead, as Brierley et al. (1971) urge, if there is evidence only of neocortical death when the rest of the body is alive in some sense. Neurological tests of death advocated by the Harvard Committee determining that no parts of the brain are alive (Beecher et al., 1968) are safer.

The report of the Harvard Committee requires negative responses for four kinds of neurological test:

(a) "total unawareness to externally applied stimuli and inner need and complete unresponsiveness";

(b) "no spontaneous muscular movements or spontaneous respiration or responses to stimuli such as pain, touch, sound, or light";

(c) "absence of elicitable reflexes";

(d) "flat or isoelectric EEG."

"All of the above tests shall be repeated at least 24 hours later with no change" (Beecher et al., 1968, pp. 337–338). Of course, these cautions are necessary only for patients being otherwise sustained on life-support systems.

Second, we should seriously consider conditions in which there might be a moral obligation to end a person's life. The significance of this recommendation is to reverse the trend of calling a person dead on dubious brain-death criteria and then turning the respirator off: the argument sometimes made is that if the respirator were turned off before the declaration of death, the doctors might be charged with murder. Perhaps they should take responsibility for euthanasia; the justifying arguments would then have to be made public and assessed (see Beecher et al., 1968; Veatch 1972).

Third, the perspective of physicians having to decide whether someone is dead is insurmountably at variance with the person's anticipation of his own death. The definition of death is entirely different from the meaning of death. The meaning of death as faced in advance, and of dying as suffered through, determines a person's orientation of his own finitude. For most affairs, the meaning of death for a person is far more important than the definition of the state of death and the determination of when it has occurred. But the physician, in trying to make the latter decision, cannot be guided by what the patient himself would have said, because the patient's views would invariably have been oriented to the moral meaning of life—whether to live or die. In a situation of potential euthanasia, the doctor may have to make that decision too, and the patient's views would be highly relevant. But the question of whether a person should die is not the same as whether he is in fact dead. My own subjective feeling is that the question whether to die is the easier one, because the validity of the answer depends so much on the will of the person deciding about himself. The question of what it is for a human being to be dead is a question of dumb fact, however hard to interpret. It is a pedestrian question, unglamorous, unedifying, difficult, and very important.

REFERENCES

Beecher, H. K., *et al.* A definition of irreversible coma: Report of the Ad Hoc Committee of the Harvard Medical School to Examine the Definition of Brain Death. *Journal of the American Medical Association*, 1968, *205*, 337–340.
Black, H. C., (Ed.). *Black's law dictionary* (4th ed.). St. Paul: West Publishing Co., 1951.
Brierley, J. B., Graham, D. I., Adams, J. H., & Simpson, J. A. Neocortical death after cardiac arrest. *Lancet*, September 11, 1971, pp. 560–565.
Neville, R. C. *The cosmology of freedom.* New Haven: Yale University Press, 1974.
Veatch, R. M. Brain death: Welcome definition . . . or dangerous judgment? *The Hastings Center Report*, 1972, *2* (5), 10–13.

Artificial Prolongation of Life:
Means and Morality

DAVID HENDIN

David Hendin, who has a B.S. (1967) and an M.A. (1970) from the University of Missouri, is a journalist and an author. He is Special Projects Editor for Newspaper Enterprise Association, and writes the nationally syndicated newspaper column "The Medical Consumer." Mr. Hendin has received the Medical Journalism Award of the American Medical Association, the Howard W. Blakeslee Award of the American Heart Association, and a Certificate of Commendation of the American Academy of Family Physicians. He is the author of Everything you need to know about abortion *(1972),* Save your child's life *(1973),* Death as a fact of life *(1973), and co-author of* The doctor's save-your-heart diet *(1972).*

I did not have a great deal of difficulty when I sat down to sort out my thoughts on the topic "The Artificial Prolongation of Life: Means and Morality"—not much trouble until I returned to the last word of the title again . . . and again. The word "morality" has always caused problems for me.

Since I am neither a philosopher nor a theologian, and I have no formal training in either the practice of law or the art and science of medicine, and possess not even the honored educational degree which allows me to be referred to as "doctor," how am I supposed to be able to understand the true meaning of that word, "morality"? What is morality?

Some thought leads me to believe that I learned its meaning early, in the very first year of my Sunday school studies. The teacher told us a story which I never forgot, the story of a pagan who came to the great Rabbi Hillel and with great scorn said to the sage:

"I hear you are such a great teacher. If that is so then you should be able to teach me the whole of the Torah while I stand on one foot."

Rabbi Hillel agreed, and in a firm, gentle voice he answered: "Do not unto others as you would not have others do unto you; that is the whole Torah, the rest is commentary. . . ."

These few words, I believe, teach us the meaning of the whole of the Torah—and the holy books of the other great religions as well—but they also seem to me to be as good a place as any to begin one's understanding of morality. And now that we have at least that beginning in common, let us take a brief look at what we are calling "the artificial prolongation of life" to see how it affects our lives as well as our deaths.

IS ARTIFICIAL PROLONGATION OF LIFE MORAL?

Perhaps it is best to begin by asking the question which seemingly goes right to the heart of the matter: Is the artificial prolongation of life moral?

Many will answer: "Certainly not—why prolong the agony of those terminally ill individuals who are near death anyway. We must be more humane and stop prolonging meaningless life." If someone should answer my question in that way, you can be sure that within moments another would rise to say—as if we have never heard it before—"Who are you to play God? Only He must say when one should live and when one should die."

Those who harp on this argument, however, seem to be suffering from a kind of tunnel vision. But in the past few years we have become so accustomed to talking about the terminally ill and the dying that when someone mentions "the artificial prolongation of life," one immediately envisions the terminally ill cancer patient, wracked with pain, waiting for the merciful end to come at any moment, his every organ riddled with malignant cells.

The individual who immediately sees artificial prolongation of life as immoral, as well as the one who says that life must be prolonged, visualize an aggressive young physician subjecting this poor dying soul to all of what have today come to be known as the modern obscenities of dying—tubes in nostrils, needles in veins, pounding on the chest and electrifying of a tired heart in an attempt to revive it. But the truth of the matter is that the terminally ill and dying patient is not, as a general rule, the most common recipient of what we call today the "artificial prolongation of life."

WHAT IS ARTIFICIAL?

Let us get down to the basics. What is the artificial prolongation of life? What is artificial? Perhaps at this time, in the United States of America, a better question would be: "What is *not* artificial?"

For only a few decades of a history which stretches back millennia has man had penicillin, insulin, or vaccinations against a score or more diseases. Must we call these things artificial? It is, after all, *natural* for a child to succumb to the virulent rabies virus after having been bitten by a rabid dog or other animal. Is it, then, an artificial prolongation of life to inject this child with Pasteur's vaccine? It is *natural* for men to fight with each other. When such natural acts occur, and men receive wounds which fester and swell, should we avoid administering something which would *artificially* prolong a life, such as penicillin?

Surely you will say that such medication should not be withheld, even though it may constitute an artificial prolongation of life. Some may even argue that such a life-saving action is really natural and not artificial after all.

What, then, I ask again, is artificial?

Students of history will recall the humane movement, which began in Europe with the founding of the first "Humane Society," in Amsterdam in 1767 (Ackerknecht, 1968). Others followed, and in 1780 in the United States the Philadelphia Humane Society was formed. These societies were the forerunners of today's humane societies, the major difference being that the first humane societies concerned themselves with the welfare of people instead of dogs and cats.

A physician of the time, Benjamin Waterhouse, was invited to give a lecture to the Massachusetts Humane Society in 1790. He declared that "To blow in one's own breath into the lungs of another is an absurd and pernicious practice" (Thomson, 1963, p. 48). Today, of course, the once controversial "humane" practice is called mouth-to-mouth resuscitation and is commonly practiced and taught to physicians and laymen alike. It has been responsible for saving many thousands of lives. I guess those lives have been saved, or prolonged, artificially. At least, in the eighteenth century to try to resuscitate a drowned child with mouth-to-mouth breathing was as artificial a medical act as one could perform. Today, however, knowledgeable people consider such treatment second nature, for we know that a child who has just drowned has precious minutes of life remaining if quick action is forthcoming.

This background, then, leads us to two points crucial to our discussion. (*a*) What is considered to be "artificial" is likely to change often. Indeed, as we progress toward the twenty-first century, the "artificial" becomes the "natural" with an alarming degree of frequency. (*b*) The "artificial prolongation of life" is not something reserved exclusively for terminally ill and dying patients. In fact, in the vast majority of situations in which life is prolonged with some "artificial" means, we are dealing with individuals suffering from *acute* rather than *chronic* health conditions.

When an individual suffers an acute threat to his or her life, such as massive infection, shock, or drowning, we refer to "artificial prolongation of life" as "the miracles of modern medicine." But when an individual suffers in the terminal phases of a chronic illness or injury, and the technologies of "artificial prolongation of life" are fruitlessly applied, we refer to them as "the modern obscenities of dying."

I believe that the above observations are rather significant, lest we forget the accomplishments of modern medicine. As we become increasingly concerned with dying, we must also remember that we are dealing with a continuum and not with a particular moment in time. At the other end of this continuum is birth; and in between are life, and the young, and the healthy. Ever since I began writing my book *Death as a fact of life* (Hendin, 1973), I have been asking people to pay more attention to the dying. I continue to make that request, but now I also feel obliged to remind others, as well as myself, that we must not omit the rest of the continuum from our field of vision.

ARTIFICIAL PROLONGATION OF LIFE IN THE DYING PATIENT

With all the above as background, then, let us examine the relevance of artificial prolongation of life vis-à-vis the dying patient.

Medical Viewpoints

As Joseph Fletcher has pointed out, the old-fashioned question faced by physicians was "May we morally do anything to put people out of hopeless misery?" (Fletcher, 1960, p. 140). Today the issue has shifted, and now the question is "May we morally omit doing any of the ingenious things we *could* do to prolong people's suffering?" (Fletcher, 1960, p. 140).

The Oath of Hippocrates is cited frequently in this regard. The first passage of the oath is germane to our discussion and runs as follows:

> I will follow that method of treatment which, according to my ability and judgment, I consider for the benefit of my patients and abstain from whatever is deleterious and wrong.

Yet as one physician has asked:

> How can it be judged to be to the benefit of a patient to cheat him of
> peace while being powerless to restore him to consciousness? Only a
> person who thinks of human life in terms of a senseless specimen of
> protoplasm in a test tube can see any merit in such a course. After
> all, consciousness alone means life to human beings [Hendin, 1973,
> p. 74].

It must also be noted that Hippocrates lived some 2,500 years ago and
could scarcely have visualized modern machines which can supplant the
vital efforts of lung and heart. And he certainly could never have predicted the ethical questions the use of such equipment poses.

The questions we must ask are difficult ones. Is it possible that
twentieth-century man, who basks in the glory of his achievements, has
been guilty, in some cases, of misusing his glorious creations? Has he
reached the point where the healers, the technologists, and the rest of
us are subject to that famous rebuke: "We shall have to learn to refrain
from doing things merely because we know how to do them"?

The patient, particularly the terminally ill and dying patient, who may
be unconscious all or part of the time, must be able to trust his physician not only to care for his life in the best way he knows how, but also
not to put him through unnecessary pain, agony, and stress. As early as
1798 a British physician, Dr. J. Ferriar, cautioned that the physician

> should not torment his patient with unavailing attempts to stimulate
> the dissolving system, from the idle vanity of prolonging the flutter of
> the pulse for a few more vibrations: if he cannot alleviate his situation,
> he will protect his patient against every suffering. . . . When things
> come to the last and the act of dissolution is imminent . . . he should
> be left undisturbed [quoted in Hendin, 1973, p. 83].

Court Decisions

Such a philosophy has been reaffirmed by American courts several times.
Early in 1972 a Milwaukee court upheld that 70-year-old Mrs. Gertrude
Raasch, who refused to sign papers authorizing the removal of her gangrenous leg, be allowed to die "in God's own peace" (quoted in Hendin,
1973, p. 69).

The Raasch case began when the administrator of the hospital in
which the woman was staying came to court to testify that Mrs. Raasch,
who was scheduled for her third major operation in six weeks, and her
second in ten days, had refused to authorize the amputation which doctors said was necessary to save her life. Mrs. Raasch had spent the last
seventeen years in and out of hospitals and nursing homes; she had no

living relatives, and her leg had already been amputed to mid-calf because of the gangrenous infection.

After hearing the hospital administrator's testimony, Judge Michael Sullivan said, "The court is in the position of determining . . . whether the lady shall live. . . ." But he noted that "It is not the prerogative of this court to make decisions for adult competent citizens, even decisions relating to life and death" (Hendin, 1973, p. 67).

Thus the judge had proclaimed that his primary job with relation to the case in question was to determine whether the patient involved was competent or not. After interviewing the woman he said: "it was obvious that she didn't want any more surgery." He then added that there was "absolutely no evidence of incompetence on the part of Mrs. Raasch. . . . I'm positive we're doing the right thing—we will leave Mrs. Raasch to depart in God's own peace" (Hendin, 1973, p. 69).

There are other cases in which the courts have supported the position that the patient has the final right to say what is, and is not, to be done to his or her own body.*

Religious Viewpoints

The major religions have also spoken out on this matter. The Roman Catholic view, as expressed by Pope Pius XII (1957), is well known. If life is ebbing hopelessly, the pope said, doctors may cease their efforts, thus "permit[ting] the patient, already virtually dead, to pass on in peace."

In a 1961 article in the *Hebrew Medical Journal*, Rabbi Immanuel Jakobovits says that "Jewish law sanctions the withdrawal of any factor —whether extraneous to the patient himself or not—which may artificially delay his demise in the final phase."

* This paper was prepared before the Karen Quinlan case became a court issue. The following are the facts in this case. Karen Quinlan lapsed into a coma on April 14, 1975, and was kept alive thereafter by a respirator. The Quinlans signed a form authorizing the attending physician and St. Clare's Hospital in Denville, N.J., to turn off the machine. The medical authorities decided against doing so, apparently because they feared a malpractice suit. The Quinlans then asked the court to declare Karen incompetent and to appoint her father, Joseph, her guardian so that he could give instructions for the respirator to be turned off. This request was denied by a lower court ruling (Judge Robert Muir, of the Morris County Superior Court, November 10, 1975). On March 31, 1976, the New Jersey Supreme Court (7–0) ruled that the mechanical respirator might be disconnected if her attending physicians and a panel of hospital officials agreed that there was "no reasonable possibility" that she would recover. The court also ruled that there would be no civil or criminal liability if the mechanical device was removed following the above guidelines. The court appointed Miss Quinlan's father her guardian and empowered him to seek physicians and hospital officials who would agree to remove the respirator. When the respirator was removed, the patient continued in a coma, but did not die. She was removed to another hospital facility.—Ed.

A few years ago, Fulton J. Sheen, then Auxiliary Bishop of New York, said:

> If the doctor told me that extraordinary means would be needed and I was lying with a body full of tubes to keep me alive, I would ask him to take them out. There is no moral difficulty in such a situation [quoted in Let the hopelessly ill die? 1968].

Yet, in spite of the statements of the courts and of prominent religious spokesmen of our times, it is still no easier in many cases for physicians to make decisions concerning the artificial prolongation of life. The primary reason for this is that in living, and in dying, few things are black or white.

Who is Helplessly Ill and Dying?

An acquaintance of mine, the late Ralph Trout, was a dying man. He had survived a series of crippling heart crises, and had one foot in the grave. Yet in May of 1969 Dr. Norman Shumway transplanted another's heart into Trout's chest and the man lived for about five more years. Before he died, a year or so ago, Ralph received a second heart transplant. And when that heart failed, he received a third. He might have lived another five years. If he had, few would question the advisability of the last two transplants. But they gave Ralph little time indeed; he died quickly after the third transplant. Should that artificial measure have been taken? Should the first transplant have been performed? It, too, was "artificial."

Dr. George R. Minot is another case in point. In 1921, at age 36, he was found to have diabetes. The only therapy then available was diet, and Minot fought a losing battle over the next two years. He might have died soon, too. But in 1923 insulin became generally available. Minot responded favorably to the treatment with the hormone and continued his work. In 1934 he won the Nobel Prize for his development of a treatment for pernicious anemia in human beings. The Nobel work was for the most part carried out after Minot's life was artificially prolonged by insulin (Glaser, 1970).

You see, it is very nice for us to be able to say that these "modern obscenities of medicine" offend the dignity of the dying—and that is probably true, except for the dying who are actually saved. And some would argue that if only one in a hundred, or one in a thousand, lives could be saved it would be a worthwhile effort.

The over-used statement is still true: "While there's life, there's hope." And the ever changing face of modern medicine gives even more weight to the cliché.

If, as was the case with Ralph Trout, the decision over such "heroic measures" is made by the patient when he or she is lucid, then that is one thing. But when a patient is unconscious, who will make the decisions—the decisions over life and death? As Cassell (1973) has noted, this is not simply a decision which a physician makes hastily.

In the process of care, especially in cases that lead to difficult moral decisions, a number of minor ethical matters have been handled along the way—matters that involve both fact and value, in which both patient and doctor interact in making decisions. In that process both patient and physician have informed each other of how each feels, and the interaction helps form the basis for the next decision [Cassell, 1973, p. 56].

Interaction between the Patient and the Physician

I would stress that interaction. If it is missing, then the physician lacks a vital input, significantly affecting his decisions. Continuing, Cassell asks: "Where does the physician get the right to ethical decision-making?" (Cassell, 1973, p. 61). He himself supplies the following excellent answer:

From its very origins, the art of medicine has combined both care for the body and values about life and health. Such concern for morality is not a generalization of expertise but an accepted part of the physician's role, and is so recognized by the society, though largely in a covert manner. The doctor derives his right to ethical decision-making from the society and from the individual patient [Cassell, 1973, p. 61].

What society must help to make crystal clear, however, is that the individual patient—even before he or she becomes a patient—understand the various implications involved in such a decision-making process. It is not absurd for discussions on these subjects to be held in the home, the church, and the school, in addition to the doctor's office.

Then, when we educate ourselves and our doctors to our feelings and beliefs we can only hope for the best. Let me add quickly here that we are not now talking about any sort of euthanasia or mercy killing. We are simply wondering when we should stop.

"I pray you take no more trouble for me. Let me go quietly," begged George Washington on his deathbed, after repeated bleedings, purgings, and blisterings (Elliott, 1974, p. 83).

We can only hope that the physicians of today and tomorrow will act in concert with *our* individual and collective desires. We are re-educating physicians that it is not their hell-bent duty to preserve "life" regardless of other considerations. Still, there are those who can clearly benefit from such heroic medical measures. Can we determine in advance which person will benefit from medical efforts and which will suffer? The answer is no; we can only make educated guesses, and as time passes our guesses may improve.

To improve our accuracy I should suggest that a good question to ask is: What is life when there is no chance of rehabilitation? This question, along with continued education, is crucial. Educating people to the intricacies of medicine and medical matters is, however, a lot to hope for; so, like it or not, we must conclude that much responsibility for these decisions will remain in the hands of the physicians. If the physician involved is one who actively considers such matters, then the chances are good that he will make a wise decision. But it is the job of the public to keep the physicians on their toes. Beware of the lazy ones who wish to make their decisions while standing on one foot.

REFERENCES

Ackerknecht, E. Death in the history of medicine. *Bulletin of the History of Medicine*, 1968, *41*, 19–23.

Cassell, E. Making and escaping moral decisions. *Hastings Center Studies*, 1973, *1*, 53–63.

Elliott, N. *The gods of life*. New York: Macmillan, 1974.

Fletcher, J. The patient's right to die. *Harper's Magazine*, 1960, *221*, 139–143.

Glaser, R. J. Innovations and heroic acts in prolonging life. In O. Brim *et al.* (Eds.), *The dying patient*. New York: Russell Sage Foundation, 1970.

Hendin, D. *Death as a fact of life*. New York, Norton, 1973.

Jakobovits, I. The dying and their treatment in Jewish law. *Hebrew Medical Journal*, 1961, *2*, 251ff.

Let the hopelessly ill die? *U. S. News and World Report*, July 1, 1968.

Pius XII. Morality of pain prevention. *Catholic Mind*, 1957, *55*, 260–278.

Thomson, E. The role of physicians in the Humane Societies of the eighteenth century. *Bulletin of the History of Medicine*, 1963, *37*, 43–51.

Truth-Telling and Decision-Making in the Case of the Terminally Ill

NED H. CASSEM, S.J.

Father Ned H. Cassem, S.J. received his A.B. (1959) and his M.A. (1961) degrees from Saint Louis University. His M.D. (1966) is from Harvard Medical School, and his B.D. (1970) is from Weston College, Cambridge, Massachusetts. Father Cassem is Associate Professor of Psychiatry at Harvard Medical School, and Director of Psychiatric Residency Training at Massachusetts General Hospital. In reference to the present paper, it may be mentioned that Father Cassem is Project Supervisor, Pastoral Encounters with the Disabled and Dying, Youville Hospital, Cambridge, and Boston Theological Institute; Chairman, Subcommittee for Utilization of Resources for Hopelessly-Ill Patients, Massachusetts General Hospital; and a member of the Advisory Board of the Foundation of Thanatology, New York. He is a frequent contributor to professional journals and to collections of professional papers published in book form, and has written extensively on Care of the Dying.

Without honesty any human relationship is destined for shipwreck. Accordingly, knowing the truth about his illness is listed as one of the basic rights of the terminally ill person (Chiles, 1967). If truthfulness and trust are so obviously interdependent, how can there be so much con-

201

spiracy to avoid truth with the dying? For the paradoxical fact is that
for the terminally ill both the need for honesty and the avoidance of the
truth are rampant.

THE NEED FOR HONESTY WITH PATIENTS

Sir William Osler is reputed to have said "A patient has no more right
to all the facts in my head than he does to all the medications in my
bag." Let us say that a routine blood smear has just revealed that its
owner has acute myelogenous leukemia. If he is 25, married, and the
father of two small children, should he be told the diagnosis? Obviously,
you would say. What if he is 80? What if he had had two prior psychotic
breaks with less serious illness? What if his wife tells you he once said
he never wanted to know if he had a malignancy? The plot thickens.

*Empirical Studies Show that Most Patients Want to be Told the
Truth of Their Condition*

Most empirical studies in which patients were asked whether or not they
should be told the truth about malignancy have indicated that patients
have an overwhelming desire for the truth. When 740 patients in a
cancer-detection clinic (prior to diagnosis) were asked if they should be
told their diagnosis, 99% said that they should be told (Kelly & Friesen,
1950). Another group in this same clinic was asked after the diagnosis
had been established, and 89% of them replied affirmatively, as did
82% of another group who had been examined and found free of malignancy. Gilbertsen and Wangensteen (1962) asked the same question of
298 survivors of surgery for gastric, colon, and rectal cancers and found
that 82% said that they should be told the truth. The same authors approached 92 patients with advanced cancer, judged by their physicians
to be preterminal, and were told by 79% that they should be told their
diagnosis.

   How many do not want the truth or regard it as harmful? Effects of
blunt truth-telling have been empirically studied in both England and
the United States. Aitken-Swan and Easson (1959) were told by 7% of
231 patients explicitly informed of their diagnosis that they resented
the frankness of the consultant who did so. Gilbertsen and Wangensteen
(1962) observed that 4% of a sample of surgical patients became quite
emotionally upset at the time they were told, and appeared to remain so
throughout the course of their illness. In an effort to study the importance of truthfulness, Gerle, Lunden, and Sandblom (1960) studied 101
patients, of whom one group, along with their families, were told the
frank truth of their diagnosis, while in the other group an effort was

made to maintain a conspiracy of silence with family and physician excluding the patient from discussion of the diagnosis. Initially greater emotional upset appeared in the group where patient and family were told together, but the authors observed in their follow-up that the emotional difficulties in the families of those patients "shielded" from the truth far outweighed those where patient and family were told the diagnosis simultaneously. In general, then, empirical studies do not support the myth that truth is not desired by the terminally ill or harms those to whom it is given. Honesty sustains the relationship with a dying person rather than retarding it.

> Dr. Hackett tells of a woman he saw in consultation, a housewife of 57 with metastatic breast cancer now far advanced. She reported a persistent headache which she attributed to nervous tension and asked why she should be nervous. Turning the question back to her, he was told, "I am nervous because I have lost 60 pounds in a year. The priest comes to see me twice a week, which he never did before, and my mother-in-law is nicer to me even though I am meaner to her. Wouldn't this make you nervous?" He said to her "You mean you think you're dying." "That's right, I do," she replied. He paused and said quietly "You are." She smiled and said "Well, I've finally broken the sound barrier; someone's finally told me the truth" [Hackett & Weisman, 1962].

Not all patients can be dealt with so directly. A nuclear physicist in our hospital greeted his surgeon on the day following exploratory laparotomy with the words "Lie to me, Steve." Individual variations in willingness to hear the initial diagnosis are extreme. And diagnosis is entirely different from prognosis. Many patients have told me that they were grateful to their physician for telling them that they had a malignancy. Very few react positively to being told they are dying. In my experience "Do I have cancer?" is a not uncommon question, while "Am I dying?" is a rare one. The latter question has been more common among patients who are dying rather rapidly, such as those in cardiogenic shock.

Honest Communication Does Not Preclude Subsequent Denial

We must also remember that honest communication of the diagnosis (or of any truth, for that matter) by no means precludes the avoidance or even frank denial of the truth of it later. In two studies in which patients had been told outright their diagnosis (and the words "cancer" or "malignancy" had been used), they were asked three weeks later what they had been told. Of one sample group 19% (Aitken-Swan & Easson, 1959), and, of the other, 20% (Gilbertsen & Wangensteen, 1962) denied that their condition was cancerous or malignant. Likewise Croog, Shapiro, and Levine (1971) interviewed 345 men three weeks after myocardial infarction and were told by 20% that they had not had a heart attack. All had been explicitly told their diagnosis. It is surely clear that in order for a person to function effectively truth's piercing voice must occasionally be muted in, or even excluded from, awareness. I once spoke with a man on four successive days who had a widely spread bone cancer. On the first day he said he did not know what he had and did not like to ask questions, on the second that he was "riddled with cancer," on the third that he did not really know what ailed him, and on the fourth that even though nobody likes to die that was the lot which now fell to him.

The Challenge of Truth-Telling

Truth-telling is no panacea. At times we are tempted to accept the delusion that honestly telling a person his diagnosis guarantees smooth sailing in the remainder of the relationship. As though telling a person he has a cancer were the quickest way to his heart. Communicating an honest diagnosis is simple compared with the challenge of communication which comes afterward. Do we in fact waste so much emotion over the question of truth-telling only to avoid discussion of the endless succession of tongue-tied moments which come afterward? Is truth-telling then helpful? Of course. Is honesty essential to the relationship with a dying person? Of course. Does lying help? Almost never. But when we have accomplished all these things we have achieved only the smallest portion of the care of the dying person. Telling the truth, after all, is only the way to begin.

DECISION-MAKING AND THE TERMINALLY ILL

During the last 70 hours of his life in Siskiyou General Hospital, California, Emil Loloiva accumulated a medical bill in excess of $10,000. His treatment included two unsuccessful cardiac operations. After his death, the county administrator rejected the hospital's claim for the part of the bill related to those last three days.* This is possibly the first lawsuit against a hospital alleging that certain life-saving treatments of terminally ill patients are unjustified.

In the course of every terminal illness the time may come when patient, family, and physicians must confront the question: Shall medical technology be used to save him or should he be allowed to die? When is medical treatment, in fact, abuse? Eliot Slater (1973) pointed out

* *American Medical Association News*, December 16, 1974, p. 2.

that the two goals of medicine—the relief of suffering and the preservation of health—can become, in an irreversible illness, mutually contradictory. How often might this possibility arise? In England 68% of all deaths occur after long illnesses, predominantly stroke and cancer. At least half those individuals are over 75 years of age (Vickery, 1974).

Three myths seriously obstruct the decision-making process when the above questions are raised about an irreversibly ill person. Caught between the crossfire of euthanasia societies and pro-life groups, physicians are often blamed for not accepting oversimplified solutions to complex or insoluble problems. Three of the most common misguided notions about critical illness are the following. (*a*) *Medical care of the sick has been dehumanized by advanced technology.* Although it is a convenient misplacement of responsibility, this statement is patently false. Technology never dehumanized anybody. Human beings dehumanize other human beings. The tongue can be as devastating as a laser. (*b*) *"Natural" death occurs with "dignity."* As reassuring as this maxim might be, it masks the separation, loss, debilitation, anguish, helplessness, organ failure, and pain which are as naturally associated with dying as energy, vitality, and a sense of well-being are associated with healthy living. (*c*) *God gave life; He will determine when it is to be taken away.* God, it seems, was wise enough to leave this responsibility to lesser beings. This maxim suggests that all technology available to prolong life must be used simply because it is available. If one acts according to such a principle, technology uses him, not he technology. Decisions made according to such reasoning only intensify the problems of the sick. Apparently the good of the patient is not considered, and he, like the physician, is presumed to have no choice in the matter.

Slogans ring hollow in intensive care settings themselves. Ingelfinger (1973) expressed it well when he said "As there are few atheists in fox holes, there tend to be few absolutists at the bedside." A general approach to decision-making is proposed here, based on a plea to let the decision-making process be as complicated as the reality itself. The approach is organized around three questions and five checkpoints (Cassem, 1975).

The first two questions are: (*a*) Can this illness be reversed? In other words, what are the chances of this person's restoration to health? Ideally we should want a mathematical probability, somewhat similar to the predictions calculated by Shubin *et al.* (1974) for patients in cardiogenic shock. Such probability curves are at present difficult to find. (*b*) If some restoration of health occurs, will the result justify the effort? How much cortical function will the accident victim regain? With the dialysis patient, does the post-dialysis state justify the repeated removal of excess urea, potassium, and other substances from the bloodstream? Or, to reword it: When do the life-saving efforts become "grave inconveniences" and thereby render the means used "extraordinary"?

In answering these questions attention to five checkpoints or aspects of the situation is necessary.

Technological

What, in fact, can be done for the sick person? Because of certain anti-technological paranoia which is currently fashionable (by which medical treatment is regarded as sadistic or looked on as at least unnecessary procedures reserved for "guinea pigs" who unwittingly fall into the hands of physicians), many are biased against life-saving procedures. Some years ago, when the cardiac surgeons at our hospital began to replace aortic valves in persons in their 70s and 80s, there were protests and accusations of unwarranted brutality to the old. Yet experience has demonstrated that aortic valve replacement can effect dramatic improvement in the quality of life of persons in this age range and therefore should not be denied them (Austen *et al.*, 1970). We had a similar experience with the introduction of the intra-aortic balloon pump (Cassem & Hackett, 1972).

Socioeconomic

How limited are the resources of the family? Of the community? Of society? Many years back when bloodbanking was in its infancy a hemophiliac patient in the hospital, hemorrhaging severely, was literally using all the blood in the bank. A special meeting was called to discuss the dilemma, which resulted in an agreement that transfusions would continue for the man regardless. The anecdote reminds us that resources are limited and their distribution quite vulnerable. In parts of Canada a hospital is told at the beginning of the fiscal year how much it has to spend and given the responsibility and freedom to spend it in any way it sees fit. One woman with a metastatic bone cancer told me that she wanted the family savings spent on her son's medical school education and not on elaborate care for herself. In a country so wealthy, particularly where so much is spent on the destruction of life, it would be indeed difficult to justify curtailment of medical treatment on economic grounds alone. But even here resources are limited. At one large general hospital, for example, a cost accounting was made for patients undergoing emergency surgery for ruptured abdominal aortic aneurysm. Of 62 patients, four survived, at a cost of approximately $130,000 per survivor. Others have calculated that if all the patients in this country who could use dialysis were to do so, by 1980 the budget for dialysis would consume 20% of our Gross National Product.

Moral/Ethical

When the decision is made, is it based on or guided by norms which are applicable to human personhood in general—i.e., can the reasons be generalized? Certain principles have been commonly accepted by many ethicists: e.g., life is not an absolute good nor death an absolute evil; there is no obligation to prolong life in irreversible illness by extraordinary measures; any means which causes serious inconvenience to the patient (family) is extraordinary; medications which hasten death may be used as long as they have a primary beneficial effect (which morphine has, for example, while potassium chloride does not). The ethicist is very likely to insist that any decisions must rest, not on the disposition of the persons choosing, but on norms which are constitutive of human personhood in general (e.g., the direct taking of a human life is wrong).

Legal

All too often we talk about decision-making as though the dying person himself had nothing to say about it. One man, still intubated after thirty days in the intensive care unit, took paper and wrote for his family: "Above all, no extraordinary means!" The patient is the first and most important person to be consulted under such circumstances. Often he may be comatose, but when conscious, patients should have more to say about what is done to them than anyone else. What if the patient says that he or she wants to be allowed to die? If the person (*a*) knows what treatment can offer, (*b*) is not psychotic, (*c*) is not treatably depressed, and (*d*) is not suffering such pain that death seems preferable (and were the pain to be relieved, his desire to die might dissolve), then he is within his rights to refuse (further) treatment.

Psychological

What motives bias the decision to save or let die? Would a hopelessly ill patient be allowed to die because he arrived in an emergency ward at 2 A.M., an undesirable time to begin surgery? Or because he was not covered by third-party payers? Or was not a good "teaching case"? A 62-year-old woman lay dying in the coronary unit, a heart attack having left her in congestive heart failure and shock. Angiography had shown that her vessels were inoperable, and her physician left orders that she was not to be resuscitated. After ten days several nurses began to complain rather angrily that she continued to receive pressors to maintain her blood pressure, even though without them she would develop pulmonary edema (a most unpleasant way to die). Probing uncovered the fact that they were quite impatient because she was taking so long to die. She was an abrasive, demanding woman who had always been difficult to get along with, as her family verified. They, too, seemed to resent her not having the courtesy to make her exit sooner. Feelings such as this inevitably contaminate the decision-making process. Open, honest communication among patient, family, physicians, and nursing staff helps to ensure that such feelings do not bias the decision.

THE FINAL QUESTION

Answering the first two questions accounts for almost all the energy expended in arguments about treating the hopelessly ill. One of the strongest incentives to prolong these disputes is the nearly complete avoidance of the third and final question. (c) When the decision has been made to let the person die, how do we conduct ourselves in the face of imminent death? Almost every admission to an intensive care unit requires this encounter for patient and staff. Admission is justified, in fact, by the danger to life present should the patient remain elsewhere. In treating the critically ill patient, some talk as though making the decision to escalate or limit treatment solves the problem. It is rather then when the task becomes more difficult. How are we to take care of the individual for whom further efforts to save are inappropriate? He may remain fully conscious, or, if he is not, his family are. While some treatment efforts are modified or withheld, others must now be intensified. Preparation and support of the family throughout illness are as much a part of our responsibility toward them as providing semi-miraculous technologies is. While medical advances seem to justify being called miraculous, it may be an even greater miracle that, when reversal of illness is no longer possible, personnel can be found who will stand by the dying person to the end.

Whenever a person lies mortally ill, it is to be hoped that he, his physician, his family, and the hospital staff can share the burden and together confront the realities which often dwarf them all. Although there are some heroic measures which need not be used for irreversibly ill patients, some always remain necessary: namely, extraordinary sensitivity, extreme responsibility, heroic compassion. For care itself must continue to the end of life and never cease to be total, even when major facets of it are fully limited or stopped.

REFERENCES

Aitken-Swan, J., & Easson, E. C. Reaction of cancer patients on being told their diagnosis. *British Medical Journal*, 1959, *1*, 779–783.

Austen, W. G., De Sanctis, R. W., Buckley, M. J., Mundth, E. D., & Scannell, J. G. Surgical management or aortic valve disease in the elderly. *Journal of the American Medical Association*, 1970, *211*, 624–626.

Cassem, N. H. (s.j.). Ever say die? *The Linacre Quarterly*, 1975, *42*, 86–88.

Cassem, N. H. (s.j.) & Hackett, T. P. Sources of tension for the CCU nurse. *American Journal of Nursing*, 1972, *72*, 1426–1430.

Chiles, R. E. The rights of patients. *New England Journal of Medicine*, 1967, *277*, 409–411.

Croog, S. H., Shapiro, D. S., & Levine, S. Denial among male heart patients. *Psychosomatic Medicine*, 1971, *33*, 385–397.

Gerle, B., Lunden, G., & Sandblom, P. The patient with inoperable cancer from the psychiatric and social standpoints. *Cancer*, 1960, *13*, 1206–1217.

Gilbertsen, V. A., & Wangensteen, O. H. Should the doctor tell the patient that the disease is cancer? Surgeon's recommendation. In *The physician and the total care of the cancer patient*. New York: American Cancer Society, 1962. Pp. 80–85.

Hackett, T. P., & Weisman, A. D. The treatment of the dying. *Current Psychiatric Therapies*, 1962, *2*, 121–126.

Ingelfinger, F. T. Bedside ethics for the hopeless case. Editorial. *New England Journal of Medicine*, 1973, *289*, 914–915.

Kelly, W. D. & Friesen, S. R. Do cancer patients want to be told? *Surgery*, 1950, *27*, 822–826.

Shubin, H., Weil, M. H., Afifi, A. A., *et al*. Selection of hemodynamic, respiratory, and metabolic variables for evaluation of patients in shock. *Critical Care Medicine*, 1974, *2*, 326–336.

Slater, E. New horizons in medical ethics. Wanted—A new approach. *British Medical Journal*, 1973, *1*, 285–286.

Vickery, K. O. A. Care of the dying: Euthanasia. *Royal Society of Health Journal*, 1974, *94*, 118–126.

VII
PROBLEMS OF DYING:
THE TAKING OF LIFE

The Medical Profession: Euthanasia

ERIC J. CASSELL

Eric J. Cassell received his B.S. degree from Queens College of the City University of New York, his M.A. from Columbia University, and his M.D. from New York University School of Medicine. Since 1971, Dr. Cassell has been Clinical Professor of Public Health at the Cornell University Medical College. He has published extensively in professional journals with particular emphasis upon Health and the Urban Environment, and on Caring for the Dying. Dr. Cassell is a Diplomate, American Board of Internal Medicine; a Member, New York Academy of Sciences; and a Fellow, Institute for Society, Ethics and the Life Sciences, Hastings-on-Hudson, New York.

The definition of euthanasia has evolved over the past several centuries. From its earliest meaning as a hoped-for gentle death, it came in the nineteenth century to stand for intervention which would ease the pangs of the dying. In our own time, the word has been extended to include actively ending the life of the dying person.

EUTHANASIA: ACTIVE AND PASSIVE

Thus, we now distinguish two forms of euthanasia. The first, called passive euthanasia, means allowing the terminally ill person to die without continued efforts to maintain his life. Turning off the respirator when it alone sustains a hopeless being is one example. Another would be not treating an otherwise fatal infection in an unconscious patient, one

213

doomed by stroke or other disease. And, more recently, allowing a patient to refuse therapy which would extend his life, but promise only continued pain and suffering. In such a case, people speak of prolonging dying rather than of prolonging life. In the last few years, the dying patient has been recognized to have rights, within the constraints of faith, in the mode of his death. The so-called Living Will is a document in which a person places a morally, but not legally, binding obligation upon his physician to respect his wishes in the manner of his death.

Active euthanasia, for which mercy killing became a synonym in the 1920s, means actively terminating the life of the dying person. Originally applied to only the hopeless sufferer, including the malformed newborn, this concept, too, has been broadened considerably. People now ask whether a just and merciful society should not gently end the life of someone who requests it in honest anticipation of fatal suffering. Physicians, by virtue of their knowledge, would be called upon, in this belief, to be the agents of mercy.

From my personal experience, it is clear that in the past few years passive euthanasia has become less a debated issue and more the standard of behavior. Physicians more and more often respect the wishes of the dying and their families, and more freely step aside in the face of inevitable death. It is my sincere wish and belief that passive euthanasia will subside as an issue requiring its own name and will become simply good medical practice.

This is not to deny that many problems remain to be resolved in the care of the dying, but simply to show that the awareness of those problems and of the need to find solutions is increasing. The growing acceptance of passive euthanasia by society and physicians does not extend to active euthanasia; yet the advocates of active euthanasia are responding to a felt need, for which, if one feels their response to be wrong, another must be offered.

I should like to examine some of the underlying issues in euthanasia to see what light can be shed on the problem.

THE UNDERLYING ISSUES IN EUTHANASIA

It seems to me that ideas of euthanasia are a response to a widespread social belief that it is the sick person's privilege to invoke the social contract in order to ensure that his death be allowed, or caused, by others as a morally right act. The social respect for this claim comes, I think, from the same wellspring from which medicine as a social and a socially necessary function has arisen. For both in euthanasia, with respect to the dying, and in medicine, with respect to the care of the sick, the person derives his right to call upon others, not solely because he cannot do for himself, but because the frailty of the body is universally recognized.

The sick role, which legitimates the claim of the patient on the group to help him recover, is assigned by physicians because of their knowledge of both the body and the social rules. The euthanasia movement, in its farthest extension, would also have the physician legitimate the claim of the hopeless patient even prior to terminal suffering, in order that he or she might die with the active help of the group. In spite of the fact that both euthanasia and medicine seem to have the same origin in the human condition, I must state categorically that I believe that, under no circumstances, should physicians be the intentional agents of death as part of their socially approved function. Further, since I am personally aware of situations where doctors may be driven by mercy actively to cause death, I believe such situations should remain as lonely, painful, difficult, and unsanctioned as they are at present. Perhaps society will evolve a profession whose function is medical killing. But it would be terrible and destructive for physicians to serve both as healers of the sick and as active agents of death.

But how does one resolve the paradox that both euthanasia and medicine have the same origin in mercy, and yet deny medicine a role in active euthanasia? Before going further, I shall dismiss the often cited argument that the preservation of life is an overriding good. In modern medicine, because of the power to resuscitate and prolong life, the meaning of that unquestioned truth has often become obscure and uncertain. It is commonly said that technological medicine has failed in its pursuit of immortality. That is only partly true. Technological medicine has shown us, *not* that the body cannot be kept alive forever, but rather that the body is often hardier than the person. The person, it turns out, is more fragile than the body.

The problem remains, however, that the person facing an awful death has just claims on society for relief. Paradox or not, a latent recognition of that just claim has always existed in medicine and the Western tradition, and has had to be dealth with. This recognition has been associated with attempts to deal with the meanings of *hopeless, helpless,* and *suffering.*

I believe that the question of euthanasia arises whenever hopeless, helpless suffering exists or is anticipated. Bodily illness is, however, an essential prerequisite. Should a political prisoner be condemned for life, and, as a consequence, be a hopeless sufferer (although of sound body), or should someone suddenly lose all his loved ones and be suffering and helpless in his grief, euthanasia would not be advanced as a solution to either sufferer's problem. Suicide, perhaps, but not euthanasia. The archetypical human horror is the wounded soldier, left behind on barbed wire, dying in pain, slowly and alone in the night.

I shall examine the concepts of helplessness, hopelessness, and suffering, to show how attempts to deal with their meanings have been society's response to the just call for a merciful death. For each of the words, one finds both a medical and a spiritual response. Each is difficult to define, because each contains an element of the subjective.

Helplessness

Helplessness may be viewed as the state in which a person is no longer able to assert himself as a person, or to be the person he feels himself to be. To put it more simply: it is that condition in which an individual loses control over his existence. The loss of control which accompanies illness may be the central fear of the sick person. So basic is the terror of helplessness and the loss of control that men have developed elaborate mechanisms to deny it presence. The denial of fate is one such mechanism. For the sick, the helpless possibility that an illness resulted from fate is often denied by the search for an attributable and self-inflicted cause. Until quite recently, sickness was considered punishment for sin. Today, it is still common for those around the sick person, and the patient himself, to look for some reason why it is the patient's fault that he is sick. When illness is punishment for transgression, the threat which the sick person's helplessness poses for the group is mitigated. The sick person ceases to be a helpless being who must be rescued from, or shown mercy for, his helplessness, and symbolically becomes a warning to those who would transgress.

For the physician or other medical attendant, the patient's helplessness does not pose the same threat as it does to the other members of society. Often the helplessness and loss of control over the surroundings so characteristic of the ill are used to facilitate treatment. The sick do not do; they have done to them. While utter passivity in patients is rarely considered desirable, it is certainly too often true that everything in the treatment situation serves to emphasize the patient's helplessness and his lack of control. Think of the patient endlessly ringing the bell for the nurse in the middle of the night, impotent at the end of an electric cord. Necessary and justified as such a scene may occasionally be, it represents the sick, helpless and with no control over their existence.

Thus do we deal with the first term of the euthanasia triad—helplessness. The spiritual world, secular or otherwise, may attempt to deny helplessness, blaming the sick for their sickness. The medical world is so constructed as almost to require the helplessness.

But we have grown beyond both views. The sick do not make themselves sick. Or if they do, it is in an entirely different dimension from that of punishment for sin. Further, the well cannot know the extent to which illness and technology can reduce one to a decisionless being, devoid of consciousness and will. It is in recognition of this terrible power of modern medicine that the issue of passive euthanasia has become less absolute and more a question of degree. No one wishes to be recognized by heartbeat alone. Or circulation. Or pulse. Technology has taught that meaningful life is not its abstraction on a biological score sheet, but rather one's presence as a determinant being.

For physicians it now must be clear that whatever permanently suspends an individual's control of his life destroys that life. Doctors recognize as an overriding ethic: *above all, do no harm.* The body alone is not meant in that aphorism; it includes the person. The act which removes control, without real promise of its return, does harm to the person, without whom the body has no meaning.

Suffering

Suffering is as difficult to define as helplessness. The meaning of the word varies from person to person, attaining precision only at the moment of its presence. Even then, only the sick person can say whether he is suffering. Physical pain, for example, is only one source of the suffering of the sick. Grief, and the disconnection from the group, foulness in sight or smell, utter dependency and helplessness—all can be causes of suffering as potent as physical pain. Suffering implies the inability of the individual to transcend the source of suffering. The ability to return to wholeness, to intactness of person, appears to be denied the sufferer. As the source of suffering continues, dignity is eroded and pain becomes ever less tolerable. It is common to hear the well suggest that the person in pain will "get used to the pain," but that rarely happens. As pain continues, not only does it become less bearable, but added insults to the integrity of the person are ever harder to tolerate. In such situations, nurses or doctors may not understand why the patient with severe or continuing pain begins to shrink from injections or other minor pains which he or she previously accepted with equanimity.

I believe that the person who is suffering because of illness has a legitimate claim on the group for relief. Like the helplessness of the ill, the sufferer's distress resonates within those around him. People feel the need to respond, to help, to give relief, if only to relieve their own discomfort.

The immediate response, to be repressed before it finds expression in speech or act, is to do away with the hopeless, helpless sufferer. Put him out of his misery. It is simply intolerable for the onlooker.

But if there is some way to deny the reality of the suffering, or to give it transcendent meaning, then the concept could be relieved of its force. Again, there is both a spiritual and a medical response. Since so much of man's term on earth has been marked by suffering, the attempt to understand and give meaning to it has preoccupied the spiritual life. The spiritual response is to give meaning to the agony. To attach to the suffering something which does not diminish the sufferer, but enlarges him.

Indeed, it does seem to be true that people often grow and deepen in response to sickness. Many emerge from illness with a new appreciation of life. In terminal illness, an earlier concern for things, position, or even bodily discomfort may subside, leaving the dying person free to love and be loved, peaceful in dying as much as in living. In such people, rarely is the bystander aware of suffering. The spiritual response, however, is more concerned with the reward after death than the reward in life. And this comfort is afforded as much to the group around the sufferer as to the sick person himself. There seems to be an implication that to deprive the sufferer of his suffering would be to deprive him of his reward.

Whatever the present state of faith, mortification of the flesh has fallen from favor. There are few who still find suffering a good in itself. It is hard to know which came first in the Western world, a diminution of religious faith or a relative decline of physical suffering, but it is true that the instances of an abiding belief in God and in an afterlife appear to have decreased in frequency. This attenuation of belief, with its coincident decline in the value of suffering, may also have contributed to the comparatively recent greater acceptance of passive euthanasia. Our society has lost many of the defenses which made it possible for us to tolerate the physical suffering of others.

The medical response to suffering is to provide relief. An ancient aphorism points out that while cure may be rare, relief is always possible. Modern technological medicine is well known for its cures, but less well known is its incredible power to relieve symptoms. Not only pain, but vomiting, anxiety, depression, diarrhea, and other symptoms which contribute to suffering—all can be controlled. There need exist only the will to do so. It is paradoxical, then, that the modern physician is so poorly trained in the control of symptoms. One reason is that the control of disease, not the relief of human suffering, is the philosophical focus of medicine. Doctors are not people who simply care for other people; they have a system of thought and training which has evolved over centuries, and which has been very effective. It is understandable though sad, that the historical evolution of the profession should have drawn modern medicine away from its roots in the human condition.

It might be argued that no system of thought can protect the doctor from the daily reality of the suffering around him, but this is not true. Doctors learn to listen to people in pain without suffering that pain themselves. They are not helpless at the bedside of the sufferer; they have things they can do. That ability to do things is part of their protection. But when physicians feel that they have nothing to offer, they, sad to say, often avoid the patient. Doctors' avoidance of the dying has been the subject of much comment recently, and yet since physicians feel that their role is in the treatment of disease, it is natural that they would avoid the dying, who represent only failure and frustration.

Society then can protect itself from suffering by a spiritual and medical response. Spiritually, the group can mitigate hopeless suffering by giving it a transcendent meaning. Today, when the transcendence of suffering is cast into doubt, society can seclude the sufferer in what William May (1973) calls the "Hider Goddess" of the hospital. The physician, on the other hand, is protected against the suffering of others because he has the tools to relieve it, and when his tools fail, he has the ability not to perceive it.

But suffering, as I noted earlier, is an intensely subjective term. It cannot be measured by the intensity, duration, or quality of pain. Nor can it be predicted with any certainty for a particular illness or patient. Suffering seems to require the inability of the person to maintain himself as a person in the face of pain or other disease. Suffering is compounded greatly, as is pain itself, by the patient's fear of it. But it is hard to know of what this fear is compounded. Perhaps the underlying basis is the fear of "not being able to take it"—a fear of the loss of control and the dissolution of the integrity of the person. One hears how terribly Freud suffered from the pain of his cancer at the end of his life. But he adamantly refused pain-relieving medication because he did not want his thinking to be interfered with. He could not have suffered as they say, because the intactness of Freud's person and the continuation of his work were of more importance than was his pain, until very near the end.

Such facts lead to an inescapable conclusion: that the physician who does not constantly help his patient remain in control, who does not actively help his patient control fear, does harm no matter what his stance toward the patient's disease. It is people who suffer, while bodies are only in pain. The power which modern technology has placed in the doctor's hands still fails him, and by definition will always fail him, in the face of the dying. Yet that same power in the service of the person can enlarge the person, not by his suffering, but above his suffering.

Hopelessness

Hopelessness is the most difficult of the three terms to define. On its face, it seems so simple. A sick person who knows he will die is said to be without hope. No one believes that euthanasia should be operative if there is still hope. We say of cancer that hope is extinguished by the word. How odd. After all, one does not just dissolve when cancer is diagnosed. No, but the word promises pain and suffering; it is the end of the future. How much future? Old people, even very old people, do not seem hopeless even though they are going to die and they know it. Patients who die well, even when they are not old and know they are going to die, do not act as if they were hopeless. Is man only a becoming, rather than a being, animal? That would be sad. Does taking away the future take away the present? That seems unlikely. And yet both spiritual and medical responses to hopelessness are directed at returning the future, not enlarging the present.

The most obvious spiritual answer to hopelessness is the promise of an afterlife. There is hardly a culture which does not provide some means to promise that death is not the end. It is sad that we seem to be a culture which has lost faith in eternity. Robert Jay Lifton (1973, 1976) has written extensively on symbolic immortality, showing the numerous ways in which men attempt to transcend death: in their children, their work, their gods—all of them ways of transcending the finiteness of the body.

The medical and scientific response to hope is also obvious. "Where there is life, there is hope." Hope of continuing life. Radical vitalism, the attempt to keep the body going no matter what the price, is a medical expression of this drive. In most of such medical expressions of hope, life is seen as the totality of heartbeats. This is the opposite of the spiritual response to hopelessness. There the soul, the expression of the person, is to be transcendent. For science, the body is to be transcendent, and there is no soul. Both spiritual and scientific responses come from the same culture and thus, as opposing as they seem, they may have the same root. The possibility arises that the common basis of these two contrasting responses to the loss of hope is the need to transcend the finiteness and confinement of the body.

I believe that the loss of hope occurs whenever the body is seen as winning, whenever the person cannot rise above or get free of the narrowing confines of the body. The image of euthanasia in its farthest extension finds the person calling upon the group to kill him in anticipation of hopelessness, helplessness, and suffering. Then his person will have won, will have escaped the hangman's noose of existence.

From infancy we struggle to free ourselves from the constricting bonds of body, to struggle free of its limitations. It rests there in the background, ever waiting. Every night it wins, and every day we overcome and rise above our physicality. We forge ourselves as persons, in part from the success of our battle with the body. In death, the body inevitably wins. The loss of hope, then, is what signals its ultimate triumph.

But if that is the case, then hope can be restored by methods other than those which promise immortality. Indeed, the suspicion arises that active euthanasia itself, especially in that representation which promises death as a right act at the hands of others in anticipation of hopeless, helpless suffering, is a response to a need previously fulfilled by faith. That form of euthanasia becomes a societal answer as effective as immortality to the body's demands of finitude. "My body did not win; I won by being killed before the issue was joined."

Earlier I noted that passive euthanasia, allowing a person to die, has become a less absolute issue in the last few years in recognition of the power of modern technology. It seems to me that the area of discussion is not whether man should be rescued from the misplaced mercy of man, for surely experience has informed us that there are limits to the endurance of such mercy. Rather, I believe that the real issue is whether man is such an impoverished creature that all his solutions should be external to himself.

In examining helplessness and suffering, I have tried to show that they achieve their awfulness by the destruction or effacement of person. The loss of hope seems similar. I believe that the war with the body is not won by attempting to overcome the claims of the body through spiritual or physical immortality. Not in this age, when both claims are in doubt. The triad of euthanasia (helplessness, hopelessness, and suffering) is defeated by whatever maintains the person in control of his body, in its finiteness. Death, in the fullness of its time, is not the enemy. Helplessness and suffering are the enemy. The loss of hope is the enemy.

Spirituality, represented by a personal, self-related God with a promise of heaven, has lost favor in this society. But man has his own inner spirit, and in sickness and death it need not be told of its impoverishment by the constant search for outside solutions to inner human needs.

CONCLUSION

I understand the fear of pain and suffering which looks to physicians for solution. After all, doctors have at their hands agents which might bring on easy death. And I know from experience situations which seem to allow no other form of humanity. But they are rare indeed, and it is not the rare which is being addressed here, but the commonplace.

From his earliest days the physician learns a fear of harming patients. That fear influences his actions to a degree which no layman can know, because no layman has such power to harm. I can imagine nothing which would be so destructive to doctors as men, or to medicine as a profession, as giving physicians the right to kill. It does not matter how much society seems to need such fatal services, the price is simply too high.

But, further, I believe that the challenge is better met in other ways. We are all familiar with a medicine attuned to disease, not to persons, but things are changing. The need for a medicine of the person is perceived, but change is hard. It is not even clear to most people what they mean by person, because modern psychological or sociological explanations of mechanisms obscure holistic understanding. But medicine is a profession which has spent its history struggling under the handicap of insufficient knowledge, forced by human needs to work with inadequate tools. These times are no different.

If common to helplessness, suffering, and hopelessness is the need to maintain the patient in control, free of fear, with the person intact until death or clouded consciousness close over, then doctors have the ability to do that. If, as I believe, the social origins of euthanasia and medicine are one—namely, the universal fear of the entrapment of the body by illness—then active euthanasia is not necessary. What is necessary is an enlarged understanding of medicine. Such a change in medicine will not require that doctors do harm, for that is antithetical to medicine, but, rather, that medicine return to the service of the person.

REFERENCES

Lifton, R. J. The sense of immortality: On death and the continuity of life. *American Journal of Psychoanalysis*, 1973, *33*, 3–15.
Lifton, R. J. *The life of the self*. New York: Simon & Schuster, 1976.
May, W. Attitudes toward the newly dead. *Hastings Center Studies*, 1973, *1* (1), 6.

The State: Capital Punishment

DONALD R. CAMPION, S.J.

> *Father Donald R. Campion, S.J., a native New*
> *Yorker, was born in 1921. He completed under-*
> *graduate work at Saint Louis University and made*
> *his theological studies at Woodstock College,*
> *Maryland. His doctorate in sociology is from The*
> *University of Pennsylvania, where he published a*
> *statistical study on capital punishment which has*
> *been cited in many legislative hearings on penal*
> *reform. In addition to his writings in* America,
> Commonweal, Theological Studies, *and other*
> *periodicals, Father Campion has contributed to*
> *more than half a dozen books on social theory,*
> *the sociology of religion, and ecumenical or in-*
> *terreligious affairs. He joined the staff of* America
> *in 1965, and was named editor-in-chief in 1968, a*
> *post which he held at the time of the Institute.*
> *Currently, he is in Rome, serving as Director of*
> *the Jesuit Press and Information Service.*

In the light of a story featured on the front page of *The New York Times* today * about an event which occurred only yesterday in Saudi Arabia, I take it for granted that capital punishment is not yet—you will pardon the expression—a dead issue. Moreover, as the week of June 16 began, odds were high that the newspapers would be head-lining a long-awaited decision from the United States Supreme Court on

---

* This paper was delivered on June 19, 1975, the day after the execution, mentioned later in the above paragraph, of the assassin of the king of Saudi Arabia.—Ed.

the constitutionality of the death penalty in this country.* The issue, then, is contemporary. It is also complex and loaded, one which takes many twists and turns through the worlds of law, philosophy, sociology, theology, the administration of justice, criminology, and even the area of deeply felt and sometimes quite raw human feelings. Much of this complexity, I suggest, can be discovered in reflecting on the scene reported in the *Times* of a throng of 10,000 Saudis silently watching the decapitation of the 27-year-old prince–assassin, and the subsequent cries from the witnesses: "God is great" and "Justice is done."

THE THEORY OF CAPITAL PUNISHMENT

There was a time when, for most of mankind, the taking of life by the state through capital punishment posed no problem. The records we have of most ancient societies—those of the Middle East, for instance—tell us of laws which punished certain offenses by the death penalty. Greece and Rome in early times had similar enactments. One may have questioned whether Socrates deserved the sentence he received, but *not* whether the state had a right to execute a criminal under death sentence imposed by competent public authority. If capital punishment posed a problem for men up to relatively modern times, it was in the area of safeguarding against excessive bloodletting (an extension of the *lex talionis* or "only one eye for an eye" principle) or of ensuring that sentence and execution were carried out by proper authorities and not by the crowd or mob.

The historical significance of a limitation on judicial penalties such as that put down in the very ancient code of Hammurabi becomes clearer when we realize that the story of capital punishment is one which describes an irregular pattern. The frequency with which capital punishment is invoked in a given society may vary from age to age, and the tendency is not always toward more mercy or less cruel forms of execution. "Exotic" penalties appear at different times and are often related more to the nature of the offense and, perhaps, the effort of a given group of people to express indignation or revulsion in the presence of an offense against religion or perhaps a special person such as that of a king. Thus, after the seemingly enlightened attitude of the early Middle Ages toward capital punishment, we find in France during more modern times the use of a penalty such as "pressing" (in which a person was literally ground to death under a large stone) invoked for an attempt on the life of the king.

---

* This decision was delayed by a year and did not come until July 2, 1976, when the Supreme Court ruled that the death penalty as such did not involve cruel and unusual punishment and was constitutional.—Ed.

It is true that, in addition to the criminal under sentence of death and his or her friends and supporters, the death penalty occasionally raised problems for scattered individuals. Among the early Christian Fathers one finds an occasional questioning of the right of the state to take life in this way. But the more standard view relied for support on provisions spelled out in the Hebrew Bible or a saying of St. Paul's on the state's right to use the sword. Eventually, jurists and philosophers offered further justifications and, it should be added, limitations for use of the death penalty.

In the various nations or peoples of Europe up to the eighteenth century, a mixture of Christian insight and tribal custom had its impact on the use of the death penalty for graver crimes or misdeeds, whether secular or religious in nature. In certain instances, the result was a mitigation of the death sentence by reducing it to compensation payments (among certain Germanic peoples) or to a form of temporary banishment-*cum*-pilgrimage to a holy place such as Jerusalem, Rome, or Compostella. But for Christian princes and peoples these were only modifications of an unquestioned right to take life under certain circumstances. It was true, they would say, that Jesus enjoined "if someone strike thee on the right cheek, turn to him the other also" (Mt 5:39). But still St. Paul had proclaimed: "But if thou dost what is evil, fear, for not without reason does it [civil authority] carry the sword. For it is God's minister, an avenger to execute wrath" (Rm 13:4). And in the Middle Ages, though St. Thomas Aquinas argued that "In this life penalties should rather be remedial than retributive" (*Summa theologica*, 2a 2ae, 66, 6), he also concluded that "If a man be dangerous and infectious to the community, on account of some sin, it is praiseworthy and advantageous that he be killed in order to safeguard the common good" (*Summa theologica*, 2a 2ae, 64, 2).

THE PRACTICE OF CAPITAL PUNISHMENT

So much for theory regarding capital punishment. What about practice? Here the picture up through the sixteenth and seventeenth centuries varies from place to place, from era to era, and also with respect to the designation of capital crimes as well as the method of judgment and the modes of execution. In some sectors of Europe, for practical purposes, the death penalty at times disappeared. The rise of the national state, however, seems often to have been paralleled by a rise in the number of capital crimes on the law books and in the use of the penalty. English law, about which much has been written by scholars, recorded a rise in the period from the sixteenth to the eighteenth centuries to a total of more than 200 capital crimes ranging from high treason to economic crimes involving as little as a few shillings. It should be noted, however, that then as now there was a difference in the number of possible capital offenses, the number of convictions, and the number of actual executions. With that qualification entered, it remains true that the use of capital punishment increased in certain lands. Thus, although George Fox in a 1659 pamphlet did not call for total abolition, there is something of a landmark quality about his insistence that death be used "only for murder."

The movement to question the use of capital punishment and to work for its abolition in modern society began a century later with the publication in 1764 of Cesare Beccaria's enormously influential essay *Dei delitti e delle pene*. Although his basic philosophy of the state did not win wide adherence, his attack on the death penalty as cruel, unreasonable, and ineffective proved powerful in influencing official policy in several nations during the remainder of the eighteenth century, and in North America, largely through its impact on Dr. Benjamin Rush, the Pennsylvania pioneer in prison reform.

The nineteenth century witnessed the abolition of capital punishment in various European and Latin American nations and in certain of the states in the United States. In some instances, it is true, such abolition was later reversed, but the trend seemed to be more and more in the one direction. But World War I and the rise of authoritarian states in Europe brought a reversal of that trend. Despite the efforts of various church and other groups working for abolition, it was not until after World War II that such labor again proved effective in influencing public policy. Here, a major force was the Royal Commission on Capital Punishment in the United Kingdom (1953), which gathered evidence and held hearings from 1949 to 1953. It is safe to say that in the course of these extended hearings and the reports which followed on them one can find everything which can be said for or against capital punishment at the legal, sociological, criminological, philosophical, or religious levels. Other countries, notably Canada in the mid-1950s (Joint Committee of Canadian Senate and House of Commons on Capital and Corporal Punishment and Lotteries, 1956), have conducted similar studies, but the sides remain drawn and the evidence on both sides remains substantially the same.

A study of the nature of capital offenses in different societies is a fascinating project in itself. Even today, one comes on interesting indications of national attitudes or ideological sensitivities revealed in the criminal codes of different lands. Where capital punishment is still inflicted, it is quite often imposed for treason or for the murder of police officials. It is interesting that today in the Soviet Union one still finds the greatest use of this extreme penalty for "economic" offenses, a pattern similar to England's in its early industrial period.

More detailed studies have been made with regard to specific issues such as the deterrence value of the death penalty, its impact on a judicial system, the fairness of administration of justice where the death penalty exists, and the like. But these remain, in my judgment, refinements of knowledge which has already been available to the public for some time. There is, I believe, genuine merit in the observations made almost a decade and a half ago by Sidney Hook in his contributions to a symposium on capital punishment:

> Is there anything new that can be said for or against capital punishment? Anyone familiar with the subject knows that unless extraneous issues are introduced a large measure of agreement about it can be, as had been, won. For example, during the past 150 years the death penalty for criminal offenses has been abolished or remains unenforced, in many countries; just as important, the number of crimes punishable by death has been sharply reduced in all countries. But while the progress has been encouraging, it still seems to me that greater clarity on the issues involved is desirable: Much of the continuing polemic still suffers from one or the other of the twin evils of vindictiveness and sentimentality [Hook, 1961, p. 278].

It should be noted that Hook himself would allow for the taking of life by the state in two very specific instances: when a criminal under a life-term sentence asks for execution instead of that sentence, or when a convicted murderer repeats his offense within prison with apparent impunity.

A few statistics about trends in the United States over the past generation will support part of Mr. Hook's claim. From 1930 to 1976, a total of 3,859 executions were carried out under civil authority in the United States. Taken by decades, this total breaks down as follows:

Period	Number of Executions
1930–1939	1,667
1940–1949	1,284
1950–1959	717
1960–1964	181
1965	7
1966	1
1967	2
1968—	0

While I am citing these figures let me add a further breakdown which bears, I believe, on the ultimate issue of the abolition or retention of the death penalty. In the period from 1930 to 1976, of those executed by civil authority 1,751 were white, and 2,066 were black.

ARGUMENTS FOR AND AGAINST CAPITAL PUNISHMENT

As for the arguments pro and con, one can describe them as ideological and pragmatic on both sides. Very briefly, all arguments for retaining the death penalty derive in one way or other from: the need for retribution; the need to vindicate justice; the need to rehabilitate (?); the need to deter; the need to safeguard society from further crime by the same criminal. On the other side, it seems to me that the arguments turn on these points: the appropriateness or inappropriateness of the state's exacting vindication; the effectiveness of capital punishment to deter; the availability of other ways to safeguard society or the common welfare; the undesirable consequences in the way of a corruption of the judicial process; the inequities in the administration of capital punishment across economic, racial, and other lines; the revulsion aroused in most cultures by the inflicting of the death penalty as evidenced in the trend to make execution as private as possible.

CONCLUSION

Why has capital punishment come to be a problem in modern society? My personal opinion is that it results from a heightened sense of human dignity both of the criminal and of the judge or executioner as much as from any other single factor. It is this, I believe, which has influenced the churches, including the Catholic Church, gradually and often quite slowly, to argue against the retention of the death penalty as an instrument of justice in human society. When all is said and done, it seems to me a sign of health that a people should turn away from a procedure which involves them unnecessarily in a judgment and action which are so irreversible and so final in their consequences.

REFERENCES

Hook, S. Contribution to: Symposium on capital punishment given by the District Attorney's Association. *New York Law Forum*, 1961, 7, 249–319. Hook's contribution, pp. 278–283.

Joint Committee of Canadian Senate and House of Commons on Capital and Corporal Punishment and Lotteries, 1953–1955. *Final report*. Ottawa: Queen's Printer, 1956.

Royal Commission on Capital Punishment, 1949–1953. *Report*. London: Her Majesty's Stationery Office, 1953.

The Individual: Suicide

WILLIAM W. MEISSNER, S.J.

*Father William W. Meissner, S.J. received his
A.B., M.A., and Ph.L. degrees from Saint Louis
University, his S.T.L. from Woodstock College,
Maryland, and his M.D. from Harvard University.
Father Meissner is a psychiatrist and a member of
the American Psychiatric Association and the
American Psychoanalytic Association. Currently,
he is a Staff Psychiatrist at both the Massachusetts
Mental Health Center, and the Cambridge Hospital,
and is Assistant Clinical Professor of Psychiatry at
the Harvard Medical School. In addition to a
constantly increasing number of articles in professional journals and other periodicals, Father
Meissner is the author of the following books:*
Annotated bibliography in religion and psychology (*1961*), Group dynamics in the religious life
(*1965*), Foundations for a psychology of grace
(*1966*), The assault on authority: Dialogue or
dilemma? (*1971*), The paranoid process (*1975*),
and co-author of Basic concepts in psychoanalytic
psychiatry (*1973*).

There is perhaps no enigma more perplexing or more confounding than
that of suicide. The enigma of suicide and the motivations of the suicidal
impulse have escaped our capacity to understand and consequently have
frustrated our abilities to predict and prevent the suicidal event. Suicide
has been defined as "the human act of self-inflicted, self-intentioned
cessation" (Shneidman, 1973). As a human act, therefore, suicide em-

229

braces a multitude of underlying motivational states, both conscious and unconscious, and is influenced by multiple factors, no one of which can be regarded exclusively as the basic cause. Factors which come into play and which influence suicidal behavior are at a most critical level certainly intrapsychic and psychological, but they are also strongly influenced by interpersonal events, social forces, economic crises, cultural influences, and a host of other determinants which exhaust the capacity of scientific thinking to detail and integrate.

My purpose here is to sketch, however briefly, various dimensions of the phenomenon of suicide. I shall first discuss the typology of suicide and try to establish some basic terminology. I shall then present a few of the basic statistics and the general theoretical orientations to the understanding of suicide. The major focus, however, will be on the formulation of the dynamics of suicide and some subsequent inferences regarding the role of moral issues in the evaluation and understanding of it.

TYPES OF SUICIDE

The descriptive categories of suicidal behavior have been broken down in a variety of ways (Beck & Greenberg, 1971). The first important distinction is that between committed suicide and attempted suicide. *Committed suicide* refers to one of the generally recognized modes of death—natural, accidental, suicidal, or homicidal—which are involved in the certification of actual deaths. In this usage the term generally implies that the victim had consciously intended the lethal act to result in his own death. *Attempted suicide*, however, is complicated by the issue of intent. Stengel (1968) defines a suicide attempt as "any non fatal act of self-damage inflicted with self-destructive intention, however vague and ambiguous."

A second important distinction has to do with the seriousness of the suicide attempt. Other than cases of successfully completed suicides, *serious attempts* may be regarded as those in which the individuals express a definite intention to die, but the suicidal act is aborted through some unforeseen circumstance. Other less serious attempts, as in cases where the attempters gamble with death or when the suicidal intent is uncertain even to themselves, must still be regarded as serious enough to pose a definite risk to life. Even attempts which involve a minimum of suicidal intention and are perpetrated for consciously or unconsciously manipulative motives cannot be regarded lightly. I shall return to this aspect later in regard to the question of intentionality.

An important area of consideration in reference to the understanding of suicide is that of *subsuicidal phenomena*. Menninger (1938) described subsuicidal phenomena in terms of *chronic suicide*, which includes asceticism, martyrdom, addiction, invalidism, and psychosis; *focal suicide*, which involves acts of self-mutilation, malingering, polysurgery, multiple accidents, impotence, and frigidity; and, finally, *organic suicide*, which refers to the operation of psychological factors in organic disease states, particularly the self-punitive, aggressive, and erotic components. Moreover the role of self-destructive impulses in alcholism and drug addiction, the neglect of medical care for chronic and debilitating diseases such as hypertension and diabetes, and even the role of suicidal impulses in the victims of homicides has been carefully studied.

Seen in the broader context of subsuicidal phenomena and *suicidal equivalents*, it becomes plain that the incidence of suicidal behavior and suicidal impulses in the human race is by no means minimal; nor is its significance to be underestimated. The questions raised by this self-destructive dimension of human existence are indeed profound and perplexing. They touch upon some of the most basic theological, philosophical, social, psychological, and moral questions about human nature and human existence. We can wonder indeed whether the suicidal impulse and the incidence of serious committed suicide can ever be meaningfully reduced beyond a certain level. In discussing Freud's views on the death instinct, Litman has made the following comment:

> My experience is in agreement with Freud's general schematic view. Deep down there is a suicidal trend in all of us. This self-destructiveness is tamed, controlled, and overcome through their healthy identifications, ego defenses, and their constructive habits of living and loving. But when the ordinary defenses, controls, and ways of living and loving break down, the individual may easily be forced into a suicidal crisis [Litman, 1967, p. 339].

STATISTICS

The problem with evaluating the statistics on suicide is that the data are largely unreliable, and the categorizing of them is complicated by the problems in clear definition of the types of suicide. Most suicide statistics are social statistics; that is, they are collected by government or state agencies for specific purposes. The data are manufactured, by and large, by coroners and physicians. Suicidal deaths are notoriously underrepresented and vary considerably from country to country, not only in terms of the varying rates occurring in respective countries, but also in terms of the cultural influences which dictate when self-inflicted deaths are to be regarded as suicidal or not. There are also problems of the "false positives," in the sense in which a non-suicidal act may be counted as a suicide, and of the "false negatives," when a committed suicide may be deliberately camouflaged or misclassified. Moreover, the critical data for determining whether a given death is suicidal or not may be lacking.

The suicide rate in the United States is generally estimated at between 10 and 12 per 100,000 of the general population. The number of suicides annually is about 25,000 but because of the difficulties in reporting and identifying actual cases of suicide, the incidence is estimated by most experts to be at least twice that. The tenuous character of the data notwithstanding, suicide must be ranked as the second highest cause of death for white males between the ages of 15 and 19 and the fifth highest cause of death for the same group between the ages of 10 and 55. The high rate of suicide in the earlier age group is probably a reflection of the fact that other killers such as heart disease or cancer do not affect this group very significantly. The rate of committed suicide is higher among males at all ages and tends to increase with age. Among females the rate of attempted suicide is higher at all ages. In general, women attempt suicide more frequently than men (in a ratio of about 3 to 1), but the men outdo the women in committed suicides (again in a ratio of about 3 to 1). Some recent evidence suggests that the ratio for committed suicides seems to be moving toward a more equal proportion between the sexes. For many years the suicide rate among whites in the United States far outstripped that of blacks, but over the past decade the suicide rate for blacks seems to be drawing closer to the rate for whites. Anywhere from 10% to 15% of deaths certified by coroners or medical examiners are equivocal, between suicide and accident, as to the actual mode of death. The ratio of attempted to committed suicides is estimated at 10 to 1.

The most serious aspect psychiatrically in dealing with suicide is the recognition of suicidal patients and the prevention of suicidal behavior. There are a number of indices which point to the increased potentiality for serious suicidal risk. The first is the association with psychiatric illness, particularly severe depressions, both psychotic (unipolar) depressions and bipolar affective disease, otherwise known as manic-depressive psychosis. The association with schizophrenia also increases the potentiality for suicide. Moreover, the period of apparent recovery from severe depression has been described as a period of increased suicidal risk (Shneidman & Farberow, 1957). Clinical improvement may frequently be a sign that the patient has decided on a suicidal solution to his difficulties. Other important indicators of presuicidal risk include alcoholism, drug addiction, and previous attempts. Almost three-fourths of all suicide victims have previously threatened or attempted suicide (Shneidman & Farberow, 1957). More than two-thirds of the patients who attempt suicide communicate their suicidal intent in one way or another, and 41% have specifically stated that they intended to commit suicide. The most common expressions take the form of a desire to die, the thought that they would be better off dead, an explicit statement of intent to commit suicide, or the feeling that their families would be better off if the patient were dead. The incidence is highest in those who are separated, divorced, or widowed. Consequently, your chances of dying by suicide are best if you are male, white, over 50; if you are separated, divorced, or widowed; and if you live alone.

THEORIES OF SUICIDE

Sociological Theories

We can turn our attention at this point to a consideration of some of the major theories of suicidal behavior. The major sociological theorist of suicide is Emile Durkheim (1897/1951). In his classic treatise, Durkheim proposed three categories of suicide: egoistic, altruistic, and anomic. Egoistic suicide is the result of the individual's failure to be integrated within his own social structure. Thus the suicide rate tends to be low in Catholic countries because religion integrates the individual into the collective life of the Church; it tends to be higher in Protestant countries where the stress is on individualism. Similarly, suicide rates drop in periods of political crisis, since in such periods society is more strongly integrated; hence individuals become more actively involved in social life and are thus less subject to egoistic suicide.

Altruistic suicide, on the other hand, is more or less the antithesis of egoistic suicide in that it represents instances in which the individual is excessively integrated with his society. Thus a suicide becomes the fruit or price of religious sacrifice or fanatical political allegiance (e.g., Japanese suicides during World War II). On the other hand, anomic suicide has to do with situations in which the accustomed relationship between the individual and his society is suddenly shattered, radically altered, or shifted in some significant manner. Thus the sudden loss of a job, a close friend, or a fortune could be the precipitating factor for an anomic suicide.

Critics of Durkheim's work have found fault with his collection of data and with the relatively frequently unexplained "exceptions" (e.g., the high suicide rate in Catholic Austria). His general approach to statistics was to employ them as explanatory rather than simply descriptive devices. For Durkheim, sociology is the positive science of social facts, the extrinsic social forces which determine human behavior. Durkheim's study of suicide rates as regularities of social behavior concludes that such regularities must mean that social forces outside the individual are at work causing the observed regularities.

The problem with much of Durkheim's approach—and with it a considerable body of subsequent sociological interpretation—is that in the search for the relevant meanings to understand social behavior, Durkheim is forced continually to supply common sense meanings to interpret suicidal actions. Thus Durkheim committed a twofold error: (*a*) trying to explain social behavior by merely external factors, and (*b*) explaining meaning by imputing the observer's own common sense understandings. The methodological weakness is critical and points to the fact that the suicidal action and the meaning of suicide are sufficiently complex and difficult to exceed the grasp of any single methodology, even one as far-reaching as that of sociology (Douglas, 1968). As Beall has commented:

> The inadequacy of statistical or actuarial correlations (whether with age, occupation, or residential area) have been pointed out by many investigators. . . . Such correlations are too simple and mechanical. Suicide is not a simple variable that can be correlated directly with another single feature of society. It involves much more than simply being detached from or integrated with society. Social attitudes, feelings of belonging, evaluation of self according to group mores, competitive interpersonal struggles, and identification of one's welfare with that of other people are important, but they are not the entire story. To attribute an increase in suicides to the development of civilization, to economic depressions, anomie or social disorganization, and then to attempt a purely sociological explanation omits the basic internal struggle that these environmental situations produce. It also fails to explain why, in these circumstances, only *some* individuals commit suicide. An examination of psychological explanations is needed to fill this gap [Beall, 1969, p. 4].

When we enter the realm of the psychology of suicide, we encounter considerable diversity and complexity. In fact, we enter a quite divergent realm of study, since the sociological phenomena of suicide are to some extent different from those of the psychological approach. Sociological studies are based primarily on the statistics of actual suicides, while psychological studies deal primarily with attempted and unsuccessful suicides. These, in fact, are quite divergent phenomena, not only descriptively but dynamically as well.

Psychological Theories

The psychological thinking about suicide derives primarily from Freud's (1917/1957) formulations in his classic paper on "Mourning and melancholia." Subsequent to Freud's formulation, thinking about suicide was dominated by the concepts of identification with the ambivalently held object which is both loved and hated, and of the turning of aggression against the self as a result of the direction of murderous hostility against the introjected ambivalent love-object. Suicide was thus viewed equivalently as murder turned inside out.

Perhaps the best known development of Freud's view was presented by Karl Menninger (1938) in his *Man against himself*. Menninger amplified the psychodynamics of hostility and divided the murderous wish in suicide into the wish to kill, the wish to be killed, and the wish to die. Gregory Zilboorg (1936, 1937) added that every suicidal case not only contains strong unconscious hostility, but also reflects an unusual lack of the capacity to relate to and love others. Similarly he maintained that the role of the broken home in the tendency to suicide demonstrates that suicide is the result of both intrapsychic and external causal developments. He further maintained that suicide is motivated by the need to oppose frustrating external forces, but even more specifically by the need to achieve immortality, thus extending the existence of the ego rather than terminating it.

Another consequence of Freud's formulations has been the general trend toward linking suicide with the dynamics of depression, particularly in terms of the model provided in Freud's original formulation. This trend was more or less reinforced by Bibring's (1953) important study of depression, which regards depression as an ego state in which the feelings of helplessness and hopelessness are the basic underlying dynamic. The role of these feelings has subsequently been highlighted in the suicidal syndrome (Appelbaum, 1963; Stengel, 1964), but the association between suicidal behavior and depression cannot be taken as absolute. A similar connection between suicidal behavior and schizophrenia has been suggested, but in spite of the fact that the psychotic process increases the suicidal risk, it is difficult to make any generalizations. The schizophrenic reaction may, in fact, be a defense against suicide (Farberow & Shneidman, 1961).

Subcategories of Suicide

In the attempt to bring more specific understanding to the dynamics of suicide and to avoid oversimplistic, if easy, generalization, there has been an attempt to divide suicidal behavior into a variety of subcategories. Surveying a fair amount of this literature, Beall (1969) comes to the conclusion that there seem to be three main suicidal syndromes, two having to do with attempted suicide and one with completed suicide. In the first form of suicide attempt, the syndrome is characterized by psychopathic acting-out, in which the behavior is more or less impulsive and aggressive, and there is little evidence of guilt. The suicide attempt itself tends to adopt a more passive method and usually comes without much advance warning. This form of suicide attempt is usually not very harmful and tends to occur among men. A second form occurs primarily in women with an hysterical personality style. Again the behavioral mode is primarily passive, but there is an increased amount of guilt used in a manipulative fashion, the method tends to be dramatic, and the attempt comes with clear and definite warnings to elicit rescuing maneuvers from important figures. This is closer to the pattern of manipulative suicide described by Sifneos (1966).

In contrast, completed suicides tend to occur more frequently among professional and managerial classes. In these cases the conflict is more internal, the behavior is restricted rather than impulsive or aggressive, and the personality tends to be obsessive–compulsive with a good deal of underlying guilt over dependency wishes. Generally, if a warning is given, it is not dramatic, and the method chosen for suicide tends to be more painful. The suicide attempt when it occurs is serious, and the result is usually fatal. The interplay of socioeconomic determinants and personality styles in these descriptive types of suicide reflects once more the interplay of social and psychological factors in the determination of patterns of suicidal behavior.

Another important aspect of the suicidal action is that it can be regarded as a form of communication. There is a "cry for help" which is implicit in every suicidal action (Farberow & Shneidman, 1961). Though the cry for help plays a prominent role in many suicidal actions, particularly in attempts of a less serious and manipulative nature, there are also other cases in which the cry for help is too implicit to play a much observable role. The basic issue is the extent to which the suicidal individual has resolved the underlying dilemmas of life and death, and the extent to which the balance has been tipped in favor of the forces of life as opposed to those of death.

Notion of Lethality in Suicide

An important and critical notion which has been added more recently to the vocabulary of suicide is that of "lethality." Lethality was originally described by Shneidman (1969) as the probability of an individual's killing himself in the present or in the immediate future, or as the "deathfulness" of the act. Weisman (1971) has gone on to distinguish basically three forms of lethality: (*a*) lethality of intentionality, pertaining to ideation and involvement; (*b*) lethality of implementation, having to do with factors of risk and rescue; and finally (*c*) lethality of intercession, in connection with available resources, relief, and reorientation. Weisman goes on to comment:

No one attempts suicide in a vacuum, and no one investigates suicide without an implicit concept of lethality. Clinicians who treat suicide attempts tend to define lethality according to the damage inflicted. Psychiatrists and psychologists who deal with demographic and psycho-social factors are apt to emphasize ideas, moods, and cultural and social involvements. This is the lethality of intentionality. Workers who are engaged in preventive activities view lethality in terms of the person's available resources and supports. This is the lethality of intercession, or, more properly, non-intercession [Weisman, 1971, p. 228].

Thus lethality must be distinguished from the degree of discomfort or distress in the patient. It has to do, rather, with the probability of the patient's committing suicide. Any given adult, at any given time, may have more than one aspect of his lethality. There may be a more-or-less long-range, chronic, pervasive, and characterological orientation toward death or suicide, which functions as an integral part of his psychological makeup and affects his philosophy of life and other aspects of his general functioning. At the same time he is capable of a more acute and rela-tively short-term exacerbation of lethality. Clinically this is, in fact, what is meant by saying that a patient has become suicidal. Both aspects are crucial for the clinical evaluation of the suicidal risk in any patient. A patient may be highly disturbed and distressed, caught up in the acute turmoil of a schizophrenic episode, and yet not necessarily be suicidal. The opposite is in fact all too often true; a patient may not manifest any noteworthy degree of distress, but may indeed go on to kill himself. It is specifically the increase in lethality which kills the patient. It is the identification of lethality and the preventive protection of patients during periods of exacerbated lethality which are the major problems in dealing with suicidal behavior.

Intentionality in Suicide

Related to lethality is the issue of intentionality in suicide. In this regard deaths may be regarded as intentioned, subintentioned, or unintentioned (Shneidman, 1973, 1975). In this sense, the death is intentioned or intentional when the subject plays a direct, conscious role in bringing it about. Death is unintentioned when the subject plays no effective role in it and when the death results from independent physical events, whether traumatic or biological. Between these polar categories, there lies the large and relatively uncharted area of subintentioned deaths. These are cases in which the subject plays some partial, implicit, or unconscious role in bringing about his own death. I have discussed this category al-ready, particularly in regard to Menninger's concepts of chronic, focal, and organic suicides. Suicidal intent can vary from the more or less non-serious and manipulative suicidal gesture (Sifneos, 1966) to the most serious, severe, and unalterable commitment to death. Even here, one must be cautious. The terms "manipulative" and "gesture" are unfortunate, since they often lead clinicians into a state of mind which minimizes or makes light of the inherent suicidal potential of these patients. Frequently enough, such patients actually do commit suicide, some unintentionally, some perhaps subintentionally, and a few even, finally, intentionally.

Moreover, suicidal intentions can be determined by the most complex and often unconscious of motives. Hendrick describes a classic case in which a young woman attempted suicide as a regression to an erotic and idealized relationship with her brother in which the suicide represented the fulfillment of her wish for identification with him rather than the consequence of it. The brother had been an aviator-hero in the First World War who had reached his moment of highest phallic achievement in a flaming death over the fields of France. As Hendrick comments:

> This suicidal attempt, in contrast to depressive suicides, represents a different escape from aggression, libidinal frustration, and anxiety, rather than an act of self-punishment. It is not a consequence of identification, but an effort to fulfill the need to solve this terrible crisis in the patient's life by achieving an identification with the act of a hero [Hendrick, 1940, p. 42].

In the light of such cases it becomes abundantly clear that the suicidal intention is various and variously motivated. In some cases it may express the dynamics of self-punitive, self-destructive impulses—along the lines of the more classical Freudian analysis—while in other cases it may express the deepest, unconscious wishes and needs for self-fulfillment and self-expression. It is Weisman (1971) who points out that intentionality is not equivalent to the wish to kill oneself or to the suicidal intent. Motives for attempting suicide are as obscure as, if not more obscure than, the motives for any behavior. The expression of suicide intent is often a reliable clue to a high degree of lethality, but they are by no means related; more commonly those who attempt suicide try to mask or deny their wishes or present their ambivalence and equivocation. Rather, intentionality is a form of consciousness which distinguishes purposeful human activity from merely reflexive or stereotype behavior. It is the human way of making sense out of our experience and the ambiguities of life. Lethal intentions, then, have reference to "transient belief-systems that impel people to anticipate greater pain and to terminate existence" (Weisman, 1971, p. 229).

THE DYNAMICS OF SUICIDE

My purpose in this section is quite specific. I should like to link some of the aspects of suicidal behavior with a more general frame of reference which I have described at some length elsewhere in terms of the "paranoid process" (Meissner, 1975). The paranoid process is envisioned as a fundamental process in the organization of developmental experience and defensive and adaptive functioning, which underlies the experiential continuum reflected, at one extreme, in the mature and integrated functioning of a stable human identity and, at the other extreme, in the most severe and pathological forms of human dysfunction. The paranoid process is based essentially on the mechanisms of introjection, and its correlative projections, and the elaboration of a cognitive frame of reference, the paranoid construction, which serves to sustain and integrate the rest.

Introjection in the Dynamics of Suicide

I should like to focus here on the notion of introjection since it is central to the understanding of the dynamics of suicide and, in fact, serves as the focal point of derivation for the other aspects of the paranoid process. Introjection refers to the aspect of the paranoid process through which the subject's inner world and the organization of a sense of self are achieved. That organization takes place specifically through the internalization of objects in such a way as to provide the nucleus of the sense of self. These internal objects carry with them into the subject's inner experience of himself all the defensive and developmental vicissitudes which were embedded in the original external object relationships. This understanding of the basic introjective mechanism of the paranoid process is crucial, since, as we shall see, it underlies some of the basic dynamics of the suicidal impulse.

One of the central and most critical aspects of the pathogenic organization of the introjects has to do with the victim-introject. We are already familiar through the work of Anna Freud (1936) with a related but quite different aspect of the introjective economy in terms of her description of the "identification with the aggressor." Identification with the aggressor is, in fact, basically an introjective function which serves very specific developmental and defensive purposes. The victim-introjection, however, is a necessary precursor and correlative component of the introjective dynamics to the aggressor-introject.

The purpose of identification with the aggressor is to ward off aggressive impulses by externalizing them and identifying with the aggressive external source. The mechanism consequently implies the defensive ability to separate self and object images by projection of these aggressive drives onto external objects, while at the same time a portion of these same drives is temporarily taken into the self. Consequently, the externalization partially spares the immature and vulnerable ego from the destructive effects of unneutralized aggression.

In the course of development, when a fixation takes place at this level of the victim-introject, it serves to impede the capacity to move on into and beyond the stage of identification with the aggressor, and thus creates conditions in which the organization and functioning of the superego are impeded. The basic postulate underlying this view of introjective development holds that when the infant's primary love-object, particularly the mother, fails to provide a reliable aggressive resonance, especially when the child is between 6 months and 15 months of age—Mahler's (1965) practicing phase—the conditions are set up in which it becomes relatively impossible for the immature ego of the infant to neutralize these aggressive drives and to discharge them in a sufficiently fused form against the mothering object in such a way as to provide a safe area of projection away from the child's own threatened and fragile ego.

Need for the Mother to Accept the Child's Aggressive Impulses

The manner in which the child works through the interlocking processes of introjection and projection is in some degree at any rate a function of the interaction between himself and the mothering figure. The child deals with the inner forces of evil or destruction which he feels within him (Winnicott, 1958, p. 207) by projecting them onto the significant figures in his environment. The capacity to project these aggressive and destructive impulses becomes a matter of vital concern to the emerging development of the child's inner world. These impulses, left awash in the child's inner world, threaten to fragment and destroy his emerging sense of self. As long as they persist, he is in the position of ultimate self-victimization and dissolution. Projection provides the mechanism of escape. Orgel comments:

> Restitutional attempts are made, to a greater or lesser extent, to create counteraggression in the sought-for objects. Such a relationship, even if it is with someone who can safely be hated or an aggressor with whom one can safely identify, or to whom one can masochistically submit, provides an external object upon whom one may rid oneself of quantities of aggression that threaten ego fragmentation and self-destruction [Orgel, 1974, p. 532].

The question, then, is whether the significant objects, the objects of the child's dependence and love, can allow themselves to be the adequate objects for the discharge of the child's destructive impulses. This is a difficult matter, but nonetheless crucial. This can only be accomplished to the degree that the mothering figure in particular is capable of tolerating and absorbing the child's aggressive impulses without being destroyed by them and without allowing the loving relationship with the child to suffer dissolution or distortion. The critical element here is the extent to which the mother can tolerate her own aggressive destructiveness, her own feelings of hate which are generated in response to the child's aggressive initiatives. Winnicott comments as follows:

> A mother has to be able to tolerate hating her baby without doing anything about it. She cannot express it to him. If, for fear of what she may do, she cannot hate appropriately when hurt by her child she must fall back on masochism, and I think that it is this that gives rise to the false theory of a natural masochism in women. The most remarkable thing about a mother is her ability to be hurt so much by her baby and to hate so much without paying the child out, and her ability to wait for rewards that may or may not come at a later date [Winnicott, 1958, p. 202].

Consequently, it is to some extent the mother's capacity to be a good hater of her child which provides the context within which the child can emerge from a state of passive victimhood to a position of being able to discharge noxious and threatening aggressive impulses so as to provide the matrix within which he can make the important developmental step in the direction of identification with the aggressor. As I have already noted, this developmental progression is critical in the formation and integration of a more stable superego and the institution of more consistent structural barriers to regressive pulls.

The Emergence of a False Self in the Child

I shall return to this issue in more pragmatic terms in a few moments, but I should like to shift the ground at this point to another aspect of Winnicott's view of the development of the child. Winnicott (1960/1965) has addressed himself to the formation of what he calls a "false self." Where the dynamics we have been describing fail, the consequence is the emergence of a false self, which is usually based on the child's compliance as a defense against undischarged and unneutralized aggression. This forces a split in the child's emerging sense of self, between the true self and the false self, and forces the child's development in the direction of an evolving and progressively adaptive elaboration of the false self. The price is in the frustration and strangling of any true growth of the inner and real sense of self.

The child's compliance is, of course, sought for and reinforced by many forces around him. It brings immediate rewards from the adults on whom the child is so dependent for love and sustenance, and these adults can very easily mistake the child's compliance with their wishes for real growth. True inner development, then, can be bypassed by a series of introjections so that what becomes manifest is a false acting self, a copy of the significant objects with whom the child relates and complies. The true or essential self, however, becomes hidden and deprived of the roots of meaningful living experience. Those who are caught in this destructive web may seem to function well and adaptively and to be leading normal and healthy lives, but at some point they may seek actually to end those lives which have become so false and unreal. It is worth considering the extent to which our child-rearing practices, our social and cultural mores, our socially reinforced expectations, and even our systems of morality and religious belief, contribute to this inner undermining and splitting of the child's emerging personality and to the erection and enforcement of the false self.

From another point of view the false self can be seen as in part a struggle to cope with the dangers and difficulties of the outer world. It thus serves often quite specific and important defensive needs. At times it can represent an often heroic struggle to stay alive. The price which it pays is the sacrifice of creativity, vitality, and originality to the more pressing needs for safety and for ensuring external supports. To pick up the thread of our earlier observations: if the important care-taking objects cannot tolerate and respond meaningfully and lovingly to the child's emergent aggression, the child is forced into a position of compliance and into the internal divisions which lead to the formation of the false self.

The Role of the False Self in Suicide

It is the persistence of this false self which can have a powerful impact in setting the stage for suicidal acting-out. This implication has been clearly stated by Winnicott:

> Let us say that in the severe case all that is real and all that matters and all that is personal and original and creative is hidden, and gives no sign of its existence. The individual in such an extreme case would not really mind whether he or she were alive or dead. Suicide is of small importance when such a state of affairs is powerfully organized in an individual, and even the individual himself or herself has no awareness of what might have been or of what has been lost or is missing [Winnicott, 1971, p. 69].

I am reminded at this juncture of a case in my own recent practice of a young woman whose early experience was one of constant rejection and devaluation from a hostile and rejecting mother. The whole pattern of her life was so carried out around the internalization of that malignant and devaluing maternal figure that my patient felt that there was nothing good, nothing strong, nothing worthwhile in herself. Her constant complaint to me was that there was no hope, no future for her, and that it were better had she not been born. Moreover, the whole pattern of her external life had been structured around the attempt to appease the mother's expectations and to gain some measure of acceptance from her. She had turned to nursing as a career as a result of her mother's suggestion that she do so, since her mother felt that she did not have the brains or ability for much of anything else. The false-self pattern is, of course, considerably more complex than simply a matter of career choice, but my patient reviles, is disgusted by, and is caught up in hopeless despair over, almost every aspect of it. Her only alternative as she sees it is suicide. It seems clear to me at this juncture that a suicidal action on her part will have two clear implications: (*a*) it will destroy the false self built upon her lifelong compliance with her mother's wishes and her seeking for her mother's acceptance, and (*b*) it will realize in the fullest measure the sense of victimhood which she senses within herself and within her life experience.

My patient represents many of the aspects of what Guntrip, building on the basic notion of the false self, has called "schizoid suicide." The schizoid suicide differs somewhat from the depressive suicide in which the impulse to self-destruction is angry and hostile. Schizoid suicide is, rather, the result of an apathy toward real life which can no longer be accepted. There is a quiet but tenacious determination to fade from the scene and to give up the struggle. The death of the false self carries with it the hope of a rebirth of what is more authentic and creative in the subject's own existence. Guntrip writes:

> Schizoid suicide is not really a wish for death as such, except in cases where the patient has utterly lost all hope of being understood and helped. Even then there is a deep unconscious secret wish that death should prove to be a pathway to rebirth. . . . Whereas in depressive suicide the driving force is anger, aggression, hate and a destructive impulse aimed at the self to divert it from the hated love-object, i.e. self-murder, schizoid suicide is at bottom a longing to escape from a situation that one just does not feel strong enough to cope with, so as in some sense to return to the womb and be reborn later with a second chance to live [Guntrip, 1969, pp. 217–218].

In my patient, as in others of this sort, it is a rebirth with the hope of experiencing a meaningful accepting and loving relationship with the mother which lies at the root of these impulses. It is a relationship of loving closeness and acceptance which has been constantly desired, constantly frustrated, and never attained.

The idea which I am proposing here in a more theoretical vein is that the false self is in fact organized around the introjects which I have been describing (Meissner, 1975). In suicidal patients, in particular, the forming of a false self which clusters around a central introject of the victim provides the basic root and underlying motivation of the suicidal tendency. The suicidal impulse, then, becomes the expression of the inner unneutralized and unresolved aggressive impulses which have been solidified and embedded in the victim-introject and which form an essential aspect of the core of the individual's sense of self. It is the unresolved aggression which cannot be adequately discharged and absorbed by the significant love-objects, which must be projected onto those objects and subsequently reintrojected and internalized to become the permanent possession of the child's emerging sense of self. It is in this context, then, that the self-hate and self-loathing of such individuals take on a particular meaning. It reflects not only their own inner sense of guilt and shame because of the inner hatefulness and evil which they sense in themselves, but also the unresolved and unassimilated hatred more often unconscious than conscious in their significant love-objects.

THE THERAPEUTIC ENCOUNTER WITH A SUICIDAL PERSON

It is worth noting that the interplay between the dynamics of the victim-introject and victimization, on the one hand, and the dynamics of hatred, on the other, plays itself out not only in the developmental experience of the child but in the living experience of the adult as well. It is not merely that the suicidal patient is fixated at a point of victimization, but that there is a commitment to victimization and an adherence and clinging to the victim-introject. The clinging to the victim-introject has strong narcissistic underpinnings, the discussion of which would carry us far afield, but it can be noted that this becomes a powerful force in the suicidal patient's unconscious motivation and represents a clinging to the original intensely ambivalent object of infantile dependence. The point on which I should like to focus here, however, is that the patient's commitment to victimhood leads him to attempt to elicit and provoke the conditions of victimhood in many of his adult relationships. An understanding of these dynamics gives us some insight not only into the child's developmental experience, but also into the patterning of the suicidal patient's life experience which draws him to the brink of suicidal behavior.

If the suicidal patient carries out these dynamic processes at large in many contexts of his living experience, it is to be expected that the same dynamics can come into operation in an even more intense and provocative way in the therapeutic encounter. It seems to me that this is a point of critical pastoral interest, since in the pastoral ministry one is frequently brought into contact with suicidal individuals and one can expect that the same dynamics will operate in one's own experience of the interaction. In a sense, the patient recreates the dynamics and interplay of destructive and ambivalent impulses which were at work in the original relationship to the primary love-objects. It is essentially the undischarged and unneutralized aggressive destructive impulses which the patient projects onto the figure of the caring object and which are experienced then as hate.

This maneuver has the obvious unconscious advantage of reinforcing and consolidating the patient's position as victim. The patient reacts with a sense of inner evil, worthlessness, and primitive guilt. The defensive gain through this projective maneuver is of sufficient importance that the patient must attempt to validate it by various forms of provocative behavior. The patient then tries to arouse hatred and destructive feelings in the caring objects in a variety of behavioral and verbal attacks. The patient will discredit, devalue, criticize, and disparage his therapist. Any least sign of irritation or anger in the doctor's response will be taken as confirmation and validation of the projection. The provocations may take the form of direct physical action, involving physical assault or destruction of personal property. There may be telephone calls at particularly inconvenient and annoying times. There may be mutinous rebellion and withdrawal within the therapeutic situation.

In general, there is the abiding accusation that the therapist is inadequate, is not being helpful, is doing little or nothing to alleviate the patient's pain—in general, the constant direct and implicit assertion of the therapist's incompetence. Thus the resistance to any therapeutic inroads or effective progress can be quite rigid and intense, and may frequently take the form of a profoundly negative therapeutic response. If we remind ourselves that the suicidal patient carries out this behavior in many facets of his life experience, it is not difficult to understand how the constant reinforcement of these dynamics can lead progressively closer to a suicidal resolution.

The dynamics of this interaction have been carefully delineated in a recent contribution by Maltsberger and Buie (1974). They describe in some detail the patterns of defense which therapists mobilize in one or other degree to deal with the distressing experience of hatred elicited by the patient. Such countertransference hatred may be repressed, so that the therapist may find himself daydreaming or thinking of something else besides what is happening in the therapy. He may find himself restless, or bored, or drowsy, etc. Or the countertransference hatred may be turned against the therapist's own self, and he will begin to be filled with doubts as to his capacity to help the patient and may begin to experience feelings of guilt, degradation, a sense of inadequacy, helplessness, and hopelessness. He may even begin to experience suicidal impulses and feelings himself. This masochistic and penitential stance on the part of the therapist further impedes any possibility of the patient's unleashing directly aggressive impulses on him and only intensifies the suicidal dynamics.

A third way of dealing with countertransference hatred is to turn it into its opposite. Under these circumstances the therapist finds himself preoccupied with trying to be helpful to the patient, being excessively solicitous about his welfare and well-being. There is an anxious urgency to cure and to help. The therapist may be drawn into an excessive fear of the patient's suicide and resort to the excessive use of restrictions and even hospitalization when it may not be called for. Such a therapist cannot take the necessary reasonable risks in dealing with the patient's suicidal impulses and rage and in general cannot help the patient with these feelings.

Countertransference hatred can also be projected as a form of counterprojection to the patient's own projective operations. This would take the form "I do not wish to kill you, you wish to kill yourself." This would be accompanied by a subjective sense of anxious dread, and the therapist may become preoccupied with fantasies about the patient's potential for acting out the suicidal impulses. The therapist thus often tends to feel helpless and has considerable difficulty in deciding how much of his concern comes from the objective possibilities and how much from his own hostile feelings. There are a number of risks which operate in this position. The therapist may act out his countertransference hostility by imposing unnecessary external controls (e.g., hospitalization) which will serve to disrupt the therapeutic alliance and possibly provoke suicidal acting-out. The therapist may also, out of fear of such acting-out, run the risk of failing to recognize the objective need for protective measures. Or he may run the risk of giving up the case and rejecting the patient, feeling that the situation is hopeless when in fact it is not so. The projection may also at times take the form "I do not wish to kill you, you wish to kill me." This may be in part a recognition of the patient's own hatred, but it runs the risk of the therapist's responding to his sense of frustration with further rejection and abandonment of the patient.

And, lastly, the therapist may resort to distortion and denial of the objective reality as a way of validating the countertransference hatred. Under these circumstances the therapist tends to devalue the patient and is prepared to see him as a hopeless, bad, or dangerous case. He may then interrupt the therapy prematurely, transfer the patient to other therapists or other institutions, or discharge him prematurely from the protective environment of the hospital.

Maltsberger and Buie conclude their discussion of these patterns of defensive interaction of the dynamics of countertransference hate by making the following observations which resonate strongly with the previous comments of Winnicott's regarding the hatred of the mother for her child:

> The best protection from antitherapeutic acting-out is the ability to keep such impulses in consciousness. Full protection, however, requires that the therapist also gain comfort with his countertransference hate through the process of acknowledging it, bearing it, and putting it into perspective. Guilt then has no place in his feelings, and the therapist is free to exert a conscious loving self-restraint, in which he places a higher value on the emotional growth of his patient than he does on his own tension discharge. At the proper time, the patient can be shown how his behavior leads to an attacking or rejecting response in others. In other words, the suicidal patient's repetition compulsion to involve others in relationships of malice and ultimately to be rejected is signalled in the therapist's countertransference hate. In time it can be interpreted and worked at, provided the therapist, by accepting, tolerating, and containing the countertransference, does not join the patient in repeating his past instead of remembering it [Maltsberger & Buie, 1974, p. 632].

It is in this fashion, then, however difficult it may be to attain, that the therapist undermines the dynamics of the victim-introject and avoids the reinforcement of the false-self configuration. To the extent that the therapist can acknowledge, tolerate, and deal with his own countertransference hatred, he fails to be victimized by the patient's inherently aggressive and destructive impulses. This provides a way open for the patient to begin to deal with those earlier issues of identification with the aggressor which have been previously thwarted and which in regressive fashion have been impeded by the persistence and domination of the victim-introject.

THE MORALITY OF SUICIDE

I should like to close this discussion with a few comments on the morality of suicide. The more enlightened and humanistic view of suicide developed by contemporary moral theologians can be reflected in the following comments by Bernard Häring (1973):

> Suicide does not usually arise from such reflections, but is an act of despair. The suicide is often a person who has failed to find the meaning of his life, or realizes that, at the moment in question, he has muddled it and made it senseless through a whole series of frivolous decisions and complications. A short-circuit has plunged his life into total darkness from which he fails to emerge. At the decisive moment,

the basic instinct of self-preservation yields to tremendous frustration.

One who consciously and freely destroys his life is nothing other than a craven deserter who refuses to face the trials of the pilgrim. We must be mindful, however, that in spite of the extreme gravity of the sin of suicide, taken objectively, we may not and cannot judge the subjective guilt of anyone who has wrought self-destruction or attempted to do so. In many cases there is an acute mental disturbance. In fact, in justice and charity, we always assume this to be the case, where those whom we know to have led a virtuous life have committed suicide in a moment of deep depression or under terrible compulsion [Häring, 1973, p. 70].

Using this statement as a frame of reference, I should like to propose some questions by way of an extension of our previous discussion of the dynamics of suicide. I do not feel that I am in the position to pass judgment on such complex moral issues, but it seems to me that the process of moral investigation must take into account as much as is known about the suicidal process, and carry on the reflection within the broader contexts of the meaning of human existence and the place of death in human experience.

Attitudes toward suicide must be fitted into the context of changing attitudes toward the morality of death. At one extreme there are the radical libertarians such as Thomas Szasz (cited in Weisman, 1971, p. 222), who reproaches the psychiatric profession for defining suicide as though it were a product of mental disease. To him suicide, however misguided or misdirected, is still the product of the human will engaged in the pursuit of freedom. Consequently, the prevention of the suicidal act is an infringement of personal rights and freedoms. Such an unqualified assertion of the right to suicide stands at a diametric pole to the more conservatively Catholic view that man is only the steward of his own life the proprietorship of which belongs to God alone.

A more moderate view is that proposed by Weisman (1971, 1972) that man has a right to an "appropriate death"; that is, that just as man has the right to live his own life, so also has he the right to die his own death. In this sense the suicidal death is not an appropriate death. Too often in the context of suicidal intention, there is an inherent ambivalence, as we have seen, which directs the individual toward life as well as toward death. The choice of a suicidal resolution is the equivalent of opting for the wrong means to the right end. A suicidal patient thus mistakes the termination of a false self for an effective cure for his malady. Unfortunately it is a cure with lethal side-effects.

I personally should not care to hedge any bets on this matter. I think it is safe to say that the incidence of so-called rational suicide in which one reasonably and rationally decides upon his own death is rare indeed.

It possibly can be found in those instances of terminal and tormenting illness in which the individual can be thought of as reasonably exercising his decision and his right to an appropriate death, a death congruent with his right to die in dignity and in peace. I do not think that this is a violation of the authentic Christian teaching on suffering, although I am sure there is room here for theological argument.

It should be recognized, nonetheless, that attitudes toward death in general are changing. Inroads are being made on those attitudes which dictate the preservation of human life at all costs and by whatever technological resources are available. Increasing recognition is given to the inherent rights of patients to die in dignity and reasonable comfort. It seems to me that there is reasonable room within this context for a decision about the termination of one's own life which is both appropriate and rational. It seems inconceivable to me that a Christian morality would in such a context prescribe intolerable suffering and the inhumane degradation of the human person. It seems to me that there is a real distinction between the abuse of freedom in the suicidal act, and the determination in reasonable terms of an appropriate and dignified death as an exercise of authentic human self-determination.

Our major concern within the pastoral context, however, is that we place ourselves on the side of life, on the side of creative vitality, and that we enable the individual caught within the maelstrom of suicidal impulses and distress to hang onto the slender threads of life in the hope of some better resolution of his turmoil. If we hearken back for a moment to Häring's comments, which I take to be representative of some of the best of contemporary moral thinking on the subject of suicide, the question I should pose is one which I think gives rise to painful and distressing reflection. If we recall the discussion of the dynamics of hate and particularly of countertransference hate in the suicidal process, the question which can be raised is whether or not the moral stance does not serve to reinforce the condemnation of the suicidal person and in certain ways to express and reinforce elements of countertransference hate.

In terms of the dynamics of countertransference hate, this can only serve to intensify the suicidal dynamics and impede any efforts of the pastoral counselor to intervene effectively and to help the suicidal victim through the suicidal crisis. Rather I should wonder whether in such statements one does not hear an implicit devaluation and rejection of the suicidal victim as well as an implicit, if not often explicit, demand for conformity to a prior set of moral expectations and prescriptions. I do not suggest that this is always the case, but I should like to raise the question in a serious manner as to whether or not such attitudes, which fail utterly to respond to the core of the suicidal dynamics which

I have been discussing here, do not in fact serve to reinforce and collaborate in the maintenance and intensification of the false-self dynamics which play such a central role in the vicissitudes of suicidal intention and behavior.

REFERENCES

Appelbaum, S. A. The problem-solving aspect of suicide. *Journal of Projective Techniques and Personality Assessment*, 1963, 27, 259–268.
Beall, L. The dynamics of suicide: A review of the literature, 1897–1965. *Bulletin of Suicidology*, March 1969, pp. 2–16.
Beck, A. T. & Greenberg, R. The nosology of suicidal phenomena: Past and future perspectives. *Bulletin of Suicidology*, Fall 1971, pp. 10–17.
Bibring, E. The mechanism of depression. In P. Greenacre (Ed.), *Affect disorders*. New York: Wiley, 1953. Pp. 13–48.
Douglas, J. *The social meanings of suicide*. Princeton: Princeton University Press, 1968.
Durkheim, E. *Suicide: A study in sociology*. Glencoe, Ind.: Free Press, 1951. (Originally published, 1897.)
Farberow, N. L. & Shneidman, E. S. *The cry for help*. New York: McGraw-Hill, 1961.
Freud, A. *The ego and the mechanisms of defence*. New York: International Universities Press, 1936.
Freud, S. Mourning and melancholia. In J. Strachey (Ed.), *Standard edition of the works of Sigmund Freud* (Vol. 14). London: Hogarth, 1957. Pp. 237–258. (Originally published, 1917).
Guntrip, H. *Schizoid phenomena, object relations and the self*. New York: International Universities Press, 1969.
Häring, B. (c.ss.r.). *Medical ethics*. Notre Dame, Ind.: Fides, 1973.
Hendrick, I. Suicide as wish-fulfillment. *Psychiatric Quarterly*, 1940, 14, 30–42.
Litman, R. W. Sigmund Freud on suicide. In E. S. Shneidman (Ed.), *Essays in self-destruction*. New York: Science House, 1967. Pp. 324–344.
Mahler, M. S. On the significance of the normal separation–individuation phase. In M. Schur (Ed.), *Drives, affects, behaviour* (Vol. 2). New York: International Universities Press, 1965.
Maltsberger, J. T. & Buie, D. H. Countertransference hate in the treatment of suicidal patients. *Archives of General Psychiatry*, 1974, 30, 625–633.
Meissner, W. W. (s.j.). *The paranoid process*. New York: Aronson, 1975.
Menninger, K. A. *Man against himself*. New York: Harcourt, Brace, 1938.
Orgel, S. Fusion with the victim and suicide. *International Journal of Psychoanalysis*, 1974, 55, 531–538.
Shneidman, E. S. Suicide, lethality, and the psychological autopsy. In E. S. Shneidman & M. Ortega (Eds.), *Aspects of depression*. Boston: Little, Brown, 1969. Pp. 225–250.
Shneidman, E. S. *Deaths of man*. New York: Quadrangle, 1973.
Shneidman, E. S. Suicide. In A. M. Freedman, H. I. Kaplan, & B. J. Sadock (Eds.), *Comprehensive textbook of psychiatry* (2nd ed.). Baltimore: Williams & Wilkins, 1975. Pp. 1774–1785.
Shneidman, E. S. & Farberow, N. L. Clues to suicide. In E. S. Shneidman & N. L. Farberow (Eds.), *Clues to suicide*. New York: McGraw-Hill, 1957. Pp. 3–11.

Sifneos, P. E. Manipulative suicide. *Psychiatric Quarterly,* 1966, *40,* 525–537.

Stengel, E. *Suicide and attempted suicide.* Baltimore: Penguin, 1964.

Stengel, E. Attempted suicides. In H. Resnick (Ed.), *Suicidal behaviors: Diagnosis and management.* Boston: Little, Brown, 1968. Pp. 171–189.

Weisman, A. D. Is suicide a disease? *Life-threatening behavior,* 1971, *1,* 219–231.

Weisman, A. D. *On dying and denying: A psychiatric study of terminality.* New York: Behavioral Publications, 1972.

Winnicott, D. W. *Collected papers: Through paediatrics to psycho-analysis.* New York: Basic Books, 1958.

Winnicott, D. W. Ego distortion in terms of true and false self. In D. W. Winnicott (Ed.), *The maturational processes and the facilitating environment.* New York: International Universities Press, 1965. Pp. 140–152. (Originally published, 1960).

Winnicott, D. W. *Playing and reality.* New York: Basic Books, 1971.

Zilboorg, G. Suicide among civilized and primitive races. *American Journal of Psychiatry,* 1936, *92,* 1347–1369.

Zilboorg, G. Considerations on suicide with particular reference to that of the young. *American Journal of Orthopsychiatry,* 1937, *7,* 15–31.

VIII
LIFE BEYOND DEATH:
EXPECTATIONS OF IMMORTALITY

Immortality in Humanistic Perspective

PAUL KURTZ

Paul Kurtz is the Editor of The Humanist, *the publication of the American Humanist Association. He is also Professor of Philosophy at the State University of New York at Buffalo. In 1973 he published in* The Humanist *the four-page Humanist Manifesto II. Subsequently he issued in a separate volume* Humanist Manifestos I and II, *which he had written and which had been signed by more than 275 distinguished authors and leaders throughout the world. He is the author of* Decision and the condition of man *(1965), and of* Fullness of life *(1974); co-author of* A current appraisal of the behavioral sciences *(1964); and editor of* The humanist alternative: Some definitions of humanism *(1973). Educated at New York University and Columbia University, Dr. Kurtz has taught at Vassar College, Trinity College, Union College, The New School for Social Research, and The City University of New York.*

If there is any issue which divides secular humanism and theism, it is the question of the immortality of the soul. For humanism is primarily an ethical philosophy, and it emphasizes creating an authentic life here and now rather than worrying about the blessings of immortality. This has been the case for humanisms from classical Greece and Rome, through the Renaissance and the emergence of modern science, down to the present day.

The humanist critique of the immortality thesis is threefold: (*a*) it

255

finds the concepts of "soul" and "immortality" ambiguous, often unintelligible; (b) it can discover no adequate evidence to support claims
of immortality; and (c) it finds the so-called ethical case for immortality—the view that life or morality would have no ultimate meaning
without eternal salvation—to be self-contradictory.

I shall address myself to all three objections, but concentrate on the
last because of its psychological implications.

DIFFICULTY WITH THE CONCEPT OF SOUL

The first objection to immortality, and one which is very popular today,
is logical: i.e., the lack of a clear meaning of the term "soul." Classical
philosophers from Aristotle to Hume and Kant have raised serious
doubts about the idea of a substantial "soul" separable from the body.
Many contemporary philosophers have raised more fundamental issues.
John Dewey (1925/1958) and the behaviorists, for example, rejected
"mentalism" and the existence of a mind–body dualism as empirically
unwarranted. In recent years, Gilbert Ryle (1949), Antony Flew
(1964), Peter Geach (1969), and other linguistic philosophers have
found the concept of "soul" logically unintelligible. Ryle thinks that we
do not make any sense when we talk about "the ghost in the machine,"
and he indicts Descartes and all who hold a dualistic or Platonic view
for committing a category mistake. The human being is an integrated
unity; what we call the "soul" or the "mind" is simply a functional aspect of the physical organism interacting in an environment. If this is
the case, it is difficult to know what it means to say that something called
the "soul" survives the dissolution of the body. The notions of a "dis-
embodied self," "astral projection," or "non-material soul" are based
upon abstractions and reification and a puzzling misuse of language.

Hume (1739/1961) pointed out the problem of personal identity.
One may ask, Is there an independent substantial soul or self underlying
my particular experiences? If my body no longer exists after my death,
and if I survive it, will I remember my past self? Will I continue to have
feelings, in my limbs, genitalia, and stomach, after they are gone? How
can I have memory if I have no brain to store experiences? Will it be
I who survive or only a pale shadow? Antony Flew (1955–56) asks,
Can I witness my own funeral? As my corpse lies in its coffin, can I,
lurking in limbo, view it? Does it make any sense to say that I can see
if I do not have any eyes to receive impressions or a nervous system to
record them?

Thus many contemporary philosophers find all sorts of linguistic con-
fusions about what it means to say that an alleged "soul" survives the

body. The basic issue for them does not involve the factual claim as to whether the soul exists so much as it involves the logical puzzle about the definition of the concept itself.

This being the case, perhaps the only sense which can be given to immortality is to say with St. Paul (Rm 6:5; 1 Co 15:42–58) that at some point in the future there will be the physical resurrection of the body, including the soul. This would avoid the issue of whether the soul is separable from the body, and we merely need to say that some divine being will in the future ensure the survival of the whole human being.

INSUFFICIENT EVIDENCE FOR IMMORTALITY

To say that avoids the meaning muddle, perhaps, but it raises still more serious questions: What is the *evidence* for the claim that I can survive my death in some form, whether as a separated soul or as a being resurrected in one piece? For in truth the claim is being made that people who die come back at some time immediately after death in some form or another, or that in some remote future they will be resurrected in some new guise.

Many cultures and many individuals have no doubt believed that something survives the physical death of the body; some have thought it to be part of the world soul, others to involve personal identity. Yet, as far as I can tell, we have been unable, in the entire history of the race, to find sufficient evidence for these assertions. Here I am asking for objectively confirmable evidence. I am talking, not about hearsay, old wives' tales, unsubstantiated reports by the uninformed or the credulous, but about hard data. What would constitute a test: the ability of the dead to communicate with or influence the living, or to have some observable effects in our experience?

I do not find the so-called data of psychical research in any sense conclusive. One might claim that we cannot decisively confirm the fact *until* we die and find out; but if so we ought at least to suspend judgment until then—though it would seem to me that the preponderance of evidence from all we know about human and animal death as a biochemical phenomenon suggests the high improbability of the claim. Of course, some things do survive death in one form or another. There is the physical body, which decomposes, and the skeleton, which, under proper conditions, can be preserved for thousands of years. It may even be that much the same as urine is expelled from the bladder at death some discharged energy remains—hovers, haunts, or whatever else—for a period of time until the body is fully decomposed; but whether this discharged energy has personal consciousness or identifiable experiences is another matter. We would have to submit this to careful scientific measurement, and nothing like it has even been sufficiently verified. But if we could verify it, it would be a momentous breakthrough.

A further problem in survival concerns the time scale. Perhaps energy patterns survive only for a brief time, say ten minutes, a few years, at most a few centuries (like the alleged ghosts haunting English castles until they are released). But the claim for *eternal* survival is unverified and indeed virtually unverifiable. For how would we go about proving that something which survives death (a soul or something else) will *never* become extinct? In any case, it would be difficult for us to date any souls which we might uncover—even if we should manage to discover an incorporeal-like carbon 14 technique for dating surviving souls. If we were to uncover a very old soul, it would not necessarily be eternal. It would have had a beginning (unless one believed in reincarnation and prior existence) and most likely would not have preceded the origin of the human species in time. But, more importantly, we would have no guarantee that it would continue into the infinite future, unless by eternity we mean beyond the categories of time altogether. Such claims would at best be in the form of postulates or conjectures, not proofs. Thus the immortality thesis needs to be tested. It never has been.

It is of course apparent that belief in immortality transcends the categories of science. Of this we are reminded by immortalists. Belief in immortality is coherent only in terms of a larger metaphysical–theological system. The immortality thesis is part of a theist's general picture of the universe (which, incidentally, humanists also reject). But the point is that neither can the immortality thesis by itself be made intelligible nor has it been independently confirmed by a sufficient body of evidential data.

Thus in the last analysis belief in immortality is an article of faith, an inference from a broader view of a divine universe, an item of revealed, not of philosophical or scientific, truth. It involves faith that a divine being will in some way enable us to survive death so that we can exist throughout eternity, and/or that the divine being will resurrect the physical body and soul at some point in the future and reinstitute personal identity and memory, even though there has been a lapse of several thousand years in which worms have picked clean our brains, marrow, and flesh.

It is paradoxical that the doctrine of immortality is not peripheral to belief in the existence of God, and that it cannot simply be deduced from it. On the contrary. Belief in immortality is itself, in my judgment, central to belief in God and perhaps is even its chief psychological ground. What I mean by this is that the doctrine of immortality is not so much a descriptive claim about an alleged reality as a normative ideal which is postulated to satisfy an apparent psychological hunger. Indeed, the God-idea takes on meaning dramatically because man faces death, and God is introduced along with immortality as a solution to the problem of death. This is the existential–psychological argument for immortality which many earlier humanists such as James (1896) and Santayana (1905/1954) defended, and it involves at least three factors: (*a*) a response to the problem of death, an attempt to explain away death and overcome it; (*b*) some moral direction and focus for what otherwise seems to be a random and purposeless universe; and (*c*) psychological sustenance and support, giving courage and consolation to the bereaved and fearful, helping individuals to overcome anxiety, forlornness, loneliness, and alienation.

In this ethically pragmatic sense, the doctrine of immortality is interpreted not so much as providing normative guidance as making a descriptive truth claim about the world. To say that one believes *in* immortality as an ideal is not the same as saying *that* immortality of the soul necessarily exists in some literal sense.

CRITIQUE OF THE ETHICAL CASE FOR IMMORTALITY

Now, the secular humanist critique of the ethical argument for immortality is equally decisive, and on several grounds.

The humanist considers the doctrine of immortality to be basically morbid. It grows out of both fear of and fascination with death. The immortalist is fixated on death, yet he endeavors to deny its awesome reality. For the humanist this means a failure to face the finality of death and an inability to see life for what it really is. This attitude has all the earmarks of pathology, for one is out of touch with cognitive reality. It is an immature and unhealthy attitude, a form of wish fulfillment. It exacerbates an illusion in order to soothe the heart aching over the loss of a loved one, or to avoid accepting one's own impending termination. Death is a source of profound dread. There is an unwillingness to let go. One hopes for an opening to another life in which all one's unfulfilled aspirations are realized in fantasy. The primitive mind, not possessed of science, invested death and dying with mystery and awe. Death was unfathomable: the source of brutal suffering. The eschatological myth enables one to transcend the pain.

This mood of denial expresses a basic lack of courage to persist in the face of adversity. Immortality is a symbol of our agony before an unyielding universe, and our hope in some future deliverance. It is the tenacious refusal meaningfully to confront the brute finitude of our existence, the contingent and precarious, often tragic, character of human life. Those who believe in immortality trust that somehow someone will

260   LIFE BEYOND DEATH

help us out of our misery, however long we have to wait; that this vale of tears can be overcome; and that in the end, despite our present suffering, we will have a reunion with our departed loved ones. Immortality offers therapeutic solace; and in the past history of humankind, when disease was so prevalent and the life span so brief for the mass of people, it seems to have made some sense. Life was often "nasty, brutish, and short," and three score and ten was not the norm but the exception. Thus, the immortality myth functioned as a tranquilizer. Today, other attitudes dominate. Armed with modern medicine and technology, we can combat death in other ways. We attempt to prolong life and to make it abundant and enjoyable as far as we can—that is, until the dying process sets in, at which point many are willing to hasten its onslaught if there is great pain, and to accept the inevitable with stoic resignation.

Thus *existential courage* is a key humanist virtue. So essential is courage to life that Kierkegaard (1941) and Tillich (1952) have recognized that without it life becomes difficult and unendurable. For the humanist it is not enough to muster the courage to be—merely to survive in the face of adversity—he must cultivate the courage to *become*. In other words, the problem of life for each of us is constantly to remake our lives in spite of all the forces in nature and society which seek to overwhelm us.

For the humanist, the immortalist has forsaken full moral responsibility. For he is unwilling to take destiny—as far as he can—into his own hands. There are surely some limits on human achievement and independence. We need to make a distinction between the things within our power and those without, as the Stoics recognized; but of those within our power we have the great challenge to make the most of life, to re-create and redefine it, to extend the parameters of human power.

Here freedom of human choice and action is pivotal. The humanist is not content with simply discovering and accepting the universe for what it is, in an act of piety; he seeks to change it. Nor is the task of life to discover what our nature is (whether God-given or not) and to realize it, but to *exceed* our nature. Thus man invents culture. We are post-Prometheans, stealing fire and the arts of civilization from the gods, continually tempting and recasting our fate.

A key objection which the humanist levels against those who cling to the doctrine of immortality is the undermining of ethics. One is unable to be fully responsible for himself and others, creative, independent, resourceful, free, if he believes that morality has its source outside man. The reflective, deliberative, probing moral conscience is too vital to be deferred to the transcendent. We are responsible for what we are, and out of our compassion for other human beings and our desire to see that justice be done, we can achieve the good life here and now if we work hard enough to bring it about. It is not fear of damnation, or hope of salvation, which moves us to seek a better world for ourselves and our fellow humans, but a genuine moral concern without regard for reward or punishment. Morality is autonomous.

For the humanist, the believer has committed a grievous mistake: he has wasted much of his life. Life is short, yet it is rich with possibilities, to be lived fully with gusto and exhuberance. Those who are morbid, fearful, timid, unwilling to seize destiny, are often unable to experience fully the bountiful joys of life.

All too often those who believe in immortality are full of foreboding, laden with excessive guilt and a sense of sin. All too often the pleasures of the body, sex, and love are repressed, and a variety of opportunities for creative enjoyment denied. Many such individuals have thus bartered their souls for a future life; but if the promissory note is unfulfilled—as I think it is—then this means that they have in part lost important values in life. In retrospect their lives have often seemed barren; they have missed many chances, failed to do what they really wanted; they could not seize the opportunities because of a deep-seated fear and trembling.

Many theists believe that without immortality life would have no meaning. How puzzling and contradictory to argue so. It is a confession of their own limitations as persons. For it is, the humanist contends, precisely the doctrine of immortality which impoverishes meaning. If you believe in immortality, then nothing here counts. It is all preparatory; life is but a waiting-room for transcendent eternity. As such, this life is not fully cultivated, for only the next one counts. But life *per se* has no meaning, except what we choose to invest it with. All it presents are opportunities, which we may choose to capitalize upon, or to let pass by. The humanist says: Life is full of plans and dreams, hopes and aspirations, joy and sorrow, tragedy and achievement. It is too beautiful to be squandered in idle chanting for a morrow which may never come.

PERHAPS THE ILLUSION OF IMMORTALITY IS NEEDED

One question often raised is, Even if immortality is unintelligible or unproven, can we live without illusions? Perhaps we all have our illusions, and as soon as we outlive one myth another appears to beguile us with false temptation. The Marxist utopia-vision, for example, seems to be replacing theism as the dominant world religion. But is this inevitable? Perhaps illusion is the result of a tendency toward gullibility engrained in human nature (for the humanist, this is the doctrine of original sin). But some illusions are perhaps less false and less harmful than others.

Humanists no doubt have their own illusions; the belief that we can solve life's major problems by the use of intelligence and achieve a good life of happiness may very well be one of them. Yet some illusions become irrelevant to human interests and social needs. And the immortality myth, as powerful as it once was in the history of culture—in an era of poverty and disease—is now no longer fully relevant to human concerns.

Does belief in immortality satisfy a necessary psychological need? I doubt it. For I have found that people without belief in immortality often fear death much less and are able to accept it and face it with greater equanimity than those with such a belief. Such unbelieving individuals are able to develop some confidence in their capacities as humans, an independent moral conscience, a commitment to social justice or species welfare on this planet; and for them life can be pregnant with meaning. Such individuals need not be without "transcendent" ideals, ideals larger than they. They may believe in contributing to a better world and be deeply concerned about the future of humankind; and they have a sense of obligation to that ideal which is as powerful as any which the immortalist possesses.

The humanists may indeed believe in "immortality" in a metaphorical sense: we are devoted to the good works which will outlast us. But we strive for them not because we will be rewarded or punished by posterity, but because while we live we find our ideal goals worthwhile. We are moved now to do what we think will contribute to a better future for our children's children's children, even though we may never live to see it. We need nothing beyond that to support or sustain our moral dedication. Thus a thoroughgoing humanism does not need a doctrine of immortality to give life meaning or to provide morality with a foundation. Both meaning and morality grow out of lived experience, and commitment to the good life, as we define it, can be as powerful a stimulus to life as the traditional immortalist doctrine.

REFERENCES

Dewey, J. *Experience and nature.* New York: Dover, 1958. (Originally published, 1925.)

Flew, A. G. N. Can a man witness his own funeral? *Hibbert Journal,* 1955–56, *54,* 242–250.

Flew, A. G. N. (Ed.). *Body, mind and death.* New York: Macmillan, 1964.

Geach, P. *God and the soul.* New York: Schocken, 1969.

Hume, D. *A treatise of human nature.* New York: Doubleday, 1961. (Originally published, 1739).

James, W. *The will to believe.* New York: Longmans Green, 1896.
Kierkegaard, S. A. *Concluding unscientific postscript.* Princeton: Princeton University Press, 1941.
Ryle, G. *The concert mind.* London: Hutchinson, 1949.
Santayana, G. Reason in religion. In G. Santayana (Ed.), *The life of reason.* New York: Scribner, 1954. Pp. 179–297. (Originally published, 1905).
Tillich, P. *The courage to be.* New Haven: Yale University Press, 1952.

Immortality in Oriental Religious Perspective

ROBERT E. KENNEDY, S.J.

Father Robert E. Kennedy, S.J. received his A.B. degree from Fordham University in 1957. He spent the years from 1958 to 1966 in Japan where, after a two-year study of Japanese, he taught English in Rokko High School in Kobe, Japan. Father Kennedy completed his theological studies at Sophia University, Tokyo, in 1966, and then went on to earn a Ph.D. degree from the University of Ottawa in 1970, and an S.T.D. from Saint Paul's University, Ottawa, in 1972. In 1971, Father Kennedy joined the faculty of Saint Peter's College in Jersey City, where he is currently Assistant Professor of Theology. He is also an Associate Member of the Columbia University Faculty Seminar on Oriental Thought and Religion.

My topic, "Immortality in Oriental Religious Perspective," is broad indeed. To do it justice I should have to discuss the origin and growth, the beliefs and practices, of the Hindu, Jaina, Taoist, Buddhist, and Confucian traditions, all of which are older and at least as complex as our own Christian tradition. And so, in the space allotted, I should like to discuss the theme of immortality in only one of these traditions, the Buddhist.

I have chosen Buddhism primarily because, unlike Hinduism which is a loose but convenient term for a variety of faiths in a specific geographical area, Buddhism is the first world religion known to history.

264

It bridged all the differences which existed in the unique and creative cultures of India, Indochina, Indonesia, China, Tibet, Korea, and Japan, and is the most representative religion of Asia.

More specifically, I have chosen Mahāyāna Buddhism because it is of the highest philosophical importance and forms the basis of the beliefs held by the great majority of Asian Buddhists.

And within Mahāyāna Buddhism I have chosen Japanese Buddhism. Japan has been called a storehouse of east Asian culture since the influences pouring in from Asia over the centuries took root there and survived and can be most easily studied.

Finally, for my discussion of immortality within Japanese Buddhism, I have chosen to compare two schools of thought, Zen Buddhism and Shin or Pure Land Buddhism. I believe this comparison will be interesting because the two schools represent the two extreme positions concerning the means to immortality. Does man save himself through self-power, or is he saved by the merciful power of another (Schumann, 1974, p. 167)?

I believe the comparison of these two schools will be of further interest because they are championed by two of the most original and creative figures in the entire history of Buddhism: self-power as taught by the fiery Zen Master Hakuin, and other-power as taught by the gentle lover of the common man, Shinran.

Before I begin the comparison of these two Buddhist schools and teachers concerning immortality, there are two points which it will be helpful to recall. First, immortality, or as it is more usually called, salvation or nirvana, has several different shades of meaning. D. T. Suzuki writes that most Christian missionaries and scholars have ignored this fact and found it advantageous to stereotype one meaning which is clear to them and to use it as a key to interpret other meanings. With this warning in mind I shall dwell upon two of the most important meanings of immortality: the active nirvana of the liberated man of this world, and the static nirvana which occurs after death (Suzuki, 1963, pp. 342–343; cf. Drummond, 1974, pp. 113–127).

Finally, in order to understand the teaching of Hakuin and Shinran on immortality/salvation in their proper perspective, I believe it is necessary to study as well their teaching on the nature of man and the nature of faith.

THE ZEN MASTER HAKUIN

Let us begin then with Zen. Briefly stated, Zen is a religion with a unique method of body–mind training the aim of which is enlightenment or self-realization. Grounded in the highest teachings of the Buddha, it was brought from India to China, where the methods characteristic of Zen were evolved, and then through the centuries further elaborated in Japan (Kapleau, 1972, p. xv).

Zen is a discipline of strenuous self-effort. In order to experience the personal "awakening" which Zen calls enlightenment, the devotee must possess an overriding faith in his own abilities and in the direction of his master. His only task in seeking enlightenment is to "see into his own nature," and once this enlightenment is experienced, he should continually deepen it through the practice of meditation. This un-remitting discipline is a lifelong commitment for both student and master (Ingram, 1973, p. 187; cf. Enomiya-Lassalle, 1967, pp. 11–46).

The high point in the development of Japanese Zen was achieved in the Ashikaga period before 1400. With the beginning of the Muromachi period there was a growing secularization of Japanese culture which drew Zen in its wake. The temples, which had been centers of spiritual renewal and had radiated throughout the nation a refined and religious culture, degenerated into spiritual stagnation and moral decadence. A Zen master of this period writes:

> In bygone days, those whose hearts were awakened to faith entered the monasteries, but now they all forsake the temples. A careful ob-server readily discovers that the bonzes are ignorant. They find that to sit in meditation is burdensome. . . . They enjoy outward frills and spend much time in the decoration of their cushions. With much satis-faction they glory in their monastic robes, and though they wear the habits of a monk they are only laymen in disguise [Dumoulin, 1963, p. 185].

The one man most responsible for the revival of Zen was the great Master Hakuin who lived in the Tokugawa period from 1686 to 1769. His greatness and influence can be recognized in the fact that all present-day masters of his school trace themselves to him (Yampolsky, 1971, p. 1; Shaw, 1963, p. 14).

In his teaching, Hakuin, of course, stressed that immortality could be achieved only by the self-power of Zen, and he simultaneously sharply criticized the other-power tradition of the Pure Land school. Hakuin's criticism can be summarized in the three points which we have already mentioned: the nature of man, the nature of faith, and the nature of salvation.

Nature of Man

First, let us look at the nature of man. According to the Pure Land teaching, man is now living in the most degenerate stage of the historical process and is no longer capable of saving himself by means of the traditional Buddhist discipline and meditation. His physical, moral, and spiritual capacities are totally corrupted, and he is unable to save himself. He must rely on Amida Buddha to save him.

Hakuin would have none of this theory. He claimed that Pure Land teaching made it too easy for men not to take the responsibility for their own lives which he believed was so necessary for enlightenment. It too easily led men to grovel in self-pity and to make excuses for their failures. In short, for Hakuin this theory was simply too pessimistic about the nature of man (Ingram, 1973, p. 190).

In his appendix to his *Orategama Zokushū* he writes:

> The teaching of the Pure Land is for people of inferior or mediocre capacity. . . . men of the Zen school have superior capacities [Yampolsky, 1971, p. 153].

and in *Orategama III* he writes:

> Such people are known as destroyers and wasters of their own selves. . . . They are like fish in water who lament the fact that because of their natures they are unable to see the water, or like birds flying through the air who regret the fact that to see the air is an unattainable desire. . . . Is there anything more lamentable? [Yampolsky, 1971, pp. 99–100].

Nature of Faith

Concerning the nature of faith, Hakuin said that there is no Buddha independent of man's mind who will come to save him. Rather, salvation can be achieved only by each one's "seeing into his own nature," an experience which leads to the discovery that a man's "mind" and the "Buddha mind" are the same "mind." In other words, man discovers the Buddha nature which is within himself and all things. This realization is one of difficult self-effort requiring a man's total energy (Ingram, 1973, pp. 194–195).

Hakuin judged the Pure Land teaching to be dualistic to the core because it takes the ego into account and attaches itself to form. He believed that, at most, Pure Land teaching was merely a kind of "psychological-egolessness" in which a man devotes himself in total surrender to a Buddha conceived as objective to him and upon whom he is completely dependent for salvation. Hakuin writes:

> But non-ego is of two kinds. Take the man who is weak in body and mind. He is afraid of everybody, destroys his vitality, and is influenced by all external circumstances. He does not get angry even when reviled; he does not even care if he is rejected but always stupidly plods along

getting nowhere. . . . Such a person is a torn rice bag, bloated from gorging himself on the swill of swine, an ignorant, blind fool. This does not represent true non-ego. How much less so for the man who, relying on the power of the calling of Buddha's name, hopes to "go" to the Pure Land and thus to "become" a Buddha! What is this "going"? What is this "becoming"? If this isn't ego, then what is it [Yampolsky, 1971, 134–135]?

For Hakuin, therefore, all dualism, psychological and ontological, must be overcome. There is no ego, there is no Pure Land, and there is no Buddha "apart from a man's mind."

Nature of Salvation

Hakuin's teaching on the nature of salvation flows from his understanding of non-duality. The term he uses for salvation is ōjō, a word which literally means "death." In the Pure Land sense, however, ōjō means death to the phenomenal world of birth, suffering, and death, and rebirth after death. It is that kind of death which causes rebirth into the Pure Land (Ingram, 1973, p. 191).

Hakuin asks:

What is salvation (ōjō)? It all comes down to one thing—seeing into your own nature. . . . Is it not the innate self-nature with which you yourself are endowed, standing bright before your very eyes? If you have not seen into your own nature it will not be easy for you to see this Pure Land, yet nowadays those who practice the Pure Land teaching recite the name daily a thousand times, ten thousand times, a million times, but not one of them has determined the greater matter of salvation [Yampolsky, 1971, p. 127].

Hakuin's phrase, seeing into one's own nature, refers to the experience of enlightenment, the sudden, decisive somersault of the mind in which the empirical ego is so submerged that there is no longer "I" and "it" but only pure existence or "is-ness." The Zen novice is constantly told that the self does not exist and that its illusion should be annihilated; at the moment of enlightenment he actually experiences this as true. Though the Christian would insist that this is a misinterpretation of experience, the enlightened man has no doubt that the experience itself is one of absolute unity (Johnston, 1970, p. 20).

Hakuin writes of enlightenment:

Then the state of mind in which you are not a man, not a woman; you do not see birth, you do not see death; and in which there is only vast emptiness, where the distinction between night and day is not seen and the body and mind are lost, will many times be present. . . .

The brilliance of the real form of True Reality will appear before your eyes and a great joy . . . will burst upon you without your having sought it [Yampolsky, 1971, p. 161].

This, then, is salvation for Hakuin. He pities those who believe that Buddha is in the Pure Land and that by calling on his name they will somehow leap through space and after death be reborn in the Pure Land. Rather, for Hakuin, the Pure Land is our innate self-nature, standing bright and clear before our very eyes (Yampolsky, 1971, pp. 127–128).

It might be worthwhile at this point to mention that contemporary Zen authors still follow the lead of Hakuin in his understanding of non-duality and of salvation. Masao Abe, a disciple of the Zen Master Hisamatsu, and the Charles and May Gooding Lecturer in Buddhism at the University of Chicago in 1969, writes that life and death are not two separate things. We are not moving from life to death, but living and at the same time dying. At every moment we are all life and all death. Our life is not a movement toward death but a continual living–dying, a paradoxical and dynamic oneness of life and death.

Abe questions our usual idea of immortality and wonders whether it is not the extension of life beyond death. And if so, does this idea not presuppose life as the basis upon which one overcomes death? But then, he asks, how can one overcome death in terms of life when life and death are inseparable?

This living–dying in Zen thought is neither process nor continuity. If we realize that we are living and dying at every moment, then we will grasp that this existence itself is death. It is not death as opposed to life, but death in an absolute sense. It is called the Great Death, and at the very moment when one dies the Great Death, Great Life manifests itself, and one can live our living–dying existence without becoming shackled by it.

Our living–dying existence is without beginning, end, or history. It has no center. Accordingly, every point in history is a center. One lives Great Life through Great Death realized at every moment.

Zen, therefore, does not look for immortality of the soul, or for eternal life in the Pure Land or in the kingdom of God, but for a salvation in which living–dying itself is completely abolished. Today does not bring us closer to eternity; today, at this moment, eternity is completely manifesting itself (Abe, 1969; Kapleau, 1971, p. xiii).

SHINRAN

Until now we have been considering the Zen understanding of im-mortality according to Hakuin and his sharp criticism of the Pure Land hope of immortality. But it is time to let the Pure Land tradition speak for itself, especially since in all probability Hakuin possessed little, if any, knowledge of the teaching of Shinran in whom the whole Pure Land tradition came to fulfillment (Ingram, 1973, p. 186).

Shinran lived from 1173 to 1262. As a young man Shinran was a monk who found himself unsuited for the rigorous practices of meditation in the Tendai system. After years of serious study and sincere attempts to achieve some degree of spiritual enlightenment, he experienced only frustration and inner conflict. In 1207 he left the priesthood, married, and began to raise a family. He said of himself at this period that he was neither priest nor layman. He had lost his priestly privileges and he was a layman without experience. The hard practical problems he faced in establishing a new life for himself and his family gave him a deep sensitivity to the struggles of the common man which he had not known when he lived apart as a monk (Bloom, 1973, pp. x–xii; Suzuki, 1970, pp. 13–15).

It was in this context, then, that Shinran came to realize that the common man could attain Buddhist ideals in his ordinary life, and the guidance he gave to his disciples can be summarized under our familiar three divisions: the nature of man, the nature of faith, and the nature of salvation.

Nature of Man

Shinran's understanding of the nature of man was shaped by his own sensitive personality. He was so deeply aware of his own spiritual condition as a passion-ridden man incapable of purifying his spirit sufficiently to gain enlightenment that he concluded that no practice whatever would assure him of salvation. He called himself Gutoku, a foolish bald-headed old man, to signify his debased condition, and wrote:

> how sad that I . . . am drowned in the broad sea of lust and wander confusedly in the great mountain of fame. . . . O how shameful, pitiful! [*Shinshū Shōgyō Zenshō*, 1953, p. 80].

and again:

> This sad self who is unable to distinguish right from wrong, good from evil, who has no claim even for little deeds of love and compassion, and yet who is willing just for name and gain to pose as teacher (how shameful!) [Suzuki, 1949, p. 140; cf. Bloom, 1973, p. 29].

Shinran described existence as life within the burning house, the most prominent Buddhist description of sentient life. It seemed to him that believers performed a good act and thought this good act was the basis of their salvation, but to Shinran they were wrong for two reasons. On the one hand, they failed to take their depravity as human beings seriously, and, on the other, they did not recognize their complete need for Buddha's assistance in attaining salvation.

The cure for this mistake was to shift their attention from practices to attitude. He taught that it was entirely impossible for a person to do a good act. Whatever appeared to be good on the surface was really evil because it was ultimately intended to redound to his own benefit. No practice whatever could bring salvation. It was spawned in the web of passion and self-seeking: namely, to save himself.

Shinran's view of man was remarkable in two ways. First, he made the act of faith itself the essential basis of salvation and, secondly, he proclaimed that the act of faith was made not by the individual but by the Buddha in that person (Bloom, 1973, pp. 30–31).

And this takes us to our second point, Shinran's understanding of the nature of faith.

Nature of Faith

Faith, for Shinran, can be looked at from two standpoints: from that of the individual and from that of Amida Buddha. From the standpoint of the individual, faith means the absence of doubt. And the doubt referred to is not intellectual doubt but religious doubt by which the individual would doubt Buddha's help and would strive for salvation on his own. Doubt, for Shinran, is synonymous with the self-power attitude which he regarded as a most serious sin because it hurt both the sinners and the just. Sinners would be tempted to despair, and the just would be tempted to self-righteousness which, for Shinran, was the grand illusion.

His exaltation of faith as the only way to salvation opened a new understanding of life. If men could accept themselves for what they are, passion-ridden and incapable of changing their nature, they could reject all legalistic and meritorious practices such as monasticism, celibacy, and abstention from certain food and drink. There was no need to appease Buddhas or win them over to gain salvation. It is freely offered by Amida Buddha, and we need only to trust him.

From the standpoint of Amida Buddha, however, faith is identified with the Buddha nature. Buddha nature refers to those qualities of the Buddha, his mercy and compassion, which operate to bring men to enlightenment. It refers essentially to the Buddha's work of salvation which is realized in the faith which is aroused in men. Faith then is a reflection of the very spirit of Buddha; it is the fruit of his loving aspiration and not at all a contrivance of man's.

But if man need not strive to win his salvation, why is he encouraged to repeat the name of Amida Buddha? Shinran followed the Pure Land tradition in its teaching that the name Amida Buddha causes salvation as it mysteriously arouses faith in sentient beings when they hear it and become aware of Buddha's compassion. The basis for salvation, however, was not the finite repetition by individuals for their own salvation, but the universal repetition of the name by all the Buddhas heard by the beings in the universe. Shinran kept the practice of recitation but altered its meaning.

An important point must be made here about the meaning of these words. Buddhists often describe concepts as pointing to transcendental realities, but they do not mean that the concepts exist outside the mind of the believers as a self-subsisting, objective reality. It is just the way men usually express their thoughts that what is discovered within their consciousness is spoken of as apparently existing objectively (Matsunaga & Matsunaga, 1972, p. vii).

Hence, for Shinran, the name of Amida Buddha is not a metaphysical entity or some objective existence somewhere in the world; nor is Amida Buddha himself an objective existence located in the universe. The name spoken by the Buddha and heard by the faithful is the name heard upon the lips of men; it is the teaching in which Buddha is praised, and it is the whole tradition of compassion of Pure Land itself.

But if there is no objective Buddha to cause salvation, who causes it? Shinran answered this question in a famous work, *Jinenhōnishō,* written in his eighty-sixth year, which is regarded as the highest point of his philosophical and religious interpretation of existence. No one causes salvation. Rather, everything is caused to be; things are as they are. The individual is caused to be saved through the operation of nature, which is the working of Amida Buddha and symbolized by his vow to save all men (Suzuki, 1949, pp. 15–16).

Behind this terminology we can see the Buddhist and Taoist view of nature as the undefinable, formless reality which is the ground of finite beings. Shinran is saying that man and nature are one. He expresses this truth symbolically by saying that man and Buddha are one. The foundation for this view is that Buddha's compassionate activity is correlative with the working of nature. What is emphasized here is nature's apparently effortless activity in which nothing is done but everything happens. Therefore for man to do what is natural, what is uncontrived and spontaneous, has the highest religious significance (Bloom, 1973, pp. 39–70).

Nature of Salvation

Shinran's understanding of salvation flows naturally from his vision of faith. In spite of the way he adapted his message to the grasp of the common man, Shinran rejected the ideal of meeting Buddha at the moment of death. The Pure Land is a symbol for the ultimate goal of nirvana, and its mythological presentation is not to be taken literally. Rather, the terms Pure Land, nirvana, enlightenment, and extinction, all refer to spiritual freedom, to the end of all illusions, and to the ultimate union with the Buddha—or with reality itself. Shinran taught not only that religion is altruistic, but that reality at its very heart operates to bring beings to enlightenment in spite of their sin and ignorance. Compassion is the essence of religion because it is the essence of reality; it confronts us at every turn in compassionate individuals, in the tradition of the Pure Land, and in the name of Amida Buddha, which consoles us and arouses us to compassion for others.

Although such an insight might appear to some as the death of true religion, if religion is defined as a striving for personal salvation, in reality it means the birth of true religion in which the gratification of the ego is set aside for gratitude and praise of the divinity and for compassion toward all men.

Rebirth in the Pure Land for Shinran will be completed after death, but he absolutely rejects the possibility of rebirth for one who is attached to the Pure Land for its pleasures or who wants it primarily for himself. Rebirth means this world, now, and it means the labor to seek the salvation of all beings. The gate of entrance into the Pure Land is the gate of entrance into this defiled world. The desire for enlightenment is the desire to save all men (Bloom, 1973, pp. 82–85).

CONCLUSION

Nature of Man

In temperament and personality, Hakuin and Shinran were worlds apart. Hakuin was strong, confident, successful, an admirer of the warrior class, an ascetic who buried a number of his novices behind his temple, a master sought out by the spiritual elite who had the capacity and leisure to embark on a long program of personal development.

Shinran was sensitive, overcome by a sense of personal sin and inadequacy, fresh from failure in monastic life, beset with family problems, a layman who found hope for the ordinary man who had neither the time nor the ability to pursue the Holy Path.

Their teachings followed their personalities. Hakuin taught self-effort and insisted that all men were utterly alone in the quest for salvation. He pitied the torn rice bag of a man who was not self-reliant. Shinran taught that self-effort was the grand illusion; he wept for joy and gratitude that he was saved, and he died with the name of Amida Buddha on his lips.

Nature of Faith

The fundamental basis for Hakuin's criticism of the Pure Land tradition was that it was dualistic with its teaching of "going" to the Pure Land and "becoming" a Buddha.

But Shinran never meant these expressions to be taken literally. Far from holding a dualist position, he accused self-power devotees of putting Buddha away from them and then trying to achieve union with him by their own efforts. Such a mind set, to his way of thinking, could never produce intimacy or trust or overcome our fundamental human anxiety.

I believe that the solution to this problem lies in the character of the disagreements among Buddhist schools. Both Hakuin and Shinran agree with the basic Buddhist teaching of non-duality and non-ego. But all Buddhists recognize that the symbols used by the Buddha as means to encourage devotion in people of various abilities and inclinations had only relative truth. The disagreements among the Buddhists, therefore, though vocal and at times violent, were not as rigidly conceived as in Western religions (Bloom, 1973, p. 80; cf. Glasenapp, 1966, p. 130).

Nature of Salvation

In our introduction we divided salvation into that of the liberated man in this life, and that which occurs after death. Both Hakuin and Shinran stress that salvation is now, but they conceive it differently.

For Hakuin, the great matter of salvation is to see into our own nature, to come to enlightenment or self-realization, to experience in psychic upheaval our unity with all that is—and always is.

For Shinran, to be reborn is to have, not enlightenment, but faith. Faith is the cause of Buddhahood and faith is perfected now, though it will be realized in enlightenment immediately upon the passing of the individual in death.

And after death? Hakuin and Shinran would agree that in post-mortal nirvana the liberated one loses all individuality at the moment of death and so becomes untraceable. He has discarded everything which is not pure absolute, and since the terms of individuality no longer apply to him, it is impossible to say anything about "him." To speak of the liberated one in static nirvana means to speak of the Absolute. And to speak of the Absolute is like trying to trap a scent with one's hands (Schumann, 1974, p. 140).

REFERENCES

Abe, M. "Life and death" and "good and evil" in Zen. *Criterion,* 1969. Reprint, unpaged.

Bloom, A. *Shinran's gospel of pure grace.* Tucson: The University of Arizona Press, 1973.

Drummond, R. *Gantama the Buddha: An essay in religious understanding.* Grand Rapids, Mich.: Eerdmans, 1974.

Dumoulin, H. *A history of Zen Buddhism.* Boston: Beacon, 1963.

Enomiya-Lassalle, H. *Zen: Way to enlightenment.* Montreal: Palm, 1967.

Glasenapp, H. von. *Buddhism: A non-theistic religion.* New York: Braziller, 1966.

Ingram, P. The Zen critique of Pure Land Buddhism. *Journal of the American Academy of Religion,* 1973, *41–42,* 184–200.

Johnston, W. *The still point.* New York: Fordham University Press, 1970.

Kapleau, P. *The wheel of death.* New York: Harper & Row, 1971.

Kapleau, P. *The three pillars of Zen.* Boston: Beacon, 1972.

Matsunaga, D., & Matsunaga, A. *The Buddhist concept of hell.* New York: Philosophical Library, 1972.

Schumann, H. *Buddhism: An outline of its teachings and schools.* Wheaton, Ill.: Theosophical Publishing House, 1974.

Shaw, R. *The embossed tea kettle orategama and other works of Hakuin Zenji.* London: Allen & Unwin, 1963.

Shinshū Shōgyō Zenshō (Vol. 2). Kyōto: Kōkyō Shoin, 1953.

Suzuki, D. *Miscellany on the Shin teaching of Buddhism.* Kyōto: Shinshu Otaniha Shumusho, 1949.

Suzuki, D. *Outlines of Mahayana Buddhism.* New York: Schocken Books, 1963.

Suzuki, D. *Shin Buddhism.* New York: Harper & Row, 1970.

Yampolsky, P. *The Zen Master Hakuin.* New York: Columbia University Press, 1971.

Immortality in Judaeo-Christian Perspective

LEO J. O'DONOVAN, S.J.

Father Leo J. O'Donovan, S.J., earned an A.B. degree from Georgetown University in 1956, a Ph.L. from Fordham University in 1961, an S.T.L. from Woodstock College in 1967, and the Dr. theol. degree from the University of Münster in 1971. He has been both a Fulbright Scholar and a Danforth Fellow, and is currently Associate Professor of Systematic Theology at the Weston School of Theology, Cambridge, Massachusetts. Father O'Donovan is a member of the American Academy of Religion, the Catholic Theological Society of America, and the Society for Religion in Higher Education. He is a contributor of philo-sophical and theological articles to such journals as Theological Studies, Religion in Life, The Personalist, Continuum, The American Ecclesiastical Review, *and* Philosophical Studies.

In the Kunsthistorisches Museum in Vienna hangs a painting by Albrecht Dürer which has been called the last great homage to Roman Catholic Christianity painted by a German before the Reformation. Executed in 1511 by the same man who two years before the turn of the sixteenth century had completed his monumental woodcut series of the Apocalypse, this Vienna masterpiece presents the thronged saints of Christianity gathered in heavenly rank to adore God the Father as He holds the crucified Christ and the Spirit hovers among hosts of angels above. (Called, therefore, the *Adoration of the Trinity*, the work is nevertheless more commonly known as the All Saints Altarpiece.) No one can pause enchanted before this marvel without comparing it to a jewel. Few viewers today, perhaps, will advert to the end of a religious era thus signalized by the great son of Nuremberg who was to become so ardent a disciple of Martin Luther. Many more admirers, I suspect, after basking in the painterly glory of the work, will come finally to muse over the age-old conception of heaven which it enshrines.

God as Father, Son, and Spirit are majestically centered in the upper half of the arched format, skillfully separated from the saints by a delicate nimbus of clouds. Beneath the Trinity in two resplendent groups kneel the Blessed Virgin Mary with other Christian women and John the Baptist leading the Old Testament prophets, kings, and faithful. Beneath them are the company of the blessed, popes and emperors together with the humblest layfolk, kneeling in various postures in a graceful arc which completes the heavenly scene as it floats above a typical Dürer landscape in which he has depicted himself in miniature next to the painting's inscription. The colors are radiant, dazzlingly heightened by the gold decoration of many of the costumes. No shadow darkens the scene or clouds the upturned gaze of the saints. It is surely a unique vision of celestial beatitude.

And not really so very different, I think, from the image of heaven which many Christians still retain. When I asked a friend recently how she tried to teach her eighth graders something about heaven, she said that she asked them to draw a sketch of what they thought it might be like. Almost all the children proved to imagine a scene basically similar to Dürer's. And almost all found it very hard to answer their teacher's question whether they liked the idea. All the usual difficulties arose: Does anything at all happen there? Do we just look at God and, maybe, at each other? How can that really be happy? Doesn't it just mean that everything is "over"? And what happens to the world?

More sophisticated questions about Christian faith in eternal life scarcely reach more deeply than these first puzzlements shared by children and adults. We come indeed to ask what justification there may be for our hopes that life may finally triumph over death. We question the apparent self-centeredness of the doctrine, its egoism about personal salvation and seeming neglect of human solidarity. We recognize that many men and women who deny immortality or eternal life nevertheless contribute far more to life in the present world than we ourselves do. In terms of what William James called cash value (James, 1968, p. 360), we wonder what difference a promised heaven might make for the conduct of our present life. Is it a prize guaranteed only to those who live their lives well, its loss the final retribution for those who seem to enjoy in life a fortune they do not deserve? Do all such conceptions of a reward after life not tend in fact to devalue the seriousness of issues faced during life? In short, is Christianity's heaven not fundamentally a distraction from our own ordinary earth where alone we have the gift of life to cherish and foster?

There is no doubting the seriousness of these questions, and the still more pervasive quandary of the Christian imagination today with respect to the notions of immortality, eternal life, heaven. There is no doubt in my own mind, either, that we must be able to discover in the revelation of God's promises to us an ethical import for such ideas. Not that it is simply an ethical directive, nor even a doctrine which has an ethical component. I should say, rather, that faith in eternal life is the trusting conviction that God, the author and sustainer of all life, can marvelously bring life to fulfillment even through what is its apparently final defeat in death. This great reality for which we hope, then, casts a transforming light on everything we think and do.

The promise and event of gracious union with the redeeming creator of life is the prime reality of faith's encounter—which then gives rise, in interplay with the varied life experiences of that faith, to a doctrine and ethics of faith. God's self-revelation must always be recognized as initiating the response of a loving and hopeful community of faith which indeed bears itself differently in the world from the way it would if it had heard no such invitation. But it is because of God's approach to us that we approach our own lives and deaths differently. Moving toward a final union with God in the company of His saints is a different kind of motion, and a world destined for that absolute future is a different kind of world from one in which time is gathered up only by time itself and which is productive only of further versions of itself. In this way of understanding the matter, to speak of God's heaven is faith's way of speaking of His earth in the mode of its fulfillment, and Christians do not hope for eternal life apart from their genuine hopes for the present (Rahner, 1966a; Schillebeeckx, 1969).

IMMORTALITY AND RESURRECTION

I shall try to develop the above-mentioned viewpoint throughout this paper, but it will be helpful first of all to recall how various have been the forms in which humanity has claimed a final triumph of life over death. In terms of our deepest longings we all have intimations of what most of the ideas have meant. We need, in fact, to ask ourselves which of them are most like our own.

Do we too, for instance, look for immortality in fame or in offspring— a sort of social immortality in the community? Or with so many others before us do we think in terms of the continuation of life after death, or perhaps of the restoration of life? Do we tend to imagine an afterlife, a future life, an eternal life? Reawakening after death or reanimation after death has been a common conception, as has personal survival of death or personal revival after death. People have often spoken, and still do, of the other side of life or of entry into the other world. Great religious thinkers have puzzled over the notions of the transmigration of souls or their reincarnation. There has been the expectation of a final retribution for the justices and injustices of this life. For some, immortality or resurrection has expressed this central hope; for others, it has been heaven and the vision of God. Hebrew notions which are transferred from the Old Testament into the New include assumption, ascension, or exaltation from this life to another. Paul writes stirringly of a new creation, the creation of a new being. Several biblical passages look confidently for the establishment of a new heaven and a new earth. And the central theme of the preaching of Jesus of Nazareth seems clearly to have been repentance and conversion to the gospel of the coming kingdom of God.

To be historically realistic in this matter, we should recognize that however much these various conceptions may have in common, they are indeed different conceptions, with different historical origins and different practical consequences (Brandon, 1967). Just over twenty years ago, in a famous Ingersoll Lecture at Harvard University, Oscar Cullmann drew a sharp distinction between two of these views in an effort to recall for his audience the true hope of Christian faith. Cullmann argued for a radical incompatibility between the Greek concept of the immortality of the soul and the early Christian resurrection faith. Vividly he contrasted Socrates' serene and peaceful death, in striking harmony with his own teaching, with the fearful death of Jesus, with its agony and abandonment. For the Christian, Cullmann maintained, death is overcome, not by a quality inherent in the soul, but only by the event of Christ's passion followed by His resurrection. Jesus Himself

> can conquer death only by actually dying. . . . Whoever wants to conquer death must die; he must really cease to live—not simply live on as an immortal soul, but die in body and soul, lose life itself, the most precious good which God has given us. . . . Furthermore, if life is to issue out of so genuine a death as this, a new divine act of creation is necessary [Cullmann, 1965, p. 18].

Recalling that the typically Jewish and Christian approaches to creation and anthropology exclude all final dualism of body and soul, Cullmann thus emphasized that we must die in both bodily and spiritual dimensions before God can raise us up by a new creative act to everlasting life. Compared with the negative conception that the soul cannot finally die, resurrection would thus be a far more positive idea: "the whole man, who has really died, is recalled to life by a new act of creation by God" (Cullmann, 1965, p. 19).

Cullmann admitted an analogy between the Greek and Christian doctrines: Christians living in the Holy Spirit, which is the power of the resurrection, conduct themselves with a peace like Socrates'; everyone who has died in Christ waits with Him for the final manifestation of God's glory in "the resurrection of the whole creation" (Cullman, 1965, p. 44). But Cullman's stress was on the radical distinction between the two points of view, and a good many authors have subscribed to his contention (e.g., Cadbury, 1965; Blenkinsopp, 1970). Serious difficulties have attached to it from the beginning, however, both exegetically, with regard to the adequacy of the range of texts Cullmann employed, and systematically, with regard to his conception of death and time.

Today, in fact, the contrast seems more forced than ever. Scripture scholars continue to agree that a hope for some victory of life over death developed only late in the history of Israel. But there was early preparation for this later development through Israel's central confession of the covenant faithfulness and creative power of Yahweh. According to André-Marie Dubarle (1970), we should recognize two principal themes which bear on the eventual emergence of explicit belief in resurrection: one was faith in the justice of Yahweh and in just retribution, the other was an obscure presentiment and hope of living with God forever. A number of authors read Psalms 16, 49, and 73 as implying more than survival after death through one's children and the memory of humanity. For Dahood and others, these psalms long for a happiness and a friendship with God which may be truly lasting, although they may also be understood simply to anticipate a state restored after present danger (Dahood, 1966; Schnackenburg, 1968).

In a central chapter of Hosea the prophet speaks of Israel's revival or restoration as a nation before God (Ho 6:1–2). Ezekiel expands on this theme in the awesome vision of the valley of the dry bones (Ezk 37:1–14), a scene symbolizing the restoration of the Israelite nation (Ezk 37:11–14), but also preparing a language which could later be applied to resurrection in a more limited and proper sense. It is hard to say whether chapters 25 and 26 of Isaiah wish to describe an eternal happiness or simply a lasting peace. Even if, for reasons of modesty and caution, a metaphorical interpretation is preferred, the text is open to later use in unequivocally eschatological statements about God's final renewal of His creation—as is clear when we compare Isaiah 25:7–8 with Revelation 21:4. Much the same reserve coupled with openness seems advisable when reading the frequently discussed expression of Job 19:25.

It was only with the advent of apocalyptic literature in the second century B.C. that explicit belief in a blessed future life was announced. For many years now scholars have taken for granted this general background for the preaching of Jesus and the formation of the early Christion resurrection faith. Indeed, recent study has shown that between 200 B.C. and A.D. 100 there was far more variety and range of conception in the resurrection faith of pre-Christian Judaism than had been thought by Cullmann and those who agree with him in radically contrasting immortality and resurrection.

Investigating the various beliefs in resurrection, immortality, and eternal life expressed in intertestamental Jewish theology, George Nickelsburg (1972) has found them to group under three major traditional forms. In the first of these the tradition is based on the story of a righteous man who is unjustly accused of breaking the law and then condemned to death. Rescued at the last moment, however, he is cleared of the false charges and promoted to a high position. In the Book of Wisdom (2:4–5), this story seems to have been expanded through use of the exaltation theme from the Fourth Suffering Servant Song in Isaiah 52–53. The central figure is then portrayed as actually dying but being given a place among the saints. As Nickelsburg reads Wisdom, it speaks, not of resurrection, but of immortality, and suggests that "the righteous man does not really die, but only seems to die"; thus "immortality is the state in virtue of which [his] vindication, authentication and exaltation take place" (Nickelsburg, 1972, pp. 68, 88).

Elements of the story of the vindication of the righteous man and of the accompanying judgment of the wicked are found in the famous chapter 12 of Daniel, in which we have Scripture's first unequivocal affirmation of belief in the resurrection. But Nickelsburg sees this tradition still more clearly in 2 Maccabees 6–7, where first the aged Eleazar and then the seven brothers die as martyrs full of confidence in the Lord who has given them life in the first place. Bodily resurrection is affirmed in 2 Maccabees as God's way of saving the brothers from the gruesome death inflicted on them by Antiochus. Noteworthy is the passage's concern for individual salvation of the virtuous rather than for any form of universal resurrection. Nickelsburg also sees resurrection functioning here, as in a number of other key texts, not merely as individual vindication, but as "a restoration of community" (Nickelsburg, 1972, p. 107).

A second tradition is based on the form of a judgment scene and has its most important expression in chapter 12 of Daniel. After recounting the persecution of Antiochus, the author gives assurance of the tyrant's end, an ensuing time of great distress, and the deliverance of the people: "Of those who lie sleeping in the dust of the earth many will awake, some to everlasting life, some to shame and everlasting disgrace" (Dn 12:2). Resurrection is thus conceived as a response to the desperate situation of the readers of the book. "For Daniel," comments Nickelsburg, "resurrection is a *means* by which both the righteous and the wicked dead are enabled to receive their respective vindication or condemnation"; it has "a judicial function" and is "the prelude to the reconstitution of the nation" (Nickelsburg, 1972, pp. 19, 23).

Found similarly in such contemporary works as the Assumption of Moses and the Book of Jubilees, this form of the judgment scene gradually became generalized: the Testament of Judah 25 uses it as a customary way of describing the end of time, while in 4 Ezra 7 it serves as a dispensation of final reward and punishment rather than as the adjudication of particular injustices. In both the latter cases resurrection of the body has become a formal element within the scene as a whole rather than something hoped for in response to the particular fate of individuals such as those involved in Daniel 12 and 2 Maccabees 7. Three writings are also noted by Nickelsburg as generalizing so far as to assert a *universal* judgment and resurrection: 4 Ezra 7 and Sibylline Oracles IV, both dating from the end of the first century A.D., and Testament of Benjamin 10, the date of which remains uncertain.

Two-way theology is the third form used by intertestamental Jewish theology to speak of the final relation between life and death. With its roots in Old Testament covenant theology, this tradition speaks of eternal life and eternal death as the fundamental alternatives posed to human beings. Those who walk in God's way already share somehow in eternal life, while those who do not are proceeding toward that death which truly deserves the name.

Less concerned with either persecution or chronology, this tradition emphasizes the ultimate consequences of human action and harmonizes easily with ideas of immortality of the soul (as in Wisdom) or immediate assumption into eternal life (as in the Testament of Asher). Chronological death is not viewed so much as a problem, and hence resurrection is less likely to emerge as a solution to it. Nevertheless, the streams of two-way theology and resurrection theology did tend to converge to the extent that the latter became a generalized eschatology rather than a response to more particular circumstances and became thus primarily concerned, like the theology of the two ways, with final reward or punishment for human life in general.

Together with James Barr (1961), Martin Hengel (1968), and other recent writers, Nickelsburg thus warns us against overdrawing the contrast between Greek and Hebrew thought. Rather than any uniform conception of resurrection we find wide-ranging expressions of Jewish hope for some form of life after death. It is paradoxical that the question becomes at once more common and more complex than one might suppose. Should we really expect it to be otherwise if, as John J. Collins has suggested, the central concern of the literature we have been considering is a hope for the transcendence of death (Collins, 1974)? Is it really God's plan for human life to transcend death not only socially but individually? I think we must recognize that this question, in various forms, is also a central one for the New Testament.

THE RISEN LORD: PAUL

Of the twenty-seven books in the New Testament all but seven (2 Thessalonians, Titus, Philemon, 3 John, 2 Peter, Jude, and James) refer explicitly to the resurrection. Still more striking is the close connection regularly made between the resurrection of Jesus and the resurrection of those who are one with him through faith. Paul's expression in Romans 8:11 is typical: "If the Spirit of Him who raised Jesus from the dead dwells in you, He who raised Christ Jesus from the dead will give life to your mortal bodies also through His Spirit which dwells in you" (cf. 1 Co 6:14; 2 Co 4:14; Jn 5:21). Christ is thus "the first fruits of those who have fallen asleep [i.e., died]" (1 Co 15:20), "the first born from the dead" (Col 1:18). He lives eternally with His Father in the Spirit—not simply for His own sake, but rather so that all may be brought to life in Him (1 Co 15:22). This implication of the mutual resurrection of Christ and the Christian is particularly clear in Paul, who made it a special theme, but it may be seen in the background of the other New Testament authors as well (cf. Durrwell, 1960).

Paul is our earliest witness to the resurrection of Jesus and to the faith of the early community in Him. I follow the classical Christian view that what Paul announces again and again, from his First Letter to the Thessalonians onward (1 Th 4:13ff.), is the living presence of His personal Lord Jesus Christ with God and within the lives of believers. Rudolf Bultmann's view is well known:

> If the event of Easter Day is in any sense an historical event additional to the cross, it is nothing else than the rise of faith in the risen Lord, since it was this faith which led to the apostolic preaching [Bultmann, 1961, p. 42].

The Lord rises, so to speak, in the faith which rises in a community with radically new hope for life. But it is surely not objectivistic to look for the ground of such faith in the Lord Himself. What really happens to Jesus through His death, I would say, is what gives His disciples ground for faith, so that their preaching is based not simply on an Easter experience but on the Lord of Easter. Christian faith centers indeed in Easter, but it is the crucified Lord Himself who Easters in us—and who is the hope of the entire creation to rise one day to full life.

From another perspective, in an effort to emphasize that "resurrection" is a statement of faith communicating the disciples' profound and never wholly recoverable experience of the risen Lord, Willi Marxsen (1970) interprets the resurrection as meaning that in spite of the death of Jesus His cause continues in human history. But this justifiable concern to emphasize the relativity of any reflective expression of experience still minimizes the termination of our cognitive expressions in reality itself. There are indeed a variety of ways of expressing our faith in the risen Lord, His living entry into our lives, and the transformation He promises them in days to come. But such confessions refer to the Lord Himself as well as to His effect on human life. Our liturgical as well as our private prayer seems to me also to be irreplaceable evidence of the faith that, not only the teaching and concerns of Jesus, but Jesus Himself, lives beyond death as the final promise of all our lives. We not only believe in Jesus as He offers all human history the same call to a life of faith which He offered to His first hearers. We also believe and hope in Him as having personally transcended death and being personally and finally present to God—for the sake of a renewed humanity. All His miracles reveal the transforming power of His Father in our lives, but His personal resurrection, as Karl Rahner has written, is "the fundamental miracle which anchors our faith" (Rahner, 1963, p. 35).

St. Paul, of course, provides us in 1 Corinthians 15 not only with his own most extended reflection on the resurrection but also with a summary of the earliest Easter traditions. His compendium of these traditions in verses 3–8 speaks of the death of Christ "for our sins"; His burial; His being raised "on the third day in accordance with the scriptures"; and then a series of appearances concluding with one to Paul himself.

In the discussion which follows, Paul responds to the Corinthian gnostics who held that resurrection was already achieved for those who believe and should not be hoped for in the future. In vigorous terms Paul exclaims: "If Christ has not been raised, your faith is futile and you are still in your sins. . . . If for this life only we have hoped in Christ, we are of all men most to be pitied" (1 Co 15:17, 19). He continues his commentary on the significance of the resurrection by suggesting stages for the resurrection of the dead: first Christ is made alive as "first fruits"; then at His parousia those who are His own will be made alive; at the end will come the final reign of His Father and the destruction of death, "the last enemy" (1 Co 15:22–28). The last section of the chapter (1 Co 15:35–38) presents Paul's reflections on the risen body. Here he warns his readers against idle curiosity, but also seems to assure them that in spite of all discontinuity between our bodily existence at present and the one promised us by God in resurrection, a real relation remains between the two, what is now and what is to come. This interpretation of a much discussed passage depends on seeing a consistency of viewpoint between 1 Corinthians 15:35ff. and such other Pauline expressions as Philemon 3:21. Being with Christ in this life should be understood to tend toward its fulfillment through death in the transformation of the body of our lowliness into the body of His glory. What is asserted is thus a meaning for the temporal experience of death but also for its real eternal term—final union with Christ (Gnilka, 1968, pp. 76–93).

THE RISEN CHRIST IN THE GOSPELS

Paul hands on the primitive testimony that Christ is risen. He does not give accounts of how it happened or descriptions of what the various appearances he records were like. This seems to be typical of the earliest proclamation and preaching in the Church, and it is also the approach we find in Mark, our earliest Gospel. Reginald Fuller (1971) is among those who hold that in the original form of Mark the resurrection is proclaimed rather than narrated, while the resurrection appearances are likewise listed but not narrated. He agrees with Ulrich Wilckens' suggestion that Mark probably presupposes several visions of the risen Lord by the disciples in Galilee (Wilckens, 1968, pp. 73–74). After the visions the disciples would have returned to Jerusalem, heard Mary Magdalene's story of visiting the empty tomb, and would have seen this report as confirming their own belief that God had raised Jesus from the grave. Fuller concludes persuasively that

> the disciples received Mary's report not as the origin and cause of their Easter faith, but as a vehicle for the proclamation of the Easter faith which they already had as a result of the appearances. It is as such that the Christian historian and the community of faith can accept the report of the empty tomb today [Fuller, 1971, p. 70].

At a later stage of New Testament composition, in the Gospel of Matthew, the risen Jesus is presented explicitly as appearing to the eleven disciples in Galilee (Mt 28:16–20). Though there is evidence of Matthew's editorial work in the introduction to this scene, it seems clear that Matthew is basing himself on an early tradition of Christ's mani-festation to His disciples in Galilee. The evangelist may open the way here to fuller narration of resurrection appearances, but his primary stress is to close his Gospel with a clear indication of how the Church's mission flows from its risen Lord. Possessed of all authority, Jesus sends His disciples to evangelize the entire earth; they are to have full confi-dence in His abiding presence through all of time.

Similarly, in the Epilogue to the Gospel of John (Jn 21), Jesus appears to His disciples in Galilee (Jn 21:1–14). A variety of features in the account indicate that this narrative is based on an earlier tradi-tion than the Jerusalem appearances in John 20 (Brown, 1970, Vol. 2, pp. 1085ff.). The catch of fish at Jesus' command, inevitably recalling Luke 5:4–11, clearly has reference to the missionary charge of the disciples. In the further verses of the chapter, which continue the pre-vious story (Jn 21:15–19), the Lord's threefold question to Peter corresponds to Peter's earlier denial and establishes his charge of pastoral care in the community. In its emphasis on the foundation of the Church in the love of the risen Lord and of those who belong to Him, these verses point back to the earliest resurrection traditions.

As we have just mentioned, the appearances of Jesus in John 20 are described as occurring not in Galilee but in Jerusalem. So also are those in Luke. In these latest developments of the resurrection tradition, the primary appearances have been transferred to Jerusalem. Luke 24 records first the discovery of the empty tomb by the women and then (at least in some Western manuscripts) by Peter.

In his story of the two disciples on the road to Emmaus (Lk 24:13–35), Luke portrays as vividly as can be imagined the disillusioned grief of the disciples after the crucifixion. Jesus joins the two disciples on their earthly way but is presented as a mysteriously divine figure whom they recognize finally only in the breaking of the bread. Luke also describes another appearance to the disciples in Jerusalem which he connects with the Emmaus story by three verses (24:33–35) which significantly include a simple proclamation of the resurrection and a reference to an appearance to Peter, thus indicating that by the time of Luke's Gospel the two traditions of resurrection proclamation and appearance accounts are firmly joined together (Fuller, 1971, pp. 111ff.). In the Jerusalem appearance as well as in the one on the way to Emmaus, Luke stresses the fulfillment of Scripture and the Messiah's way through suffering to glory. By locating the chapter's events around Jerusalem he once more employs his geographical–theological perspec-tive according to which the gospel will spread in the Book of Acts from Jerusalem to all the earth. It is thus Luke who first presents developed stories of Jesus' resurrection appearances to disciples: at Emmaus, to the eleven and others in Jerusalem, and in the farewell scene at the time of the ascension as it is described in Acts 1:6–11.

Luke's attention to the gift of the Spirit through the resurrection of Jesus (Lk 24:49; Ac 1:4–5, 8) is one of several features linking him to chapter 20 of John's Gospel, though it seems most likely that the two Gospels are not so much dependent on one another as on other common traditions. In John 20, the profiled narration of the discovery of the empty tomb first by Mary Magdalene and then by Peter and the Beloved Disciple gives that event more weight than it receives anywhere else in the New Testament. Following these verses are three other appearances of Jesus narrated in the chapter: to Mary Magdalene (Jn 20:11–18), to the eleven disciples on that same day (Jn 20:19–23), and a week later to the disciples with Thomas among them (Jn 20:24–29). In spite of the fact that these latest traditions of resurrection faith describe the risen Lord in far more materialistic terms than do the earlier traditions, it is above all significant that they climax with Thomas' direct confession to the crucified and risen Jesus: "My Lord and my God!" (Jn 20:28).

THE GOSPEL OF LIFE

In view of the central role which Jesus' resurrection plays in New Testament faith, it may seem surprising that our information on His own teaching about resurrection is so sparse. Only in the test question put to Him by the Sadducees with their story of seven brothers married successively to a single woman do we have a formal discussion of resurrection (Mk 12:18–27; Mt 22:23–33; Lk 20:27–40). To be sure, Jesus defends the idea against the Sadducees' doubts. But the discussion is limited by the insincerity of the question addressed to Him. The primary intention of His answer is not so much to elaborate a doctrine of resurrection as to correct the Sadducees' reading of Scripture and their blindness to God's sovereignty (Mk 12:24). Still, the suggestion behind the story seems clearly to be a confession of God's transformative power over death, a power which promises a new form of life to those who are faithful to Him. The assertion that the God of Israel is a God not of the dead but of the living (Mk 12:27) bases itself on His promise to the patriarchs, but it should be understood in an open rather than an exclusive sense. As C. F. Evans comments:

> the emphasis in the reply is on God, on his power to transform the human creature for a non-temporal existence, and on his continuing existence as the God of the living, which guarantees the continuing existence of men. . . . What men are is what they are to God, and what they are to him will be made evident by his creative action [Evans, 1970, p. 34].

In Luke's parable of the rich fool (Lk 12:16–21) it is the hope not explicitly of resurrection but of lasting treasure before God which gives force to Jesus' words. In the story of the rich young man (Mk 10:17–22; Mt 19:16–22; Lk 18:18–23) Jesus is asked about inheriting eternal life and answers finally in terms of the way His questioner may hope to have treasure in heaven. In the discussion with the disciples which follows the story in each of the Synoptics, Jesus is presented as reflecting on the difficulty with which the rich will enter the kingdom of God. Nevertheless, he teaches that "all things are possible with God" (Mk 10:27). And for those who follow Him Jesus promises eternal life (Mk 10:30).

This connection between the kingdom of God and eternal life seems a fundamental one, though it is seldom made so explicit as it is in the pericope just mentioned. It stands behind the Beatitudes (Mt 5:3–12; Lk 6:20–23), inasmuch as Jesus pronounces the poor and the mourning blessed, not because of their present distress, but because of God's pledge to give them some corresponding share in His kingdom. In a number of the parables, even though we must exercise caution in interpreting their assumptions, a form of resurrection belief seems not only presupposed but clearly taught. Neither Luke's parable of the rich man and Lazarus (Lk 16:19–31) nor the words he has Jesus speak to the good thief on the cross (Lk 23:43) should be pressed for information about the state of the dead between physical death and final presence before God. Yet they do indicate fundamental attitudes toward life, a life in which equality is meant for all, the possibility of repentance is constant, and the transcendence of death is promised.

It also seems to me impossible to read Matthew's vision of the Great Judgment (Mt 25:31–46) without seeing in it a confession of the Father's ultimate power over all of life and death and a correlation as well between His kingdom and eternal life (cf. Mt 25:34, 46). With its implied universalism and its reference to the final separation between eternal punishment and eternal life, the scene has an echo in Luke's version of Jesus' reference to a (presumably universal) "resurrection of the just" (Lk 14:14; cf. Ac 24:15). Such expressions as they stand in Matthew and Luke may not indeed be historically ascribable to Jesus, but they were obviously judged by the early Church to interpret His preaching correctly.

In short, life with God in His kingdom, a life sown on earth but harvested finally by God, seems an ineradicable dimension of Jesus' preaching of the kingdom. We should not overlook, of course, how stringent and all-encompassing are the demands of God's kingdom as Jesus announces it. According to Matthew 18:8f., we must be ready to give up hand, foot, or eye should they turn us aside—for it is better to "enter life" lame or with one eye than in health to be cast into "eternal fire." Not that Jesus sees the body as the source of our sinfulness. But it does express the sin which we personally commit and which must be renounced if we are to be converted to the Gospel.

The rigor of serving the kingdom is still more vigorously stated in the critical expressions which summarize the law of the cross in the life of Jesus' disciples (Mk 8:34ff.; Mt 16:24ff.; Lk 9:23ff.). We must be ready to lose our lives for Christ if we hope to save them finally. These central words on the cost of discipleship may well have been elaborated in various ways in the course of the Gospel traditions. But coming as they do after the first prediction of the passion—which also, of course, shows evidence of community interpretation—there can be little doubt that Jesus intended the assimilation of the pattern of His disciples' lives to that of His own (Hengel, 1968). We may suspend judgment on whether Jesus spoke this directly of His own passion and resurrection. But we may not doubt, I think, that He taught a promise of eternal life with which no worldly possession whatsoever can compare.

Utmost reserve is in order when we ask what Jesus' own passion teaches us about the struggle between death and life. Jürgen Moltmann (1974) has centered his attention on the final words of Jesus in Mark 15:34, but I think it can plausibly be argued that we must use all the words from the cross reported by the evangelists—not indeed for a harmonized psychology of Jesus' attitude toward death, but rather for complementary expressions of the experience of His death which we all need who share His faith in the powerful mercy of the Father of life. Only through the fullest possible meditation on the cross can a real hope of resurrection dawn in us. Here I would agree with Moltmann that Jesus' actual death is what gives significance to the resurrection in which He is raised from the dead as the first of all those whom God's promise of new creation embraces (Moltmann, 1974, pp. 182ff.). Only what we freely and lovingly suffer for the sake of human life can finally be resurrected by God. Jesus on the cross thus represents our central image of the struggle with the forces of death and the lasting question whether life is overcome there or rather enters thus into its final and truest state (Gnilka, 1964, pp. 109f.). It seems essential to all the passion accounts that death is in a real sense an enemy of humanity, an enemy in a far more penetrating sense than any philosophical reflection alone might determine. But through His obedience to the Father in His passion, the Lord has changed the meaning of death so that henceforth and forever it may serve His Gospel of life.

The Gospel of John has, in fact, been called the Gospel of Life. It was written, as we are told in John 20:30, that we might believe in Jesus as the Christ, the Son of God, and thus have life in His name. The vocabulary of "life" is far more frequent here than in the rest of the New Testament, and though "life" and "eternal life" are practically synonomous in John (another word, *psyche*, is used for purely natural life), it is noteworthy that the expression "eternal life" is found seventeen times in the Gospel and six times in the First Letter of John (Brown, 1966, Vol. 1, pp. 505ff.; on Luke's use of the theme of life, cf. Léon-Dufour, 1971, pp. 279f.).

God's love for humanity is again and again expressed as the promise of eternal life through His Son: in the evangelist's reflection after the Nicodemus scene, for example (Jn 3:16), or in the chapter on the Good Shepherd (Jn 10:10), or in the prayer of Jesus (Jn 17:1–2). Indeed because of the intimate union between Jesus and His Father, who is the source of all life, Jesus can be presented as being "the resurrection and the life" (Jn 11:25). In John 5:26–29, Jesus speaks of the Father's appointing the Son as supreme judge over all humanity; a final hour is foreseen when all the dead will rise, "those who have done good, to the resurrection of life, and those who have done evil, to the resurrection of judgment" (Jn 5:29). There has been much discussion of these verses; some hold with Bultmann for strong Gnostic influence on John and the secondary character of verses 28 and 29, while others see these verses as typical of John's unified vision embracing present and future perspectives. To appreciate the passage it is crucial to realize that for John the opposed forces in human existence are not (eternal) life and death but rather life and sin. Through union with Christ and victory over sin, life is already the firm possession of the believer (Jn 6:47). But this does not mean that it cannot continue to bear still more fruit (Jn 15:1–11), or that faith does not long for that time of full union with Christ and His Father when "the river of the water of life, flowing from the throne of God and of the Lamb" (Rv 22:1) will fill the messianic Jerusalem.

THE HORIZON OF RESURRECTION

On balance, it seems that resurrection was neither a central topic nor simply a presupposition of the teaching of Jesus. It is clear enough that Jesus is not presented as having often spoken directly of resurrection. We might expect, in fact, that such an emphasis would have formalized a preaching otherwise notable for its concreteness. For Jesus' hearers as well as for ourselves, the kingdom of God makes entirely practical demands for the reform of personal and societal life. But neither is it satisfactory to portray Jesus simply as sharing with His Jewish contemporaries an apocalyptic horizon of resurrection which He presupposed in His own teaching. His Father's transcendent reality and care for the world are too central in His teaching for it to be plausible that the creation's final destiny might simply be "presupposed." Far more likely is a view of Jesus' life which sees it as bearing an openness of time to eternity, of the world to God's presence—an openness such that this eternal presence is always at issue in human life, is in fact its central issue. To speak of Jesus' attitude toward resurrection and eternal life is thus to speak of the eternal dimension to His preaching on the final meaning and reality which His Father gives in promise to our world.

For the contemporary Christian as well, the transcendent term of life is a question not so much separate from the other questions of existence as it is a dimension of them all. We seek integrity and wholeness of life in all our conduct, but we await judgment on its final wholeness from the one who is the author of life in the first place. This judgment should not so much be conceived as God's intervention after death to reward the good with eternal life or to condemn the evil to its loss. Rather, as in all God's self-disclosure to us, final judgment should be understood as our realization of the true meaning of our lives before Him, in this case in their achieved finality as adherence to Him and His Christ or as a turning away from Him and those who are His own (Rahner, 1965, 1969). There is, of course, a reciprocal priority in the hermeneutics of such judgment and salvation: without the hope of eternal life, a final judgment will not be expected; but, at the same time, without a judgment surer than our own, entry into a transformed state of life will seem only an illusory projection.

To speak of eternal life as a reward or its loss as retribution for the conduct of earthly life is fundamentally to misconstrue the relation between time and eternity. Eternal value should not be understood to be realized after temporal value but rather through it. It is in the daily conduct of our lives that their eternal value before God is being graciously realized. Eternity can ripen for us nowhere else but in time, the community of saints be established only in the present strife or concord of fellow human beings. Interpreting the preaching of Jesus on this point, Rudolf Bultmann has commented that Jesus

> promises reward precisely to those who obey not for the sake of reward. . . . The motive of a reward is only a primitive expression for the idea that in what a man does his own real being is at stake—that self which he not already is, but is to become [Bultmann, 1951, Vol. 1, pp. 14–15].

It is in this sense also that we can interpret Paul's well-known words on the practice of resurrection faith: "For those who sought renown and honor and immortality by always doing good there will be eternal life" (Rm 2:7). What we hope for, then, is not another world but the renewal, the re-creation, of the present one. What we proclaim is not the futility of life but God's reign in it. And so we do not look to be rewarded or punished for our conduct on a temporary stage of life so much as we look to become finally before God what we now through His grace are making of ourselves.

This dialectical process revealed to Christian faith and symbolized in its language of parousia, resurrection, and judgment has been effective in one way or another, one may argue, in all human aspiration to the permanence of the human spirit and to personal transcendence of death. Reflection on the immortal thrust of life inevitably falls short of expressing it adequately. But it is demanded again and again when people sense that great acts of love, self-sacrifice, justice, or fidelity have true claims to be gathered up from time and to endure beyond it (Rahner, 1966b, pp. 348ff.). This reflection has taken certain paths repeatedly, with the idea of immortality chief among them. It may be true that reflection alone invariably stumbles in its effort to justify such ideas, but the committed life from which the reflection springs nevertheless has a broader and persuasive assurance.

Someone who has known and truly loved another human being has reached deeply into eternity through that communion and rightfully has confidence that the loved one may now live in a fuller form than can be imagined on earth. "In the history we share with God," writes Juan Luis Segundo, "no love is lost" (Segundo, 1974, p. 46). Knowing the achievements or, conversely, the patient suffering of men and women who have gone before us, we rightly sense a partnership with them in accepting life's challenges and looking toward shaping it in a way which may last. Whether such a stance is called faith or not, its contradiction of death is a natural longing as well as a gracious opportunity which permeates our entire social and individual existence. When we call it Christian, we acknowledge the transformation of that existence through its being gathered into the fully inclusive humanity of someone who is wholly ours and wholly God's, Jesus of Nazareth.

We could scarcely hope in the resurrection of Jesus and through Him in our own if there had been no sense created in us that life seeks to transcend death. In this respect at no disadvantage from the first disciples (cf. Jn 20:29), we can only recognize the living Lord insofar as His Father creates in us a natural anticipation that our lives are open to something more lasting and final than can be achieved by a cumulative progress bound eventually to extinction. The hope of resurrection, of eternal life, of exaltation to God's presence arises only within the horizon of commitment to the value of human life beyond all earthly limitation, including that of death. This horizon is sighted differently at different stages of our life, from the innocent spontaneity and immediacy of childhood to the differentiated consciousness and fragmentary wisdom of old age. But it is a horizon which travels with us always, framing all our activity and setting every scene we enter.

As such, it is not merely theoretical; nor is it primarily individualistic. Where it is really allowed to dawn, individualistic rationalism evaporates, for we recognize that we can hope for ourselves only what we still more generously hope for others, and we can affirm as a lasting personal value only what we enact as a present one. Neither the history of resurrection faith in Israel nor its transformation in early Christian preaching can be properly appreciated without realizing that a community's restored life was hoped for while present reform of life was demanded. Rooting reason ever more deeply in the love which alone can guide it and the individual in the community which alone can awaken true individuality, the hope of resurrection enfleshes the bare longing for transcendent life so that marvelous names arise for it: people of God, body of Christ, temple of the Holy Spirit—names to which, it may be added, a faithful Church may hope graciously to add still others in God's good time to come.

Faith in God's eternal promise may indeed, in fact it must, be expressed through other symbols besides that of resurrection. "We must also take into consideration other New Testament languages," writes Claude Geffré, "those of life and exaltation, which have precisely the role of correcting and completing resurrection vocabulary" (Geffré, 1972, p. 21). We have seen that a variety of expressions for life's transcendence of death developed in Judaism. Their eventual convergence on the notion of resurrection does not eliminate their useful complementarity. Similarly, to mention only several of the New Testament expressions discussed above, Paul's resurrection language, the Synoptics' relation between the kingdom of God and eternal life, and the special Johannine understanding of life, mutually correct and complete each other. But all these forms bespeak the realization that our natural horizon of longing for transcendent life depends on a personal presence which at once raises this horizon before us and now guides us toward it.

It is probably helpful to understand this hope as generated in the present out of the future. This emphasis of recent eschatological theology correctly recognizes that we live only in the present, but that we live meaningfully in the present only when it has orientation, when it is going somewhere. Indeed, the future of resurrection hope is one which transcends the temporal future. But the temporal future, through its promise and call to the present, seems to provide an appropriate analogy with which to speak of our invitation from God to final communion with Him. Hope is not generated for the present, but rather in the present for the future. But we would not indeed look forward if our eyes had not already been somehow lifted up. "The Christian man knows of his future," writes Rahner, "in as much as he knows of himself and his redemption in Christ through divine revelation. His knowledge of the *eschata* is not a supplementary piece of information added to dogmatic anthropology and Christology, but simply *their* transposition into the guise of fulfilment" (Rahner, 1966a, p. 335).

Need it be stressed how easily this all-encompassing hope degenerates into delusion? We are all too aware how seeking God in all things can become an excuse for avoiding the real challenges of life. But if we are down to earth in this hope of seeking God everywhere and eventually finding all in Him (1 Co 15:28), then we learn gradually that our whole life in all its bodily and spiritual dimensions is in question. What do we wish to become of it? Are we willing to sacrifice it for what the Lord of heaven and earth may make of it?

If we value our earth as God's creation, then we will not look away from it toward a heaven purportedly presupposed by our hope and awaiting our entry (Rahner, 1963, pp. 214ff.). Heaven is rather the result of God's transformation of our humble bodiliness into the bodily glory of His Son, the transformation of this earth whose form passes away into one which will endure through His life-giving Spirit, the transformation of the cities in which we struggle into a heavenly Jerusalem. To practice faith in this eternal life is to take hold of our lives and our world only so that we may restore them wholly to their original author. Seeking heaven is authentic only on the condition that it is sought as the true future of the earth we seek. And because this search is one in which God always goes before us, we may undertake it with a combination of urgency and of joy possible only to those who know their lives are mastered not finally by themselves but by another. It is then that we can confess with St. Paul:

> If God is for us, who is against us? . . . For I am sure that neither death, nor life, nor angels, nor principalities, nor things present, nor things to come, nor powers, nor height, nor depth, nor anything else in all creation, will be able to separate us from the love of God in Christ Jesus our Lord [Rm 8:31, 38–39].

REFERENCES

Barr, J. *The semantics of biblical language.* London: Oxford University Press, 1961.

Blenkinsopp, J. Theological synthesis and hermeneutical conclusions. In P. Benoit & R. Murphy (Eds.), *Immortality and resurrection.* New York: Herder & Herder, 1970. Pp. 115–126.

Brandon, S. G. F. *The judgment of the dead.* New York: Scribner, 1967.

Brown, R. E. *The Gospel according to John* (2 vols.). Garden City, N.Y.: Doubleday, 1966, 1970.

Bultmann, R. *Theology of the New Testament* (Vol. 1). New York: Scribner, 1951.

Bultmann, R. New Testament and mythology. In H. W. Bartsch (Ed.), *Kerygma and myth.* New York: Harper, 1961. Pp. 1–44.

Cadbury, H. J. Intimations of immortality in the thought of Jesus. In K. Stendahl (Ed.), *Immortality and resurrection.* New York: Macmillan, 1965. Pp. 115–149.

Collins, J. J. Apocalyptic eschatology as the transcendence of death. *Catholic Biblical Quarterly,* 1974, *36,* 21–43.

Cullmann, O. Immortality of the soul or resurrection of the dead? In K. Stendahl (Ed.), *Immortality and resurrection.* New York: Macmillan, 1965. Pp. 9–53.

Dahood, M. *Psalms* (3 vols.). Garden City, N.Y.: Doubleday, 1966.

Dubarle, A.-M. Belief in immortality in the Old Testament and Judaism. In P. Benoit & R. Murphy (Eds.), *Immortality and resurrection.* New York: Herder & Herder, 1970. Pp. 34–45.

Durrwell, F. X. *The resurrection.* New York: Sheed & Ward, 1960.

Evans, C. F. *Resurrection and the New Testament.* London: SCM, 1970.

Fuller, R. *The formation of the resurrection narratives.* New York: Macmillan, 1971.

Geffré, C. Où en est la théologie de la résurrection? *Lumière et vie,* 1972, *21,* 17–30.

Gnilka, J. Die biblische Jenseitserwartung: Unsterblichkeitshoffnung—Auferstehungsglaube? *Bibel und Leben,* 1964, *5,* 103–116.

Gnilka, J. *Der Philipperbrief.* Freiburg: Herder, 1968.

Hengel, M. *Nachfolge und Charisma.* Berlin: Topelmann, 1968.

James, W. *The writings of William James: A comprehensive edition* (J. J. McDermott, Ed.). New York: Random House, 1968.

Léon-Dufour, X. *Résurrection de Jésus et message pascal.* Paris: Seuil, 1971.

Marxsen, W. *The resurrection of Jesus of Nazareth.* Philadelphia: Fortress, 1970.

Moltmann, J. *The crucified God.* New York: Harper & Row, 1974.

Nickelsburg, G. W. E. *Resurrection, immortality, and eternal life in intertestamental Judaism.* Cambridge: Harvard University Press, 1972.

Rahner, K. *Hörer des Wortes.* Munich: Kösel, 1963.

Rahner, K. *On the theology of death* (2nd ed.). New York: Herder & Herder, 1965.

Rahner, K. The hermeneutics of eschatological assertions. *Theological investigations* IV. Baltimore: Helicon, 1966. Pp. 323–346. (a)

Rahner, K. The life of the dead. *Theological investigations* IV. Baltimore: Helicon, 1966. Pp. 347–354. (b)

Rahner, K. Guilt—responsibility—punishment within the views of Catholic theology. *Theological investigations* VI. Baltimore: Helicon, 1969. Pp. 197–217.

Schillebeeckx, E. The interpretation of eschatology. In E. Schillebeeckx & B. Willems (Eds.), *The problem of eschatology.* New York: Paulist, 1969. Pp. 42–56.

Schnackenburg, R. *Christian existence in the New Testament* (2 vols.). Notre Dame: University of Notre Dame Press, 1968.

Segundo, J. L. *Our idea of God.* Maryknoll, N.Y.: Orbis, 1974.

Wilckens, U. The tradition-history of the resurrection of Jesus. In C. F. O. Moule (Ed.), *The significance of the message of the resurrection.* London: SCM, 1968. Pp. 51–76.